FIAT X1/9
OWNERS WORKSHOP MANUAL
1974-1982

Model covered:
FIAT X1/9 1300 1974-1978
FIAT X1/9 1500 1978-1982
FIAT X1/9 1500 Lido 1978

ISBN 9781855204300

BROOKLANDS BOOKS LTD.
P.O. BOX 904, AMERSHAM,
BUCKS. HP6 9JA. UK
sales@brooklandsbooks.com

FI12WH   www.brooklandsbooks.com   8W4/3068

INTRODUCTION

This do-it-yourself Workshop Manual has been specially written for the owner who wishes to maintain his car in first class condition and to carry out his own servicing and repairs. Considerable savings on garage charges can be made, and one can drive in safety and confidence knowing the work has been done properly.

Comprehensive step-by-step instructions and illustrations are given on all dismantling, overhauling and assembling operations. Certain assemblies require the use of expensive special tools, the purchase of which would be unjustified. In these cases information is included but the reader is recommended to hand the unit to the agent for attention.

Throughout the Manual hints and tips are included which will be found to be invaluable, and there is an easy to follow fault diagnosis at the end of each chapter.

Whilst every care has been taken to ensure correctness of information it is obviously not possible to guarantee complete freedom from errors or to accept liability arising from such errors or omissions.

Instructions may refer to the right-hand or left-hand sides of the vehicle or the components. These are the same as the right-hand or left-hand of an observer standing behind the car and looking forward.

ACKNOWLEDGEMENT

Our thanks are due to Fiat for their unstinted co-operation and also for supplying data and illustrations.

Considerable assistance has also been given by owners, who have discussed their cars in detail, and we would like to express our gratitude for this invaluable advice and help.

By the Autobooks Team of Technical Writers

BROOKLANDS BOOKS LTD.
P.O. BOX 904, AMERSHAM,
BUCKS. HP6 9JA. UK
sales@brooklandsbooks.com

www.brooklandsbooks.com

CONTENTS

INDEX

HINTS ON MAINTENANCE AND OVERHAUL

There are few things more rewarding than the restoration of a vehicle's original peak of efficiency and smooth performance.

The following notes are intended to help the owner to reach that state of perfection. Providing that he possesses the basic manual skills he should have no difficulty in performing most of the operations detailed in this manual. It must be stressed, however, that where recommended in the manual, highly-skilled operations ought to be entrusted to experts, who have the necessary equipment, to carry out the work satisfactorily.

Quality of workmanship:
The hazardous driving conditions on the roads today demand that vehicles should be as nearly perfect, mechanically, as possible. It is therefore most important that amateur work be carried out with care, bearing in mind the often inadequate working conditions, and also the inferior tools which may have to be used. It is easy to counsel perfection in all things, and we recognize that it may be setting an impossibly high standard. We do, however, suggest that every care should be taken to ensure that a vehicle is as safe to take on the road as it is humanly possible to make it.

Safe working conditions:
Even though a vehicle may be stationary, it is still potentially dangerous if certain sensible precautions are not taken when working on it while it is supported on jacks or blocks. It is indeed preferable not to use jacks alone, but to supplement them with carefully placed blocks, so that there will be plenty of support if the car rolls off the jacks during a strenuous manoeuvres. Axle stands are an excellent way of providing a rigid base which is not readily disturbed. Piles of bricks are a dangerous substitute. Be careful not to get under heavy loads on lifting tackle, the load could fall. It is preferable not to work alone when lifting an engine, or when working underneath a vehicle which is supported well off the ground. To be trapped, particularly under the vehicle, may have unpleasant results if help is not quickly forthcoming. Make some provision, however humble, to deal with fires. Always disconnect a battery if there is a likelihood of electrical shorts. These may start a fire if there is leaking fuel about. This applies particularly to leads which can carry a heavy current, like those in the starter circuit. While on the subject of electricity, we must also stress the danger of using equipment which is run off the mains and which has no earth or has faulty wiring or connections. So many workshops have damp floors, and electrical shocks are of such a nature that it is sometimes impossible to let go of a live lead or piece of equipment due to the muscular spasms which take place.

Work demanding special care:
This involves the servicing of braking, steering and suspension systems. On the road, failure of the braking system may be disastrous. Make quite sure that there can be no possibility of failure through the bursting of rusty brake pipes or rotten hoses, nor to a sudden loss of pressure due to defective seals or valves.

Problems:
The chief problems which may face an operator are:

1 External dirt.
2 Difficulty in undoing tight fixings
3 Dismantling unfamiliar mechanisms.
4 Deciding in what respect parts are defective.
5 Confusion about the correct order for reassembly.
6 Adjusting running clearances.
7 Road testing.
8 Final tuning.

Practical suggestions to solve the problems:
1. Preliminary cleaning of large parts - engines, transmissions, steering, suspensions, etc., should be carried out before removal from the car. Where road dirt and mud alone are present, wash clean with a high pressure water jet, brushing to remove stubborn adhesions, and allow to drain and dry. Where oil or grease is also present, wash down with a proprietary compound (Gunk, Teepol etc.,) applying with a stiff brush - an old paint brush is suitable, into all crevices. Cover the distributor and ignition coils with a polythene bag and then apply a strong water jet to clear the loosened deposits. Allow to drain and dry. The assemblies will then be sufficiently clean to remove and transfer to the bench for the next stage.

On the bench, further cleaning can be carried out, first wiping the parts as free as possible from grease with old newspaper. Avoid using rag or cotton waste which can leave clogging fibres behind. Any remaining grease can be removed with a brush dipped in paraffin. Avoid using paraffin or petrol in large quantities for cleaning in enclosed areas, such as garages, on account of the high fire risk.

When all exteriors have been cleaned, and not before, dismantling can be commenced. This ensures that dirt will not enter into interiors and orifices revealed by dismantling. In the next phases, where components have to be cleaned and keep the containers covered except when in use. After the components have been cleaned, plug small holes with tapered hard wood plugs cut to size and blank off larger orifices with greaseproof paper and masking tape. Do not use soft wood plugs or matchsticks as they may break.

2. It is not advisable to hammer on the end of a screw thread, but if it must be done, first screw on a nut to protect the thread, and use a lead hammer. This applies particularly to the removal of tapered cotters. Nuts and bolts seem to 'grow' together, especially in exhaust systems. If penetrating oil does not work, try the judicious application of heat, but be careful of starting a fire.

Tight bushes or pieces of tail-pipe rusted into a silencer can be removed by splitting them with an open-ended hacksaw. Tight screws can some-times be started by a tap from a hammer on the end of a suitable screwdriver. Many tight fittings will yield to the judicious use of a hammer, but it must be a soft-faced hammer if damage is to be avoided, use a heavy block on the opposite side to absorb shock. Any parts of the steering system which have been damaged should be renewed, as attempts to repair them may lead to cracking and subsequent failure, and steering ball joints should be disconnected using a recommended tool to prevent damage.

3. It often happens that an owner is baffled when trying to dismantle an unfamiliar piece of equipment. So many modern devices are pressed together or assembled by spinning-over flanges, that they must be sawn apart. The intention is that the whole assembly must be renewed. However, parts which appear to be in one piece to the naked eye, may reveal close-fitting joint lines when inspected with a magnifying glass, and, this may provide the necessary clue to dismantling. Left-handed screw threads are used where rotational forces would tend to unscrew a right handed screw thread.

Be very careful when dismantling mechanisms which may come apart suddenly. Work in an enclosed space where the parts will be contained, and drape a piece of cloth over the device if springs are likely to fly in all directions. Mark everything which might be reassembled in the wrong position,

scratched symbols may be used on unstressed parts, or a sequence of tiny dots from a centre punch can be useful. Stressed parts should never be scratched or centre-popped as this may lead to cracking under working conditions. Store parts which look alike in the correct order for reassembly. Never rely upon memory to assist in the assembly of complicated mechanisms, especially when they will be dismantled for a long time, but make notes, and drawings to supplement the diagrams in the manual, and put labels on detached wires. Rust stains may indicate unlubricated wear. This can sometimes be seen round the outside edge of a bearing cup in a universal joint. Look for bright rubbing marks on parts which normally should not make heavy contact. These might prove that something is bent or running out of truth. For example, there might be bright marks on one side of a piston, at the top near the ring grooves, and others at the bottom of the skirt on the other side. This could well be the clue to a bent connecting rod. Suspected cracks can be proved by heating the component in a light oil to approximately 100°C, removing, drying off, and dusting with French chalk, if a crack is present the oil retained in the crack will stain the French chalk.

4. In determining wear, and the degree, against the permissible limits set in the manual, accurate measurement can only be achieved by the use of a micrometer. In many cases the wear is given to the fourth place of decimals; that is in ten-thousandths of an inch. This can be read by the vernier scale on the barrel of a good micrometer. Bore diameters are more difficult to determine. If, however, the matching shaft is accurately measured, the degree of play in the bore can be felt as a guide to its suitability. In other cases, the shank of a twist drill of known diameter is a handy check.

Many methods have been devised for determining the clearance between bearing surfaces. Today the best and simplest is by the use of Plastigage, obtainable from most garages. A thin plastic thread is laid between the two surfaces and the bearing is tightened, flattening the thread. On removal, the width of the thread is compared with a scale supplied with the thread and the clearance is read off directly. Sometimes joint faces leak persistently, even after gasket renewal. The fault will then be traceable to distortion, dirt or burrs. Studs which are screwed into soft metal frequently raise burrs at the point of entry. A quick cure for this is to chamfer the edge of the hole in the part which fits over the stud.

5. Always check a replacement part with the original one before it is fitted.

If parts are not marked, and the order for reassembly is not known, a little detective work will help. Look for marks which are due to wear to see if they can be mated. Joint faces may not be identical due to manufacturing errors, and parts which overlap may be stained, giving a clue to the correct position. Most fixings leave identifying marks especially if they were painted over on assembly. It is then easier to decide whether a nut, for instance, has a plain, a spring, or a shake-proof washer under it. All running surfaces become 'bedded' together after long spells of work and tiny imperfections on one part will be found to have left corresponding marks on the other. This is particularly true of shafts and bearings and even a score on a cylinder wall will show on the piston.

6. Checking end float or rocker clearances by feeler gauge may not always give accurate results because of wear. For instance, the rocker tip which bears on a valve stem may be deeply pitted, in which case the feeler will simply be bridging a depression. Thrust washers may also wear depressions in opposing faces to make accurate measurement difficult. End float is then easier to check by using a dial gauge. It is common practice to adjust end play in bearing assemblies, like front hubs with taper rollers, by doing up the axle nut until the hub becomes stiff to turn and then backing it off a little. Do not use this method with ball-bearing hubs as the assembly is often pre-loaded by tightening the axle nut to its fullest extent. If the split-pin hole will not line up, file the base of the nut a little.

Steering assemblies often wear in the straight-ahead position. If any part is adjusted, make sure that it remains free when moved from lock to lock. Do not be surprised if an assembly like a steering gearbox, which is known to be carefully adjusted outside the car, becomes stiff when it is bolted in place. This will be due to distortion of the case by the pull of the mounting bolts, particularly if the mounting points are not all touching together. This problem may be met in other equipment and is cured by careful attention to the alignment of mounting points.

When a spanner is stamped with a size and A/F it means that the dimension is the width between the jaws and has no connection with ANF, which is the designation for the American National Fine thread.

Coarse threads like Whitworth are rarely used on cars to-day except for studs which screw into soft aluminium or cast iron. For this reason it might be found that the top end of a cylinder head stud has a fine thread and the lower end a coarse thread to screw into the cylinder block. If the car has mainly UNF threads then it is likely that any coarse threads will be UNC, which are not the same as Whitworth. Small sizes have the same number of threads in Whitworth and UNC, but in the 1/4 inch size for example, there are twelve threads to the inch in the former and thirteen in the latter.

7. After a major overhaul, particularly if a great deal of work has been done on the braking, steering and suspension systems, it is advisable to approach the problem of testing with care. If the braking system has been overhauled, apply heavy pressure to the brake pedal and get a second operator to check every possible source of leakage. The brakes may work extremely well, but a leak could cause complete failure after a few miles.

Do not fit the hub caps until every wheel nut has been checked for tightness, and make sure the tyre pressures are correct. Check the levels of coolant, lubricants and hydraulic fluids. Being satisfied that all is well, take the car on the road and test the brakes at once. Check the steering and the action of the handbrake. Do all this at moderate speeds on quiet roads, and make sure there is no other vehicle behind you when you try a rapid stop.

Finally, remember that many parts settle down after a time, so check for tightness of all fixings after the car has been on the road for a hundred miles or so.

8. It is useless to tune an engine which has not reached its normal running temperature. In the same way, the tune of an engine which is stiff after a re-bore will be different when the engine is again running free. Remember too, that rocker clearances on push-rod operated valve gear will change when the cylinder head nuts are tightened after an initial period of running with a new head gasket. Trouble may not always be due to what seems the obvious cause. Ignition, carburation and mechanical condition are interdependent and spitting back through the carburetter, which might be attributed to a weak mixture, can be caused by a sticking inlet valve. For one final hint on tuning, never adjust more than one thing at a time or it will be impossible to tell which adjustment produced the desired result.

CHAPTER 1
THE ENGINE

1 : 1 Description

The engine is a water-cooled, four cylinder in-line overhead camshaft unit which is mounted transversely in the car together with the rear wheel drive transmission. The engine is positioned slightly ahead of the rear wheels. The transmission final drive, which includes the differential gearing, projects rearwards from the engine transverse axis and the drive shafts are consequently in line with the axis of the rear wheels. The engine and transmission are supported as a unit on three mountings. The engine can only be removed from the car as a unit with the transmission, though the transmission can be removed leaving the engine in position. The engine in all 1300 models is of 1290cc capacity and the transmission has four forward gears and reverse. 1500 models are fitted with a 1498cc capacity version of the same engine and have a 5-speed and reverse transmission.

The overhead camshaft is driven from the crankshaft by a dry toothed belt which is tensioned by a pulley running on the plain side of the belt. The toothed belt also drives an auxiliary shaft. Skew gearing on this shaft drives the oil pump and the ignition distributor. Note, however, that on early engines the distributor is mounted horizontally at the end of the cylinder head and driven directly by the camshaft. An eccentric on the auxiliary shaft actuates the fuel pump.

Shims are fitted between the camshaft lobes and the tappets which locate over the valves. By selecting shims of appropriate thickness, valve clearances are initially set and, when necessary, adjusted.

Closed crankcase ventilation is incorporated and breather fumes are piped to the air cleaner for consumption by the engine. On relevant models, further emission control devices (as may be mandatory in countries to which the cars are imported) are provided. These, together with the closed crankcase ventilation system are referred to in **Section 1 : 15, Chapter 2, Section 2 : 10** and **Chapter 3, Section 3 : 7**.

The cast iron cylinder block is integral with the upper half of the crankcase, the lower half of which is formed by the sump. The cylinder head is of light alloy and consists of a lower section attached to the cylinder block, which carries the valve gear and sparking plugs, and an upper section attached to this which carries the camshaft in five plain bearings.

The cast steel crankshaft has integral balance weights and is provided with five plain shell bearings, all of which are pressure lubricated. Axial thrust is accommodated by the main bearing nearest to the flywheel. Similar type shell bearings are fitted to the connecting rods, which have straightcut big-end caps.

The light alloy pistons are of the auto-thermal type,

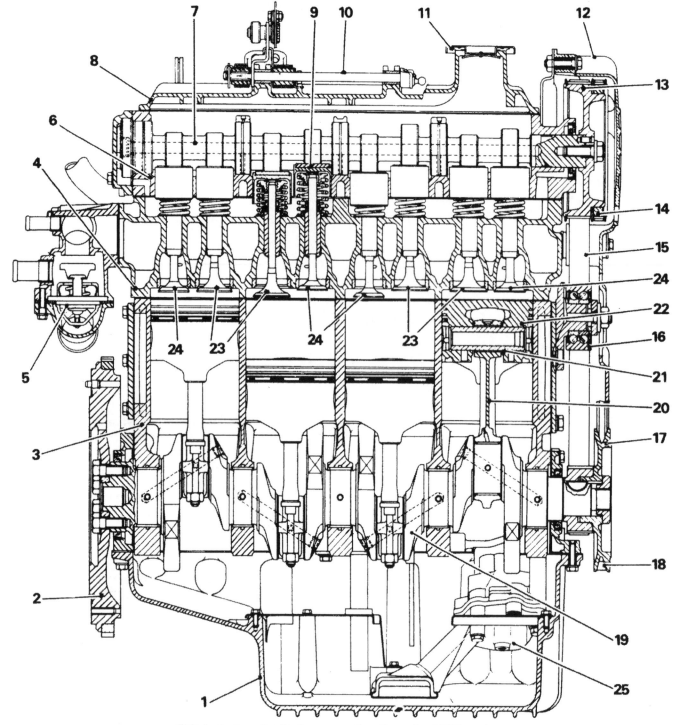

FIG 1 : 1   Longitudinal cross-section through a 1300 engine

Key to Fig 1 : 1   1 Sump   2 Flywheel   3 Cylinder block   4 Cylinder head   5 Thermostat   6 Camshaft carrier
7 Camshaft   8 Camshaft cover   9 Tappet and adjustment shim   10 Throttle relay spindle   11 Filler cap   12 Cover
13 Camshaft toothed pulley   14 Air pump toothed pulley   15 Toothed belt   16 Tensioner pulley   17 Alternator/coolant
pump drive pulley   18 V-belt   19 Crankshaft   20 Connecting rod   21 Piston (gudgeon) pin   22 Piston   23 Inlet valve
24 Exhaust valve   25 Oil pump

having integrally cast steel retaining rings and full skirts.
Two compression rings and one oil control ring are fitted to
each piston. Gudgeon pins are a free-fit in the pistons and
a press-fit in the connecting rod small-ends.

The gear type oil pump, driven by the engine auxiliary
shaft, is located in the lower part of the crankcase. Pressure
oil is fully filtered before being passed to the lubrication
points in the engine. The external oil filter is of the fullflow
type and its mounting incorporates a relief valve which

operates to return excess oil to the sump. Cross-sections
through a 1290cc capacity engine are shown in **FIGS
1 : 1** and **1 : 2**.

1 : 2 Maintenance

Oil level :

Every 500km (300 miles) or weekly, check the oil level.
Maintain the level at the upper mark on the dipstick. Use

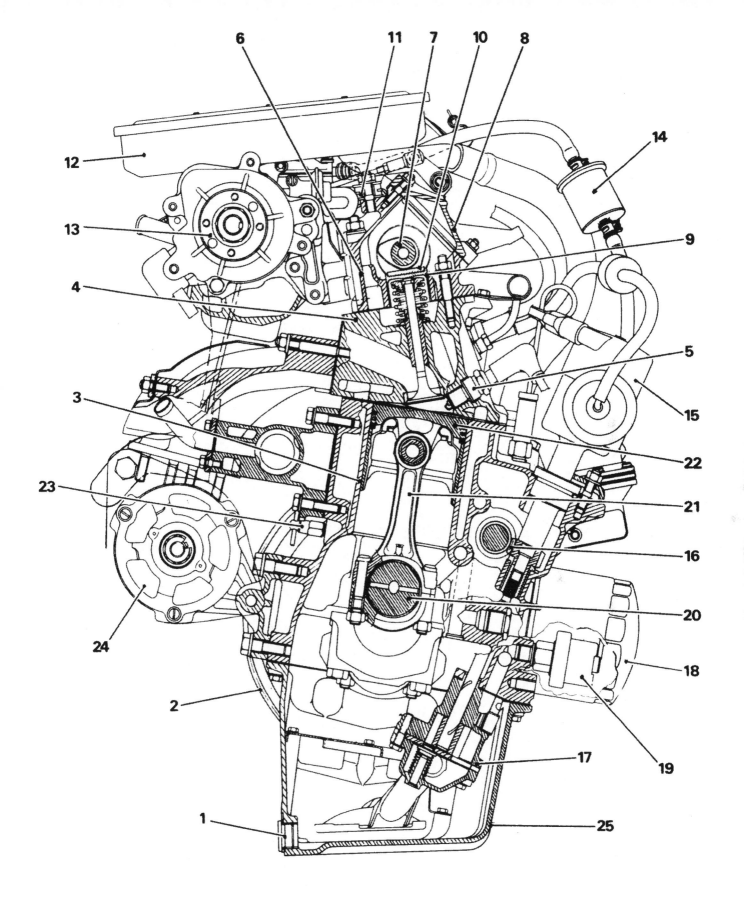

FIG 1:2 Vertical cross-section through a 1300 engine equipped with emission control systems

Key to Fig 1:2   1 Sump drain plug   2 Flywheel   3 Cylinder block   4 Cylinder head   5 Sparking plug   6 Camshaft carrier   7 Camshaft   8 Camshaft cover   9 Tappet   10 Adjusting shim   11 Carburetter   12 Air cleaner   13 Air pump   14 Fuel filter   15 Distributor   16 Skew gearing   17 Oil pump   18 Oil filter   19 Oil pressure sender unit   20 Crankshaft   21 Connecting rod   22 Piston   23 Coolant drain tap   24 Alternator   25 Oil sump

11

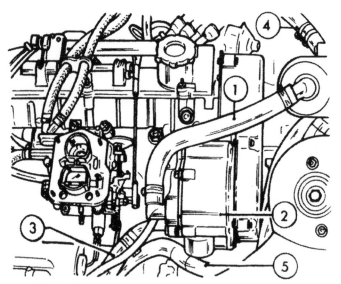

FIG 1:3 Disconnecting air pump and heater hoses

Key to Fig 1:3   1 Hose   2 Air pump   3 Hose
4 Coupling joint   5 Heater return hose

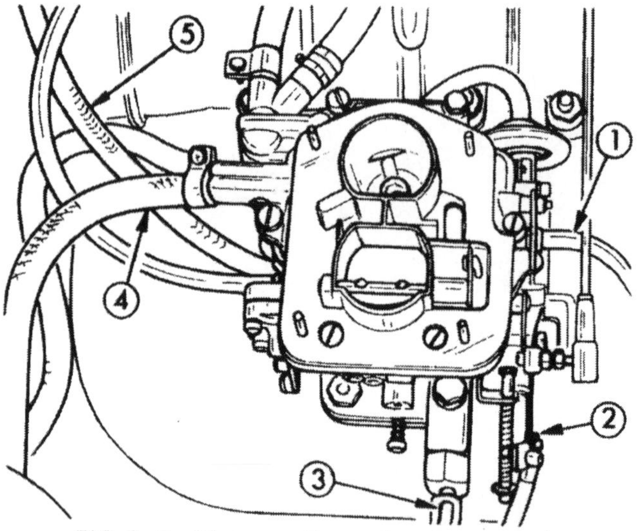

FIG 1:4 Disconnecting carburetter controls

Key to Fig 1:4   1 Hose   2 Choke linkage (not 1500 models)   3 Wiring   4 Vent hose   5 Hose

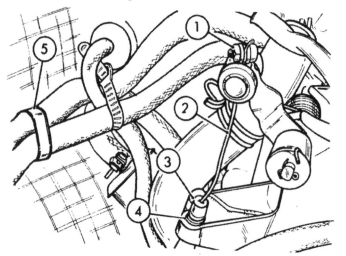

FIG 1:5 Disconnecting fuel hoses and accelerator cable

Key to Fig 1:5   1 Throttle cable bolt   2 Throttle cable   3 Seal   4 Retaining clip   5 Clamp (fuel hoses to bulkhead)

the same grade and brand of approved oil as that already in use.

Oil renewal:

Every 10,000km (6000 miles) or, in continuous stop and go (city driving) conditions or in very dusty terrain, every 5000km (3000 miles), drain and refill the sump with approved oil. Draining should preferably be carried out when the engine is warm. After draining, fit a new washer and tighten the drain plug securely. Fill the sump (refer to **Technical Data** in the **Appendix** for capacities) and, after running the engine, check the oil level.

Oil filter:

Renew the oil filter at the same time as the engine oil is being renewed. The filter renewal procedure is described in **Section 1:13**.

Air pump:

Every 10,000km (6000 miles), refer to **Section 1:15** and check the pump drive belt tension. Check the serviceability of drive belt and renew if necessary. Renew a defective air pump without delay.

Every 20,000km (12,000 miles), refer to **Section 1:15** and renew the air pump filter. Confirm that the pump is serviceable.

Valve clearances:

Every 20,000km (12,000 miles), check the valve clearances and adjust as necessary. The procedure is described in **Section 1:11**.

Emission control systems:

Every 20,000km (12,000 miles), refer to **Section 1:15**. Check security of all pipes and hoses. Service appropriate items and have other items serviced by an authorised agent.

1:3 Removing and refitting the engine

The normal operations of decarbonising and servicing the cylinder head can be carried out without the need for engine removal, as can the majority of engine servicing procedures, including the removal of piston and connecting rod assemblies. However, if crankshaft removal is necessary or attention to the cylinder bores is required, engine removal will be necessary. For some overhaul work, certain special tools are essential and the owner would be well advised to check on the availability of these factory tools or suitable substitutes before tackling the items involved. If the operator is not a skilled automobile engineer, it is suggested that much useful information will be found in **Hints on Maintenance and Overhaul** at the end of this manual and that it be read before starting work.

Owners of vehicles fitted with air conditioning (refrigeration) systems should consult a Fiat service station before attempting engine removal procedures, or any servicing procedure which involves the disconnection or removal of system components or hoses, so that advice can be obtained concerning the discharging of the system. If the pressurised system is opened, liquid

Uncontrolled release of refrigerant will cause severe frostbite or possibly more serious injury if it contacts any part of the body. For this reason, all work involving air conditioning system components should be entrusted only to a Fiat service station having the necessary special equipment and trained personnel.

Removal:

Open the front luggage compartment and disconnect the battery cables. On models with fuel evaporative emission control systems (see **Chapter 2**), loosen the fuel filler cap so that atmospheric pressure will be maintained in the fuel tank.

Refer to **Chapter 4** and drain the cooling system, then remove the cap from the expansion tank. Refer to **Chapter 2** and remove the air cleaner assembly.

Refer to **FIG 1:3**. On models with emission control system, disconnect hose 1 between air pump 2 and filter, then disconnect hose 3 from air pump. Separate heater return hose 5 at coupling joint 4, then disconnect heater hose from water pump connection. Disconnect wiring from the alternator. Remove the two bolts securing louvred protection panel at engine compartment rear bulkhead, this being below the activated carbon canister on models with emission control system.

Refer to **FIG 1:4**. Disconnect choke linkage 2 and hoses 1 and 5 from carburetter. Disconnect wires 3 and

FIG 1 : 6   Removing panels and heat shield

Key to Fig 1 : 6   1 Panel   2 Heat shield   3 Panels

vent hose 4. Disconnect the wires from the coil at their connections at the distributor, disconnect wires from oil pressure and water temperature sender units and disconnect wiring at starter motor.

Refer to **FIG 1:5**. Remove clamp 5 securing fuel hoses to bulkhead, then disconnect fuel feed and return hoses from bulkhead. Remove bolt 1 from accelerator cable 2, then slide seal 3 from cable. Remove retaining clip 4 from cable sheath. Remove cable from support. Remove bolts

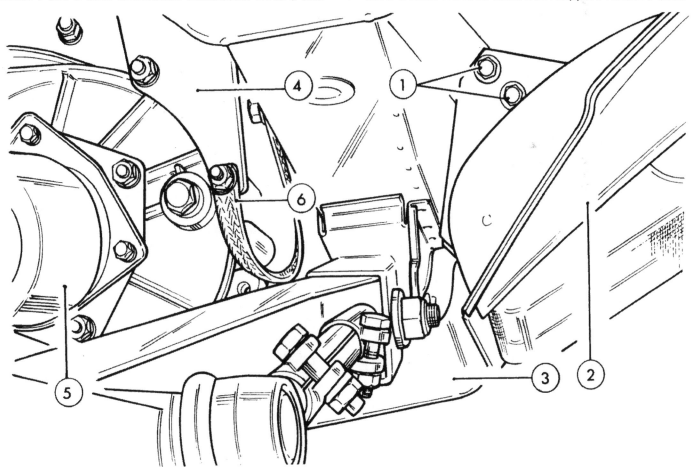

FIG 1 : 7   Disconnecting components in engine compartment

Key to Fig 1 : 7   1 Bolts   2 Silencer   3 Support   4 Bracket   5 Retaining ring   6 Earth strap

FIG 1 : 8   Disconnecting components in engine compartment

Key to Fig 1 : 8   1 Crossmember   2 Bolt   3 Control arm   4 Shims   5 Bracket   6 Bolts   7 Handbrake cable bracket

securing expansion tank at top and bottom then lift tank and allow coolant to drain into the engine. Disconnect hoses from tank at thermostat housing, then remove tank and hoses. Disconnect remaining cooling system hoses at engine connections.

Refer to **Chapter 5** and remove the clutch slave cylinder without disconnecting the hose, then support cylinder by wiring in engine compartment so that the hose is not strained.

Raise the rear of the car and support safely on floor stands for access to the underside. Remove the rear wheels. Remove the remaining bolt securing louvred panel at rear bulkhead, then remove the panel. Refer to **FIG 1 : 6**. Remove alternator heat shield 2 then remove three panels 3 from bottom of engine compartment. Remove panels 1 located inboard of each rear wheel.

Refer to **Chapter 6** and drain the transmission oil. If the engine is to be dismantled after removal, remove the sump

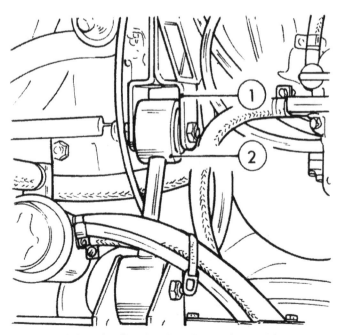

FIG 1 : 9   Bracket 1 and reaction rod 2

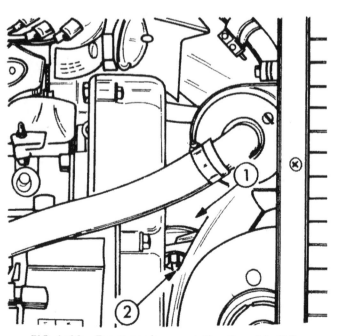

FIG 1 : 10   Front engine mounting 1 and bolt 2

14

drain plug and allow the oil to drain fully into a suitable container. Refit drain plugs after oil has drained. Disconnect the connectors for reversing lights and, if fitted, seat belt interlock system. Remove clamps as necessary to allow the wires to come free as the engine is removed. Loosen the knurled nut securing speedometer cable at transmission, then remove the cable and position away from the work area. Refer to **Chapter 6** and disconnect gearchange linkage at transmission end. Be sure to mark the connector before removing the fixing bolts then slacken the single bolt at the flexible coupling so that the coupling can be swung clear of the work area.

Refer to **FIG 1 : 7**. Remove the bolt securing earth strap 6 at body connection. Straighten tab washers at exhaust manifold flange, then remove the four nuts and tab washers. Remove the two bolts 1 at upper bracket at lefthand side of silencer 2. Remove two nuts securing silencer centre support 3 to crossmember, then remove silencer and pipe assembly. Remove two nuts and bolts retaining upper bracket 4 to differential, then remove the bracket. Remove the three bolts securing drive shaft retaining ring 5 on lefthand side, then remove the similar bolts on the righthand side. Slide the boots away from the transmission, allowing the excess oil to drain into a suitable container. Take care to avoid accidental injury on the sharp edges of sheet metal components.

Refer to **FIG 1 : 8**. Remove the nut securing handbrake cable bracket 7 at the forward end of each control arm 3. Check and record the number of shims 4 at each control arm mounting point. Remove the four bolts 6, nuts and shims 4 securing control arms 3 to body, then swing the arms downwards out of their brackets 5. Move control arms away from transmission until drive shafts are free from differential, then support drive shafts to avoid strain

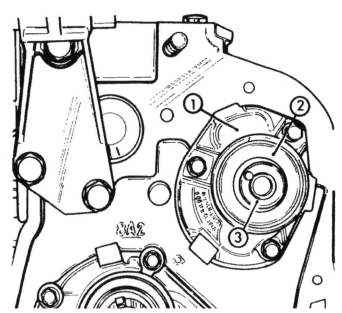

FIG 1 : 11   Auxiliary shaft flange and seal

Key to Fig 1 : 11   1 Flange   2 Seal   3 Auxiliary shaft

by wiring to the control arms. Alternatively, the drive shafts and suspension units can be completely removed for better access, as described in **Chapter 8**. Straighten the lockwashers on two bolts 2 at each end of lower crossmember 1, then loosen but do not remove the bolts.

The engine must now be supported by using a suitable trolley jack with adaptor beneath the sump and transmission, or by lowering the rear of the car until the engine weight is supported on suitable blocks of wood placed on the ground. This done, refer to **FIG 1 : 9** and, from above

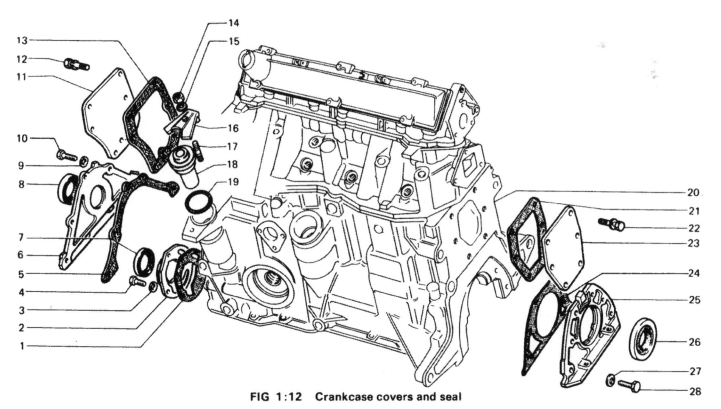

FIG 1 : 12   Crankcase covers and seal

Key to Fig 1 : 12   1 Gasket   2 Cover   3 Washer   4 Bolt   5 Gasket   6 Cover   7 Seal   8 Seal   9 Washer   10 Bolt   11 Cover   12 Bolt and washer   13 Gasket   14 Nut   15 Washer   16 Bracket   17 Stud   18 Cover   19 Gasket   20 Crankcase   21 Gasket   22 Bolt and washer   23 Cover   24 Gasket   25 Cover   26 Seal   27 Washer   28 Bolt

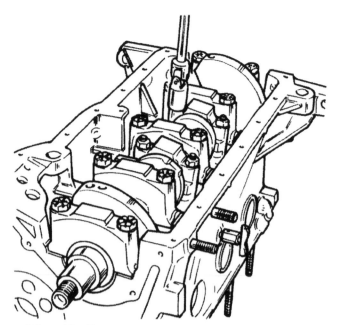

FIG 1:13   Removing main and big-end bearing caps

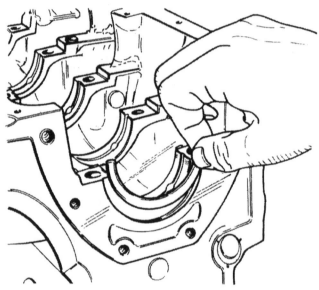

FIG 1:14   Removing crankshaft thrust washers

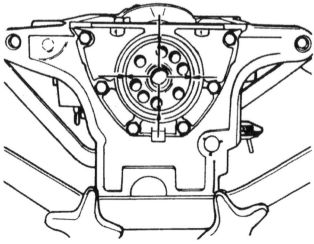

FIG 1:15   Aligning crankcase cover, flywheel side

the engine, disconnect reaction rod 2 from bracket 1 on engine. Refer to **FIG 1 : 10** and remove bolt 2 from front engine mounting 1. Check that everything linking the engine and transmission with the body has been uncoupled, removed or disconnected. Raise the rear of the car slightly, or lower the engine slightly, as appropriate, then rock the engine and transmission assembly carefully to clear front engine mounting 1. Now carefully raise the rear of the car, or lower the engine on the trolley jack, as appropriate, until the engine and transmission can be removed from beneath the rear of the car.

Refitting:

This is a reversal of the removal procedure, making sure that all component fixings are tightened to the specified torque figures. Use new tab washers, lockwashers and self-locking nuts throughout. Note that rear suspension components should be finally tightened with the car correctly laden, as described in **Chapter 8**.

1 : 4   Dismantling the engine

Remove the engine as described in **Section 1 : 3** and clean as much as possible of the dirt and oil from the engine exterior before proceeding, to prevent contamination of the internal components during dismantling. The use of an engine stand is recommended, if available. Alternatively, use suitable blocks of wood to support the engine in the appropriate attitudes for dismantling.

Refer to **Chapter 6** and separate the transmission from the engine. Drain the engine oil, if not done previously. Remove the timing belt as described in **Section 1 : 6**, then remove the belt tensioner. On models with emission control systems, remove the air pump.

Remove the oil filter, fuel pump and water pump. Remove the distributor as described in **Chapter 3**. Refer to **Section 1 : 9** and remove the cylinder head. Invert the engine so that it is standing on the cylinder head joint face, taking care to prevent damage, then remove the oil pump (see **Section 1 : 13**).

Remove the drive belt pulley from the crankshaft, then the toothed pulley, collecting the key from the shaft. Bend back the locking tab and remove the fixing bolt, then remove the toothed pulley from the auxiliary shaft. Refer to **FIG 1:11** and remove flange 1 and seal 2 from auxiliary shaft 3. Remove the pinion which drives the oil pump, then remove the auxiliary shaft. If the auxiliary shaft bearings are worn or damaged, they must be renewed by a service station having special equipment.

Mark the position of the flywheel in relation to the crankshaft, so that the original balance of the assembly can be regained when the flywheel is refitted. Lock the flywheel against rotation by suitable means, then remove the fixing bolts and lift off the flywheel.

Remove the covers, seals and gaskets from each end of the crankcase, as shown in **FIG 1:12**. Remove the big-end caps as shown in **FIG 1:13**, keeping caps and bearing shells in the correct order for refitting in their original positions if not to be renewed. Carefully scrape away any carbon ridges found at the tops of the cylinder bores, then remove the piston and connecting rod assemblies, again keeping the components in the correct order. Remove the main bearing caps as shown in **FIG 1:13**, then collect the crankshaft thrust washers from the main bearing position nearest to the flywheel, as shown in **FIG 1:14**, keeping parts in the correct order if not to be renewed. Remove the crankshaft and collect the upper main bearing shells, noting their positions.

Reassembly:

Reassembly of the engine is a reversal of the dismantling procedure, after servicing the components according to the instructions in the appropriate sections of this chapter. Renew all oil seals and gaskets and use new tab washers, lockwashers and self-locking nuts. During reassembly, all moving parts should be coated with engine oil, paying particular attention to main and big-end bearings and to the pistons and cylinder bores.

When refitting crankcase end covers, make sure that the flywheel end cover is centralised as indicated by the arrows in **FIG 1:15** and use the tabs arrowed in **FIG 1:16** to centralise the timing side cover, before tightening down.

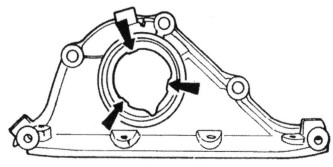

FIG 1:16   Aligning crankcase cover, timing gear side

1:5 Cylinder block

Thoroughly clean the cylinder block and examine for cracks or other damage, particularly to the machined joint faces. Check the condition of the cylinder bores. If these are scratched, ovalised or excessively worn a rebore will be necessary. If the reboring operation would remove too much metal, dry cylinder liners can be fitted. In either case, the work must be carried out by a specialist service station.

1:6 Timing belt renewal

Refer to **Section 1:8** and remove the camshaft cover. Remove the sparking plugs so that the engine can be turned easily, then align the engine so that No 4 (flywheel end) cylinder is at TDC on the firing stroke. To do this, either push the car forward in top gear or rotate the engine by means of a spanner on the crankshaft pulley nut, turning in a clockwise direction when viewed from the pulley end. The engine is correctly aligned when the timing mark on the crankshaft pulley aligns with the TDC mark on the cover, with the camshaft pulley timing mark aligned with the cast finger on the support in the case of a 1300 engine or with the pointer on the belt guard in the case of a 1500 engine and the cam lobes for No 4 cylinder pointing upwards by equal amounts. The 1300 engine camshaft pulley timing mark is visible through the hole provided in the cover. The engine will be aligned correctly once in every two revolutions. **Never turn the engine backwards as slack will develop in the timing belt and this may cause the belt to jump the pulley teeth and affect engine timing.**

Refer to **FIG 1:17**. Remove the upper bolts securing timing cover 1, then remove the righthand guard from beneath the engine and remove the cover lower securing bolt. Detach the cover.

Loosen alternator fixings 4 and 5, swing the alternator towards the engine and remove drive belt 3. With top gear selected and the handbrake applied to lock the engine, slacken the securing nut for crankshaft pulley 2. Remove the nut and the pulley, collecting the locating key.

On models with emission control systems, remove the two bolts through the rear of air pump 8 and support brackets 7, then loosen the bolt through the top of the pump. Move the pump to slacken its toothed drive belt, then remove the belt from the pulleys.

FIG 1:17   Timing cover removal

Key to Fig 1:17   1 Cover   2 Crankshaft pulley   3 V-belt
4, 5 Alternator fixings   6 Bracket   7 Support brackets
8 Air pump

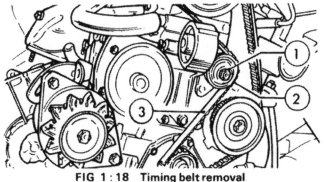

FIG 1:18   Timing belt removal

Key to Fig 1:18   1 Locknut   2 Tensioner pulley
3 Toothed belt

17

FIG 1 : 19 Timing belt, pulleys and timing marks, 1300 engine

Key to Fig 1 : 19   1 Camshaft pulley   2 Timing mark
3 Fixed timing mark   4 Tensioner nut   5 Fixed timing
mark   6 Crankshaft pulley   7 Timing mark   8 Auxiliary
shaft pulley 9 Tensioner pivot 10 Idler pulley 11 Toothed
belt

FIG 1 : 20   The 1500 engine valve timing marks

Key to Fig 1 : 20   1 Camshaft drive pulley   2 Pointer
3 Timing mark   4 Fixed timing mark   5 Pulley timing
mark   6 Belt guard   7 Camshaft pulley   8 Tensioning
pulley

Check that the timing marks are correctly aligned as previously described, rotating the engine forwards again to realign, if necessary. Refer to **Chapter 3** and remove the distributor, without turning the engine at all. Refer to **FIG 1 : 18** and loosen the idler pulley locknut 1. Push-in on the support to release belt tension, then tighten the locknut to secure tensioner in retracted position. Remove the toothed timing belt 3, first from the idler pulley then from the remaining pulleys. **Do not turn either the camshaft or crankshaft while the belt is removed, otherwise valves may contact pistons and cause serious damage.**

Install the new belt first over the crankshaft pulley, then over the auxiliary shaft and camshaft pulleys, keeping the belt taut between pulleys. Note that the camshaft pulley may have to be turned very slightly to engage pulley and belt teeth correctly. Carefully twist the belt over the idler pulley, taking care to avoid kinking or straining the belt, which may damage the internal construction. Make sure that the timing marks are still correctly aligned, removing the belt and adjusting slightly if necessary. Installation of the timing belt is shown in **FIG 1 : 19**.

Slacken idler pulley locknut 4 and allow tensioner to take up slack in the belt, then retighten the nut. Push the car forwards in gear so that the engine is rotated through half a turn of the crankshaft, then carry out the tensioner setting again as just described. Now push the car forward to turn the engine through another half turn until the TDC point for No 4 cylinder is reached, then check for exact alignment of all timing marks. If incorrect, the timing belt must be removed again and the tensioning procedure restarted. If correct, finally reset the tensioner as before, then torque tighten the idler pulley locknut.

Refit the remaining components in the reverse order of removal, tensioning air pump drive belt as described in **Section 1 : 15** (where fitted) and alternator drive belt as described in **Chapter 4**. On completion, refit the distributor and adjust ignition timing as described in **Chapter 3**.

1 : 7 Valve timing

1300 models:

Valve timing can be checked by rotating the engine until it is set at the firing point for No 4 cylinder with the mark on the crankshaft pulley correctly aligned with the TDC mark, as described in **Section 1 : 6**. The mark on the camshaft pulley should then be correctly aligned with the finger on the support (see **FIG 1 : 19**). If alignment is incorrect by a small amount, remove the timing belt as described in **Section 1 : 6**, turn the camshaft pulley slightly until correctly aligned, then refit the belt. Note that camshaft and crankshaft pulleys must not be turned independently by more than a few degrees unless the camshaft is removed from the cylinder head or the cylinder head and camshaft assembly is removed from the block, otherwise valves may contact pistons and cause serious damage.

If valve timing is to be set after engine overhaul procedures have been carried out, make sure that the crankshaft timing marks are correctly aligned, with the piston for No 4 cylinder (flywheel end) at the top of its bore, before installing the cylinder head or camshaft, whichever is the case. Note that the camshaft pulley must be fitted to the camshaft and rotated to the correct position, so that the timing marks will align as shown in **FIG 1 : 19**, before cylinder head and/or camshaft assembly

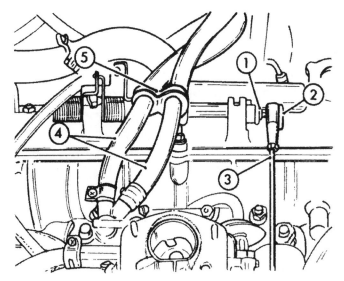

FIG 1 : 21   Disconnecting hoses and throttle linkage

Key to Fig 1 : 21   1 Ball connector   2 Clip   3 Throttle rod   4 Expansion tank hose   5 Union   6 Reaction rod

is fitted and tightened down. If this is not done, engine damage may occur. Final installation of the timing belt is described in **Section 1 : 6**. Note that the ignition timing must always be checked and reset as necessary after carrying out valve timing procedures (see **Chapter 3**).

1500 models:

Follow the procedure and warnings described earlier for the 1300 engine, but refer to **FIG 1 : 20** and note that the camshaft pulley timing mark 3 must be aligned with the pointer 2 on the belt guard.

1 : 8 Camshaft removal and refitting

Removal:

Refer to **Section 1 : 9** and carry out the necessary removal instructions to disconnect all items from the camshaft cover and housing, noting that there is no need to drain the cooling system. Remove the fixing nuts and washers and detach the camshaft cover and gasket. Remove the timing belt as described in **Section 1 : 6**.

Slacken the nuts securing camshaft housing to cylinder head alternately and evenly to avoid distortion, then remove the nuts and washers and lift off the camshaft housing assembly and gasket.

Lock the camshaft pulley against rotation by suitable means, then straighten the tab washer and slacken the pulley securing bolt. Remove bolt, washer and pulley. Remove the cover and gasket from the opposite end of the housing, noting the locations of drive gear components on early models with distributor driven from camshaft. Carefully withdraw the camshaft from housing, towards the side opposite the pulley, taking care not to damage bearings or cam lobes.

Examine the cams and bearing surfaces for wear or damage. The camshaft should be renewed if excessive wear or scoring is evident, or if the shaft is out of true. Refer to **Technical Data** for dimensions of the camshaft bearings and journals. Note that, due to the need for special equipment, the renewal of camshaft bearings should be carried out by a service station. The camshaft housing oil seal should be renewed if worn, damaged or

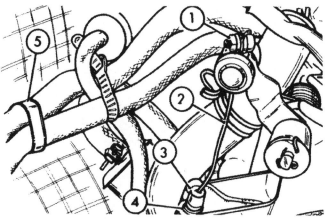

FIG 1 : 22   Disconnecting accelerator cable

Key to Fig 1 : 22   1 Stop bolt   2 Accelerator cable   3 Seal   4 Clip   5 Clamp

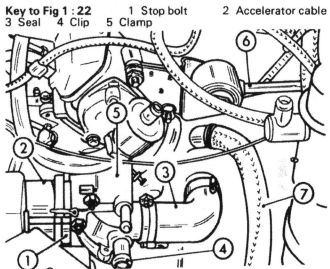

FIG 1 : 23   Disconnecting hoses and reaction rod

Key to Fig 1 : 23   1 Outlet hose   2 Inlet hose   3 Pump hose   4 Expansion tank hose   5 Union   6 Reaction rod   7 Hose

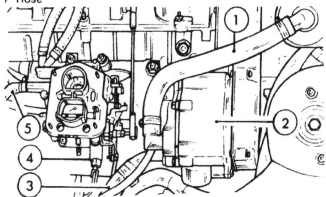

FIG 1 : 24   Disconnecting hoses and wiring

Key to Fig 1 : 24   1 Hose   2 Air pump   3 Air hose   4 Thermoswitch   5 Hose

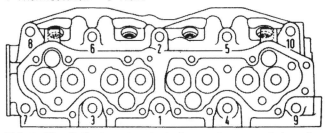

FIG 1 : 25   Cylinder head bolt and nut tightening sequence

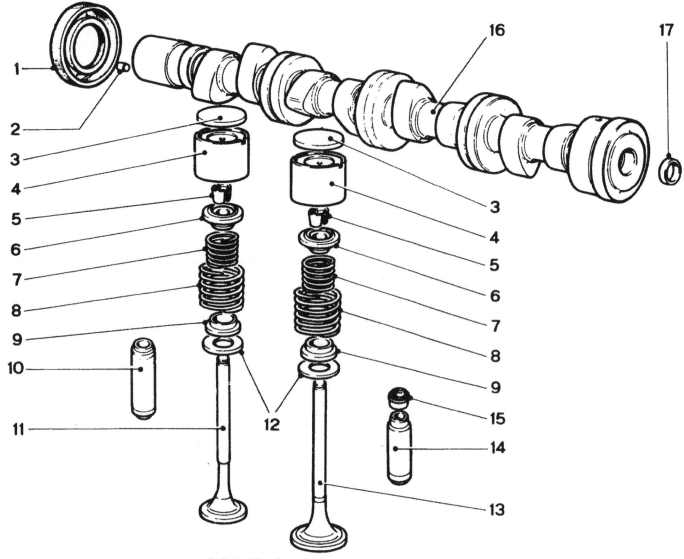

FIG 1 : 26   Camshaft and valve gear components

Key to Fig 1 : 26   1 Seal   2 Pin   3 Adjustment shim   4 Tappet   5 Cotters   6 Valve spring seat   7 Inner valve spring   8 Outer valve spring   9 Valve spring seat   10 Valve guide   11 Exhaust valve   12 Washers   13 Inlet valve   14 Valve guide   15 Seal   16 Camshaft   17 Bush

leaking by carefully removing the old seal from the bore and driving a new seal squarely into place.

Refitting:

Lubricate the cam lobes, journals and oil seal lips with engine oil, then carefully insert the camshaft taking care not to damage the oil seal. Align the pulley with the dowel on the camshaft, fit a new tab washer, tighten the bolt and lock by bending up the tab. Refit the camshaft housing in the reverse order of removal, making sure that the pulley is

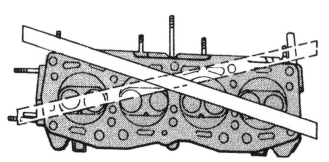

FIG 1:27   Checking cylinder head for distortion

correctly aligned (see **Section 1 : 7**) before fitting and tightening down. Use new gaskets throughout and tighten fixings alternately and evenly to avoid distortion. Before installing the camshaft cover check, and if necessary, adjust valve clearances as described in **Section 1 : 11**.

1 : 9 Removing and refitting cylinder head

Removal:

Refer to **Chapter 4** and drain the cooling system, then remove the air cleaner assembly as described in **Chapter 2**. Refer to **FIG 1 : 21** and disconnect the two fuel hoses 4 from carburetter, then pull hoses and grommets out of bracket 5. Slide spring clip 2 from ball connector 1 for throttle rod 3, then disconnect rod from connector. Disconnect HT leads from sparking plugs. Disconnect vacuum hose for distributor from fitting at cylinder head.

Refer to **FIG 1 : 22** and remove stop bolt 1 from accelerator cable 2. Slide seal 3 from cable, then remove the clip 4 securing cable to camshaft cover. Remove the cable.

Refer to **FIG 1:23** and disconnect water outlet hose 1, inlet hose 2, pump hose 3 and expansion tank hose 4 from union 5. Remove bolt securing reaction rod 6 in bracket and move rod away from work area. Disconnect hose 7 from exhaust shroud.

Refer to **FIG 1:24** and disconnect wires from thermoswitch 4 on carburetter. Disconnect hose 5 and, if an air pump is fitted, disconnect hoses 1 and 3 from air pump 2. Disconnect the exhaust pipe at the manifold flange. Remove the timing belt as described in **Section 1:6**.

Slacken the cylinder head retaining bolts and nuts in the reverse order of that shown in **FIG 1:25**, then remove the bolts and nuts and lift off the cylinder head complete with exhaust manifold, inlet manifold and carburetter. Remove and discard the cylinder head gasket.

Refitting:

Clean all traces of old gasket material from the head and block, taking care not to damage the joint face of the light alloy cylinder head. Fit a new gasket to the cylinder block, making sure that the gasket is the right way up by checking that each hole in the gasket matches the appropriate bore in the cylinder block surface. Make sure that the engine is correctly aligned as described in **Section 1:6** and the camshaft sprocket correctly aligned as described in **Section 1:7** before installing the cylinder head. Fit the head in place, maintaining camshaft sprocket alignment, then install the retaining bolts and nuts finger tight. Torque tighten the bolts and nuts, keeping to the order shown in **FIG 1:25**. Refit the remaining components in the reverse order of removal, making sure that neither camshaft nor crankshaft are turned before the timing belt has been correctly installed as described in **Section 1:6**. On completion, check ignition timing as described in **Chapter 3**, then fill and bleed the cooling system as described in **Chapter 4**.

1:10 Servicing cylinder head and valves

Dismantling:

Remove the thermostat housing complete with thermostat and remove the toothed belt protective cover. Refer to **Section 1:8** and remove the camshaft and housing assembly.

FIG 1:26 shows camshaft and valve gear components. **Note that all valve gear components must be marked or stored in the correct order for refitting in their original positions if not to be renewed.** Remove the tappets with their adjustment shims, then remove exhaust manifold and inlet manifold with carburetter from cylinder head. Discard the flange gaskets and use new ones when reassembling.

Use a suitable valve spring compressor to remove the valve gear from the cylinder head. With the springs compressed, remove the split taper collets then remove the compressor tool and collect the valve, springs, spring seats and washers.

Servicing:

Cylinder head:

Check the cylinder head for distortion, using a metal straightedge on the joint face as shown in **FIG 1:27**. With straightedge held against the surface, it should not be possible to fit a 0.05mm (0.002in) feeler gauge between the straightedge and joint face at any point. If distortion is evident, the cylinder head should be resurfaced at a specialist service station. Note that the amount of metal that can be removed in this operation is limited. After resurfacing, depth of combustion chambers should be checked using special gauge A.96216. With the shaped gauge held vertically and fitted in the combustion chamber contours, it should not be possible to fit a 0.25mm (0.01in) feeler gauge between either outer shoulder of the gauge and the cylinder head joint face. If depth of any chamber is insufficient, a new cylinder head will be required.

Cylinder head decarbonising and reseating of valves is described later.

Valves:

When the valves have been cleaned of carbon deposits they must be inspected for serviceability. Valves with bent stems or badly burned heads must be renewed. Valves that are pitted can be recut at a service station, but if they are too far gone for this remedial treatment, new valves will be required. The correct valve seat angles are quoted in **Technical Data**.

Valve guides:

Valve guides that are worn or scored must be renewed. As the guides must be pressed into or out of place, reamed to obtain the correct running clearance if necessary, then the valve seat recut to ensure concentricity, this work should be carried out by a service station having the necessary special equipment.

Valve seat inserts:

Valve seat inserts that are pitted or burned must be refaced or, if they are too far gone for remedial treatment, renewed. As either operation requires the use of special equipment, this work should be carried out by a service station. The correct valve seat angles at cylinder head inserts are quoted in **Technical Data**.

Valve springs:

Test the valve springs by referring to **Technical Data** and loading each spring by the stated amount and checking that the compressed length is not less than the figure given. Alternatively, compare the efficiency of the old springs against that of a new spring. To do this, insert both the old and new springs end to end with a metal plate between them into the jaws of a vice. If the old spring has weakened, it will close up first as pressure is applied. Make sure that the assembly is kept square to prevent the springs from flying from the vice as pressure is applied. Any spring which is distorted, or which is shorter or weaker than standard, should be renewed. However, it is recommended that if any spring is defective all valve springs are renewed as a complete set.

Decarbonising and valve reseating:

Avoid the use of sharp tools which could damage the light alloy cylinder head and piston surfaces. Remove all traces of carbon deposits from the combustion chambers, inlet and exhaust ports and joint faces. If the pistons have not been removed and cleaned during previous engine

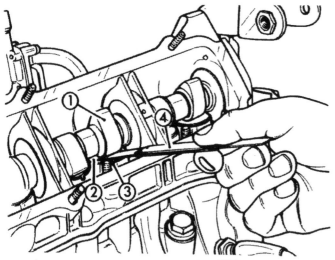

FIG 1 : 28   Checking valve clearances

Key to Fig 1 : 28   1 Cam   2 Adjusting shim   3 Tappet
4 Feeler gauge

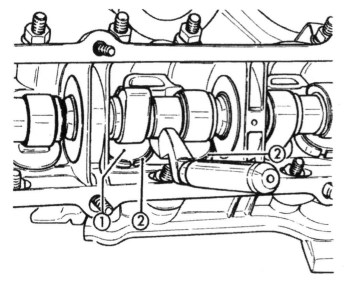

FIG 1 : 29   Adjusting valve clearances

Key to Fig 1 : 29   1 Adjustment shim   2 Tappet

dismantling, plug the waterways and oil holes in the top surface for the cylinder block with pieces of rag to prevent the entry of dirt, then clean the carbon from piston crowns. If the engine is turned to facilitate cleaning of pistons, make sure that it is correctly realigned as described in **Section 1 : 6** before the cylinder head is refitted.

The manufacturers do not recommend grinding the valves to their seats using carborundum paste in the conventional manner. Instead, valves and seats should be recut to the correct angles at a service station having the necessary special equipment. A special gauge is also necessary to check that the valve stem height above the cylinder head is correct when the work is complete.

Reassembly:

This is a reversal of the removal procedure. Lubricate the moving parts with engine oil during reassembly, paying particular attention to the camshaft lobes and bearings and the valve stems. Make sure that all valve gear components are refitted in their original positions unless renewed. On

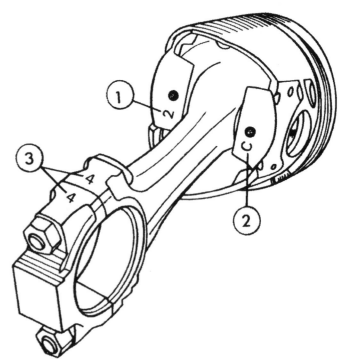

FIG 1 : 30   Piston and connecting rod assembly

Key to Fig 1 : 30   1 Piston (gudgeon) pin bore class
mark   2 Piston class mark   3 Rod/cap mating numbers

completion, check valve clearances and adjust if necessary, as described in the next section.

1 : 11   Valve clearance adjustment

The correct adjustment of valve clearances is important as it affects engine timing and performance considerably. Excessive clearance will reduce valve lift and opening duration and reduce engine performance, causing excessive wear on the valve gear components and noisy operation. Insufficient or zero clearance will again affect engine timing and, in some circumstances, can hold the valve clear of its seat. This will result in much reduced performance and the possibility of burned valves and seats. Valve clearances should be checked at the intervals recommended in **Section 1 : 2** as routine maintenance and, additionally, whenever the cylinder head has been serviced. Checking should also be carried out at any time when valve gear noise is noticed.

The valve clearances must be checked and adjusted when the engine is cold, so allow it to cool down completely before proceeding. The correct clearances are quoted in **Technical Data**.

Remove the air cleaner and the camshaft cover. Turn the engine in the forward direction by pushing the car forwards in top gear or by means of a spanner on the crankshaft pulley nut, until the cam lobe above the first valve to be checked is vertical, as shown at 1 in **FIG 1 : 28**. In either case, the engine will be easier to turn if the sparking plugs are removed first. Check the clearance between cam 1 and adjustment shim 2 in tappet 3, using a feeler gauge 4 of the correct thickness. Work in this manner until all valve clearances have been checked, noting the clearance reading for each valve as it is taken. If any clearance is incorrect, adjustment must be carried out in the following manner.

Turn the engine until the cam lobe above the valve in question is pointing downwards, holding the valve fully open. Position special tool A.60421 or similar to lock the tappet in the fully depressed position, then turn the engine until the cam lobe is vertical as shown in **FIG 1 : 29**. Use compressed air to eject the adjustment shim from the tappet, applying the air jet through the tappet slot. Alternatively, use a suitable pointed tool to remove the shim.

Note the number on the removed shim and determine the thickness required for the new shim, using the clearance measurement taken earlier. Select a new shim of the correct thickness and fit it to the tappet. Turn the engine until the cam lobe contacts the shim, then remove the holding tool and recheck the clearance. The shims must be installed with the numbered side facing the tappet and away from the camshaft. Adjustment shims are available in thicknesses from 3.25 to 4.70mm, in steps of 0.05mm.

1 : 12 Pistons and connecting rods

Pistons and connecting rods can be removed with the engine in situ, but if it is later found that attention to the cylinder bores or crankshaft journals is required, it will be necessary to remove the engine as described in **Section 1 : 3**.

Removal :

Remove the cylinder head as described in **Section 1 : 9** and the sump as described in **Section 1 : 13**. Turn the engine by means of a spanner on the crankshaft pulley securing nut to bring each big-end bearing in turn to an accessible position. Check for a ridge of carbon at the top of the cylinder bore, carefully scraping this away if necessary, taking care not to damage the bore surface. Remove the connecting rod cap nuts and detach the cap with lower shell bearing. Release the connecting rod from the crankpin and carefully push piston and connecting rod assembly through the top of the bore to remove. Keep all parts, including the bearing shells, in the correct order for refitting in their original positions and the same way round ; if not to be renewed. **FIG 1 : 30** shows piston gudgeon pin bore class mark 1, piston class letter 2 and mating numbers for connecting rod and cap 3. When the assemblies are installed, the matching numbers 3 must face towards the auxiliary shaft side of the engine.

Servicing:

Connecting rods and bearings:

Examine connecting rods carefully and renew any found damaged or distorted. If there has been a big-end bearing failure, the crankpin must be examined for damage and for transfer of metal to its surface. The oilway in the crankshaft must be checked to ensure that there is no obstruction. Big-end bearing clearance can be checked by the use of Plastigage, which is the trade name for a precisely calibrated plastic filament. The filament is laid along the bearing to be measured for working clearance, the bearing cap fitted and the nuts tightened to the correct torque. The bearing is then dismantled and the width of the flattened filament measured with the scale supplied with the material. The bearing clearance can then be read off the scale. Both main and big-end bearing clearances are

Note that each main bearing must be measured separately and that none of the remaining caps must be fitted during the operation. The bearing surfaces must be clean and free from oil and the crankshaft must not be turned during the measuring procedure. The point at which the measurement is taken must be close to the respective dead centre position and no hammer blows must be applied to the bearing or cap.

Place a length of plastic filament identical to the width of the bearing along the crankshaft journal, then fit the main or big-end bearing cap with bearing shells and tighten to the specified torque.

Remove the bearing cap and measure the width of the flattened filament to obtain the running clearance for that bearing. Clearances are given in **Technical Data**. If running clearance is too high, new bearing shells must be selected by the measurement procedure to bring running clearance to within specified limits.

If crankshaft bearing journals are excessively worn or damaged in any way, the journals must be reground to accept suitable undersize bearing shells, this being a specialist job.

Pistons and rings:

Clean carbon deposits from the piston crowns, taking care not to damage the light alloy surfaces, then gently ease the rings from their grooves and remove them over the tops of the pistons. Keep all rings in the correct order for refitting in their original positions, if not to be renewed. Clean carbon from the piston ring grooves, for which job a piece broken from an old piston ring and ground to a chisel point will prove an ideal tool. Inspect the pistons for score marks or any signs of seizure, which would dictate renewal. Refer to **Technical Data** for widths of piston rings and ring grooves.

Fit the piston rings one at a time to the bore from which they were removed, pushing them down with the correct inverted piston to ensure squareness. Measure the gap between the ends of the ring while it is positioned in the bore, using feeler gauges as shown in **FIG 1 : 31**. Remove the ring from the bore and refer to **FIG 1 : 32**. Fit the ring 1 into groove of piston 2 from which it was removed, then

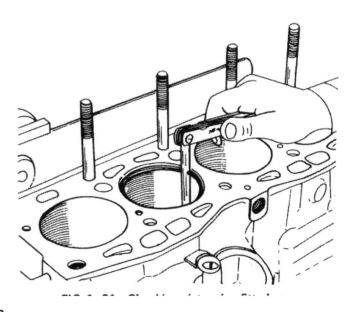

measure side clearance using feeler gauges 3. Compare the measurements taken with the figures given in **Technical Data**. If the clearance measurement in either test is at or near the wear limit, new rings must be fitted. Excessive ring clearance can be responsible for high oil consumption and poor engine performance.

Check the cylinder bores for score marks and remove glaze and carbon deposits. Badly scored or worn surfaces will dictate a rebore to accept new pistons, this being a specialist job. The fitting of new pistons to connecting rods must be carried out by a fully equipped service station, due to the need for special tools and press equipment to remove and refit the gudgeon pins. Check the clearance of each piston in its bore. To do this, measure the outside diameter of the piston and the inside diameter of the bore and compare the two figures. Piston diameter should always be measured at right angles to the gudgeon pin bore. If clearances are excessive, new pistons may be all that is required if the bores are in good condition, but if the bores are worn reboring at a specialist service station will be necessary.

Refitting :

This is a reversal of the removal procedure. Carefully fit the rings to the correct piston grooves and stagger the ring end gaps equally around the piston circumference. The positioning of the assemblies in the block varies according to which way the piston and connecting rod are fitted together. The manufacturers once instructed that the piston is fitted to the connecting rod with the number away from the piston bore offset. In this case the assembly was fitted in the block with the numbers towards the auxiliary shaft. Later instructions say the piston is fitted to the connecting rod with the numbers facing towards the piston bore offset, and the assembly fitted in the block with the numbers away from the auxiliary shaft. It is important that the piston assembly is fitted correctly with the piston bore offset away from the auxiliary shaft. The piston crown indents will be towards the manifold side of the engine. Lubricate the shell bearings and install the cap with lower bearing, making

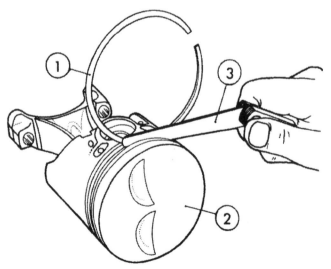

FIG 1 : 32 Checking piston ring side clearance

Key to Fig 1 : 32   1 Piston ring   2 Piston   3 Feeler gauge

sure that it is the correct way round. Fit the cap nuts and tighten to the specified torque.

1 : 13 Lubrication system
Sump removal :

This work can be carried out with the engine in situ. Raise the rear of the car for access to the underside and support safely on floor stands. Fit a suitable engine support tool or attach suitable engine lifting equipment and tighten sufficiently to take the weight of engine and transmission assembly. Remove the lower crossmember which supports the engine. Remove the drain plug and allow the sump oil to drain into a suitable container, then refit and tighten the plug.

Remove the bolts and washers securing sump to crankcase, then detach the sump and remove and discard the gasket. If necessary, remove the inner plate from sump.

Refitting :

Clean sludge from inside the sump and clean all traces of old gasket material from sump and crankcase joint faces. Install the sump, using a new gasket, tightening the fixing bolts alternately and evenly to avoid distortion. Refit the crossmember and remove the engine lifting equipment, then refill the sump with oil to the correct level on the dipstick. Run the engine and check for leaks at the sump gasket, then switch off and allow the oil to drain down into the sump before rechecking the level.

Oil pump :
Removal :

Remove the sump as described previously. Refer to **FIG 1 : 33**. Remove the three fixing bolts and detach oil pump 4 complete with strainer assembly.

Servicing :

Remove the fixing screws and detach strainer assembly from oil pump. Thoroughly clean oil and dirt from the assembly, blowing through the pipe and strainer with compressed air. Make sure that all dirt is removed from beneath relief valve 4 and pump housing 5 (see **FIG 1 : 34**). Check the relief valve spring for damage or distortion. Free length of the spring should be 40.2mm and length should not be less than 21mm under a load of 5.0daN. Renew the spring if any faults are found.

Check pump internal clearances using feeler gauges and a metal straightedge. Backlash between the two gears should be 0.15mm (0.006in), with a wear limit of 0.25mm (0.01in). Check clearance between gears and housing joint face as shown in **FIG 1 : 35**. Clearance between gear surface and straightedge should be 0.020 to 0.105mm (0.0008 to 0.004in), with a wear limit of 0.15mm (0.006in). Check geartooth to housing clearance as shown in **FIG 1 : 36**. This should be 0.11 to 0.18mm (0.004 to 0.007in), with a wear limit of 0.25mm (0.01in). Excessive clearance in any test will dictate renewal of the pump gears, pump housing or both. Renew the pump cover if the inner surface is worn or scored. When the gears are refitted to the housing, make sure that they rotate freely.

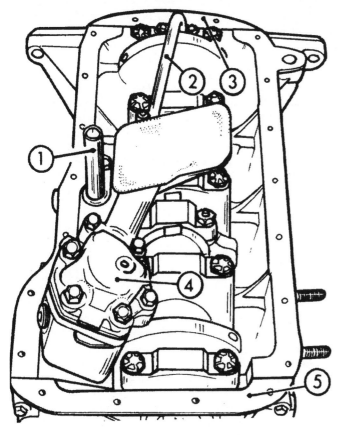

FIG 1 : 33   Oil pump removal

Key to Fig 1 : 33   1, 2 Oil return pipes   3 Flywheel end
cover plate   4 Oil pump   5 Timing gear end cover plate

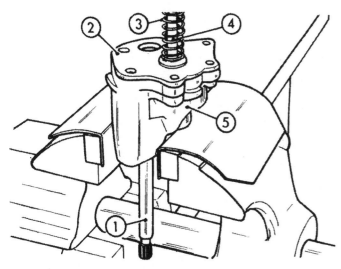

FIG 1 : 34   Oil pump with strainer removed

Key to Fig 1 : 34   1 Pump drive shaft   2 Cover   3 Relief
valve spring   4 Relief valve   5 Housing

Refitting:

This is a reversal of the removal procedure, lubricating
the pump gears with engine oil and using new gaskets
throughout.

Oil filter renewal:

The oil filter is of the renewable element fullflow type, a
bypass valve being incorporated in the filter mounting to

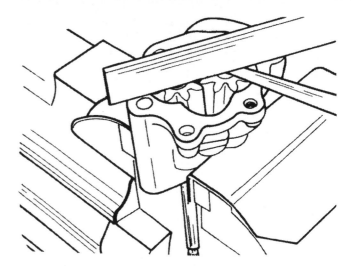

FIG 1 : 35   Checking pump gear to cover clearance

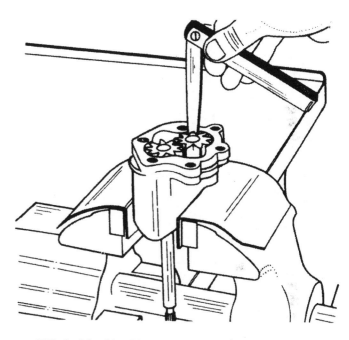

FIG 1 : 36   Checking pump gear to housing clearance

allow oil to pass directly from the pump to the engine,
bypassing the filter, if the filter element should become
blocked. The filter should be renewed at the intervals
recommended in **Section 1 : 2**.

Oil filter installation is shown in **FIG 1 : 37**. Before
removal, place an oil tray beneath the unit as some oil will
escape even if the sump has been drained. Unscrew the
filter, using a strap type tool if it proves difficult to turn by
hand. Discard the used cartridge.

Clean the mounting on the engine then lightly coat the
seal on the new filter cartridge with engine oil. Make sure
that the seal is correctly fitted, then screw the new filter
into place until it just contacts the seating. From this point,
tighten a further three-quarters of a turn by hand only. Do
not overtighten the filter or oil leaks may result. On
completion, start the engine and check for oil leaks around
the filter unit. Switch off the engine, then check and top up
the oil level.

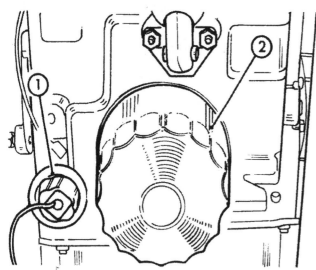

FIG 1 : 37   Oil pressure sender unit 1 and oil filter 2

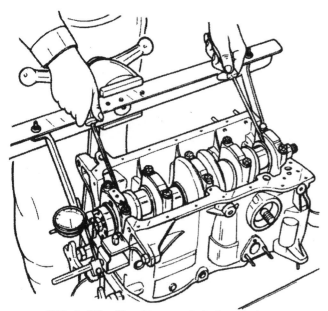

FIG 1 : 38   Checking crankshaft end play

1 : 14 Crankshaft, bearings and flywheel

Crankshaft removal :

Remove the engine as described in **Section 1 : 3**, then dismantle as described in **Section 1 : 4**. Before removing the crankshaft, check end play as shown in **FIG 1 : 38**, using a suitable dial gauge assembly. Use two screwdrivers to lever the crankshaft from one end of its travel to the other and note the total gauge reading. Alternatively, lever the crankshaft as far towards the timing gear end as possible, then use feeler gauges to check clearance between crankshaft flange and thrust washer at flywheel end. End play should be 0.055 to 0.265mm (0.0021 to 0.0104in). Excessive end float will dictate the fitting of new thrust washers when the crankshaft is refitted. Remove the fixing bolts and the main bearing caps, keeping the caps and lower shell bearings in the correct order for refitting in their original positions, if not to be renewed. Lift out the crankshaft, then collect the upper shell bearings and keep in the correct order. Crankshaft

bearing clearance can be checked by the use of Plastigage, as described in **Section 1 : 12**.

Refitting :

This is a reversal of the removal procedure, making sure that the retaining tongues of the shell bearings are free in the housings and that the shells protrude by the same amount on each side of the bearings. Fit the top half thrust washer in place, ensuring that the anti-friction face, which has oil slots, is against the crankshaft shoulder. Lubricate shell bearings and thrust washers with engine oil. Refit the remaining components in the reverse order of removal.

Flywheel :

The flywheel can be removed with the engine in situ, after the clutch assembly has been removed as described in **Chapter 5**. Mark the relationship of flywheel to crankshaft flange before removal, so that it can be refitted in its original position to retain the balance of the assembly. Lock the flywheel against rotation by suitable means, then slacken the retaining bolts. Remove the bolts and lift off the flywheel.

Examine the surface of the flywheel against which the clutch plate operates for cracks or scoring. Slight damage of this nature is unimportant, but deeper damage will dictate resurfacing or renewal. If the ring gear is damaged it can be renewed, but this work should be carried out by a service station having the necessary heating and press equipment.

Refit the flywheel in the reverse order of removal, tightening the retaining bolts alternately and evenly to the specified torque.

1 : 15 Emission control systems

Closed crankcase ventilation system :

The purpose of this system is to prevent crankcase breather fumes from escaping to atmosphere. This is achieved by piping the fumes to the air cleaner so that they are consumed by the engine. The system is fitted to all engines and is shown semi-diagrammatically in **FIG 1 : 39**. A liquid/vapour separator is included in the system and, to preclude the ignition of vapour in the crankcase from any backfiring, a flame trap is fitted. The control valve meters the passage of fumes at idling conditions but, at conditions of greater throttle openings, allows full flow of fumes.

Every 20,000km (12,000 miles), the valve and the flame trap should be washed in petrol, dried thoroughly and refitted.

The air injection and catalyst system :

This system is shown diagrammatically in **FIGS 1 : 40** and **1 : 41**. It is only provided on models exported to countries in which it is mandatory.

By injecting clean air into the incandescent exhaust gases immediately after they leave the combustion chambers, combustion of unburned hydrocarbons is encouraged and the final exhaust gases leaving the exhaust tail pipe will contain less carbon monoxide (but more of the less noxious carbon dioxide) than if the gases were untreated. By passing the exhaust gases through a

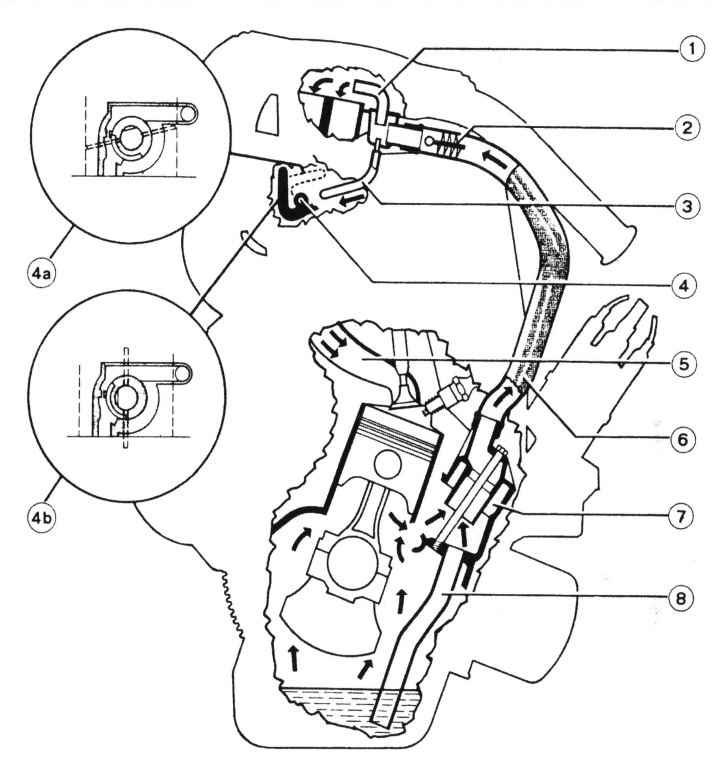

FIG 1 : 39 The closed crankcase ventilation system

Key to Fig 1 : 39   1 Emission feedback line to air cleaner   2 Flame trap   3 Air cleaner-to-control valve line
4 Control valve   4a Control valve during engine idling   4b Control valve during engine full speed   5 Intake manifold
6 Sump-to-air cleaner line   7 Cyclone liquid/vapour separator   8 Oil drain line into sump

catalyst, the nitrous oxide content of the exhaust gases is reduced and, to ensure that the renewal of the catalyst at the appropriate mileage interval is not neglected, a warning light comes on at a pre-set interval. The warning light switch is activated by a transmission driven cam which trips at approximately 40,000km (24,000 miles) after the catalyst was last renewed and the switch reset. Until this service is carried out, the warning light continues to show when the ignition is on.

The air is provided by an engine driven pump (see 13 in **FIG 1 : 2**). To ensure that the system only operates at relevant engine conditions, a diverter valve controls the supply of pumped air to the injectors.

Maintaining the correct drive belt tension, renewing the air pump filter and removing and refitting the pump are operations which can be carried out by an owner. If the serviceability of the diverter valve or other items is suspect, an authorised agent should be consulted. The renewal of

27

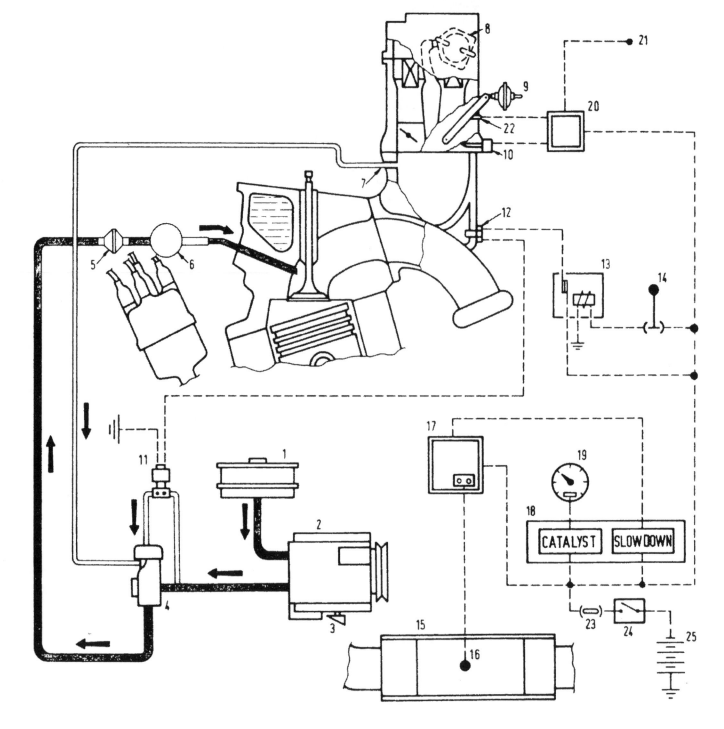

FIG 1 : 40   The air injection system

Key to Fig 1 : 40   1 Air filter   2 Air injection pump   3 Excess pressure valve   4 Diverter valve   5 Check valve
6 Air injection manifold   7 Diverter valve control signal intake   8 Automatic choke system   9 Dashpot   10 Idle
stop solenoid   11 Electro-valve (normally closed)   12 Diverter valve control thermoswitch   13 Relay   14 Gearshift
lever switch (open with transmission in neutral)   15 Catalytic converter   16 Thermocouple   17 Control unit
18 Warning device panel   19 Odometer   20 Tachometer switch   21 From ignition coil   22 Inhibitor switch   23 Fuse
24 Ignition switch   25 Battery

the catalyst and the resetting of the warning light switch should be carried out by an authorised agent.

Air pump filter renewal :

Refer to **FIG 1 : 42**. Remove wing nut 1 at the bottom of the filter housing 3. Remove and discard the filter

element 2. Install a new element, refit the housing and tighten the wing nut.

Air pump drive belt tension :

The tension of the toothed drive belt should be similar to that of the camshaft drive belt which is automatically

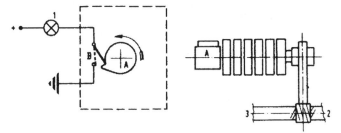

FIG 1 : 41   The catalyst warning light system

Key to Fig 1 : 41   1 Catalyst warning light   2 To
speedometer odometer   3 From transmission   A Cam
drum   B Resetting switch

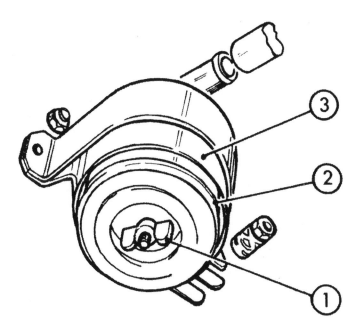

FIG 1 : 42   Air pump filter renewal

Key to Fig 1 : 42   1 Wing nut   2 Filter element   3 Filter
housing

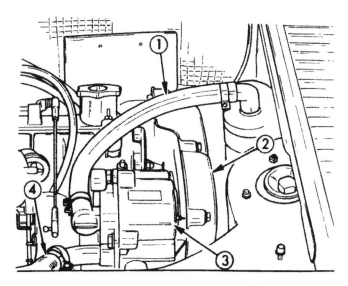

FIG 1 : 43   Air pump removal

Key to Fig 1 : 43   1 Hose   2 Timing belt cover   3 Pump
4 Hose

tensioned by its tensioner pulley. To adjust the air pump
belt tension, loosen the air pump mounting bolts, swing
the pump away from the engine, tighten the bolts and
recheck the belt tension.

Air pump removal and refitment :

Refer to **FIG 1 : 43**. Disconnect the hoses 1 and 4,
remove the camshaft drive belt cover (see **Section 1 : 6**),
remove the bolts from the support brackets at the rear of
the pump 3 and remove the bolt which secures the pump
to the bracket. Disengage the drive belt and dismount the
pump.

To refit, reverse this sequence and tension the drive belt
as described earlier.

1 : 16 Fault diagnosis

(a) Engine will not start

1 Defective coil
2 Faulty distributor capacitor
3 Dirty, pitted or incorrectly set contact points
4 Ignition leads loose or insulation faulty
5 Water on plug leads
6 Battery discharged or terminals corroded
7 Faulty or jammed starter
8 Sparking plug leads wrongly connected
9 Vapour lock in fuel pipes
10 Defective fuel pump
11 Over choking or 'pumping' accelerator pedal
12 Under choking
13 Blocked fuel filter or carburetter jets
14 Leaking valves
15 Sticking valves
16 Valve timing incorrect
17 Ignition timing incorrect

(b) Engine stops

1 Check 1, 2, 3, 4, 10, 11, 12, 13, 14, 15 in (a)
2 Retarded ignition
3 Weak mixture
4 Water in fuel system
5 Fuel tank vent blocked
6 Incorrect valve clearances

(c) Engine idles badly

1 Check 2 and 6 in (b)
2 Air leak at manifold joints
3 Slow running jet blocked or out of adjustment
4 Air leak in carburetter
5 Over rich mixture
6 Worn piston rings
7 Worn valve stems or stem bores
8 Weak valve springs

(d) Engine misfires

1 Check 1, 2, 3, 4, 5, 8, 10, 13, 14, 15, 16, 17 in (a) ; 2, 3,
4, 6 in (b)
2 Weak or broken valve springs

(e) Engine overheats (see Chapter 4)

(f) Compression low

1 Check 14, 15 in (a) ; 7, 8 in (c) ; 2 in (d)
2 Worn piston ring grooves
3 Scored or worn cylinder bores

(g) Engine lacks power

1 Check 3, 10, 11, 13, 14, 15, 16, 17 in (a); 2, 3, 4, 6 in (b); 7, 8 in (c); 2 in (d); also check (e) and (f)
2 Leaking joint washers or gaskets
3 Fouled sparking plugs
4 Automatic advance not working

(h) Burnt valves or seats

1 Check 14, 15 in (a); 6 in (b); 2 in (d); also check (e)
2 Excessive carbon around valve seat and head

(j) Sticking valves

1 Check 2 in (d)
2 Bent valve stems
3 Scored valve stems
4 Incorrect valve clearance

(k) Excessive cylinder wear

1 Check 11 in (a)
2 Lack of oil
3 Dirty oil
4 Piston rings gummed or broken
5 Badly fitting piston rings
6 Connecting rod bent

(l) Excessive oil consumption

1 Check 6, 7 in (c) and check (k)
2 Ring gaps too wide
3 Oil return holes in piston blocked
4 Scored cylinders
5 Oil level too high
6 External oil leaks

(m) Crankshaft and connecting rod bearing failure

1 Check 2 in (k)
2 Restricted oilways
3 Worn journals or crankpins
4 Loose bearing caps
5 Extremely low oil pressure
6 Damaged or faulty connecting rod

(n) Engine vibration

1 Loose alternator bolts
2 Fan blades out of balance
3 Faulty or loose engine mountings
4 Exhaust pipe mountings too tight

CHAPTER 2

THE FUEL SYSTEM

2 : 1 Description

Weber carburetters are fitted to all models covered by this manual, but carburetter type, specifications and type of choke unit (manual or automatic) vary according to year of vehicle manufacture and market territory. In standard installations, a mechanical fuel pump, operated by a short pushrod from an eccentric on the engine auxiliary shaft, supplies fuel from the tank to the carburetter through a series of pipes and flexible hoses. In certain USA models, an electrically-operated fuel pump may be fitted.

Renewable paper type air filter elements are used, contained in a casing attached to the carburetter intake. Fuel is filtered through a renewable cartridge type line filter and, additionally, through gauze type filters in fuel pump and carburetter units.

USA export models are mandatorily equipped with a fuel evaporative emission control system as described in **Section 2 : 10** to prevent fuel vapour from escaping into the atmosphere.

2 : 2 Maintenance

Idling speed :

At least every 10,000km (6000 miles), check and, if necessary, adjust the idling speed to that specified in **Technical Data** in the **Appendix**. The procedure is described in **Section 2 : 7**.

Air cleaner :

Every 10,000km (6000 miles), renew the air cleaner element as described in **Section 2 : 3**. If the car is operating in dusty terrain, this interval should be reduced to, possibly, 5000km (3000 miles) in extreme conditions.

Fuel filter :

Every 10,000km (6000 miles), renew the fuel filter as described in **Section 2 : 5**.

Throttle and choke controls :

Every 20,000km (12,000 miles), check the operation of the controls. Adjustment procedures are described in **Section 2 : 7**.

Fuel evaporative emission control system :

Every 20,000km (12,000 miles), refer to **Section 2 : 10** and have the system checked over by a fully equipped agent.

Every 40,000km (24,000 miles), fit a new activated carbon trap.

2:3 Air cleaner

To renew the air filter element, refer to **FIG 2:1** and remove the three nuts 1, then lift off cover 2. Remove and discard air filter element 1 shown in **FIG 2:2**. Wipe the

FIG 2 : 1   Air cleaner and carburetter cooling system installation (1300 model shown)

inside of casing and cover to remove oil and dirt, making sure that no foreign matter enters the carburetter air intakes, then reassemble using a new filter element.

To remove the air cleaner assembly complete, remove cover and filter element as described previously then refer to **FIG 2:1**. Loosen clamp securing air hose 3 to non-return valve 7, then disconnect hose and move it clear of air duct. Loosen clamp 5 securing air duct 4 to carburetter cooling fan 6. Remove nut and washer securing bracket 9 to engine camshaft cover, then disconnect bypass hose 8 from air cleaner. Disconnect hose from bottom of air cleaner. Release the tab washers and remove the four nuts shown at 3 in **FIG 2:2**, then remove air cleaner and fresh air duct assembly.

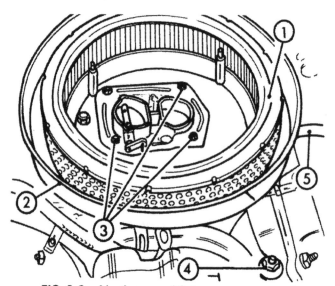

FIG 2:2   Air cleaner with top cover removed

Refit the air cleaner assembly in the reverse order of removal, using new tab washers if the originals are not in good condition. Tighten the nuts securing air cleaner to carburetter alternately and evenly, then turn up the tab washers to secure.

2:4 Carburetter cooling fan

The carburetter cooling fan operates to prevent the carburetter overheating when temperature in the engine compartment rises above a predetermined point. The fan is controlled by a thermoswitch mounted on the base of the carburetter and a relay mounted on the cooling fan support. If the fan will not operate at all, check that the vehicle interior courtesy light operates when one of the doors is opened. If the light does not operate, check the 8 amp fuse in the fusebox and renew if blown (see **Chapter 11**). If the light operates, locate the thermoswitch for the system at the rear of the carburetter. Use a short jumper lead to connect the two thermoswitch wires together. If the fan then runs, the thermostatic switch is faulty and must be renewed. If the fan does not operate, check the wiring and connections in the fan operating circuit. If these are in order the relay must be checked for correct operation, preferably by a service station having special test equipment.

Note that the carburetter cooling fan will continue to run after the engine is switched off and the ignition key removed, provided that carburetter temperature is sufficient to trigger the thermoswitch, this being normal. However, if the fan operates even when the system is cold, disconnect the grey/red wire from the thermostatic switch. If the fan then stops, the switch is faulty and must be renewed. If the fan still runs, reconnect the wire and disconnect the grey/red wire from terminal 85 on relay. If the fan still runs, the relay is defective and must be renewed. If the fan stops, there is a break in the grey/red

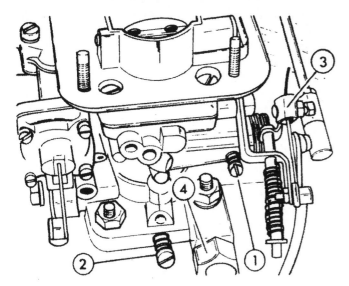

FIG 2 : 3 Typical carburetter idle adjustment screws, early USA export models

Key to Fig 2 : 3   1 Idle speed adjuster   2 Idle mixture adjuster   3 Choke control cable anchor point   4 Engine compartment cooling fan thermoswitch

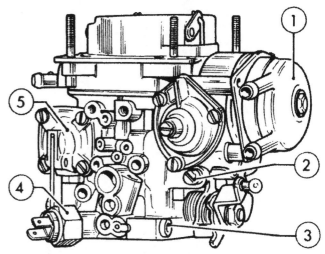

FIG 2 : 4 1500 model adjusters (34 DATR 7/250 carburetter)

Key to Fig 2 : 4   1 Automatic choke cover   2 Idle speed adjuster   3 Idle mixture adjuster (tamperproofed)   4 Engine compartment cooling fan thermoswitch   5 Accelerator pump

wire from relay to switch which must be located and repaired.

Cooling fan removal :

Refer to **FIG 2 : 1**. Disconnect wire from terminal 87 on fan relay 11. Remove the fan relay and voltage regulator 10 (if fitted). Loosen the clamp and disconnect flexible fresh air duct 4 from the fan duct. From support 13, remove two nuts at the right front and two bolts from the left rear, then remove fan and support. Remove four screws 14 securing duct to fan, then remove four screws securing fan to support.

Refit the assembly in the reverse order of removal, making sure that the black wire from the fan is under mounting nut for fan relay.

Thermoswitch removal :

Refer to **FIG 2 : 3** (1300 models) or to **FIG 2 : 4** (1500 models). Disconnect the wiring and unscrew the thermoswitch which is 4 in both illustrations. After refitting, ensure that the wiring is firm and secure.

2 : 5 Fuel filter

The fuel line filter is shown at 1 in **FIG 2 : 5**. To renew, loosen clips 2 and remove hoses 3. Discard the old filter, then fit a new one in the reverse order of removal. On completion, run the engine and check for leaks at hose connections.

2:6 Fuel pump

Testing :

Before testing the pump, ensure that the fuel tank vent system is not blocked. A blockage is indicated if the removal of the fuel filler cap results in the sound of air being drawn into the tank. If so, the vent system must be checked and cleaned.

If the vent system is clear and it is still suspected that fuel is not reaching the carburetter, disconnect the carburetter feed pipe and hold a suitable container under the end of

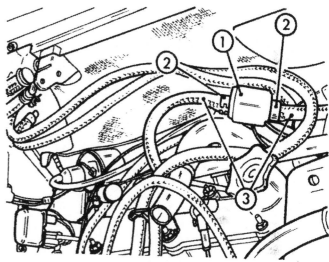

FIG 2 : 5 Fuel line filter installation

Key to Fig 2 : 5   1 In-line fuel filter   2 Hose clips   3 Hoses

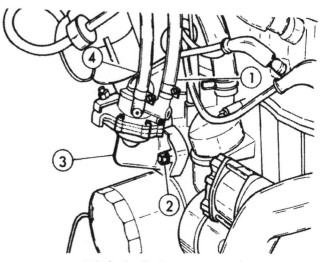

FIG 2 : 6 Fuel pump removal

Key to Fig 2 : 6   1 Inlet hose   2 Retaining nut and washer   3 Pump   4 Outlet hose

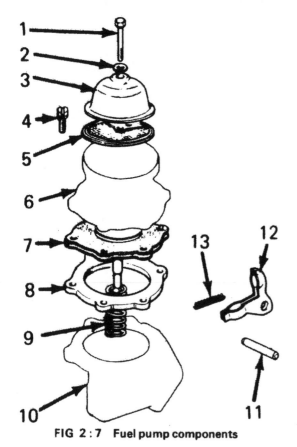

FIG 2:7   Fuel pump components

Key to Fig 2:7   1 Cover screw   2 Washer   3 Cover
4 Screw   5 Filter gauze   6 Upper body   7 Diaphragm
8 Spacer   9 Spring   10 Lower body   11 Pivot pin
12 Control lever   13 Return spring

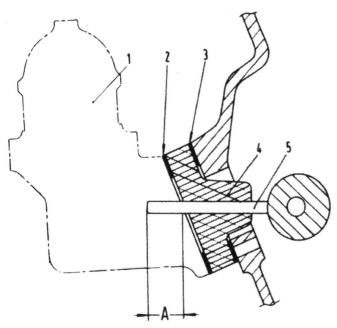

FIG 2:8   Adjusting pump pushrod projection

Key to Fig 2:8   1 Pump   2, 3 Gaskets   4 Insulator
5 Pushrod

the pipe. Turn the engine over a few times with the starter
and watch for fuel squirting from the end of the pipe,
which indicates that the pump is working. If so, check the
float needle in the carburetter for possible sticking.

Reduced fuel flow can be caused by blocked fuel pipes
or a clogged filter.

If an obstructed pipeline appears to be the cause of the
trouble, it may be cleared with compressed air. Disconnect
the pipeline at both ends. Do not pass compressed air
through the pump or the valves will be damaged. Similarly,
make sure that pipes being cleared on cars fitted with
emission control system are disconnected at both ends so
that compressed air is not passed through system
components. If there is an obstruction in the pipe leading
from the fuel tank, remove the tank filler cap before
blowing the pipe through from the opposite end.

If the pump delivers insufficient fuel, suspect an air leak
between the pump and the tank, dirt under the pump
valves or faulty valve seatings. Also check for leaks at the
pump cover seal and fixing screw washer. If no fuel is
delivered, suspect a sticking valve or a faulty pump
diaphragm.

Test the action of the pump valves by blowing and
sucking at the inlet and outlet points. Do this with the
pump in situ, using a suitable piece of pipe connected to
the pump inlet and outlet in turn. It should be possible to
blow air in through the pump inlet but not to suck air out,
and it should be possible to suck air out of the pump outlet
but not to blow air in. If the valves do not work properly
according to this test, or if the pump is defective in any
other way, the pump should be removed and serviced.

Removal :

Refer to **FIG 2:6**. Slacken the clips and detach inlet
pipe 1 and outlet pipe 4 from pump unit, plugging the
pipes to prevent leakage. Remove two nuts and washers 2
securing pump to engine, then remove pump 3 and collect
two gaskets and insulator.

Servicing :

Note that the fuel filter in the pump can be removed and
cleaned without the need for pump removal. To overhaul
the pump, dismantle the unit into the order shown in **FIG
2:7**. Thoroughly clean the filter and chamber with clean
petrol, using a small brush to remove stubborn deposits. If
the filter will not clean up or is damaged in any way it
should be renewed.

Check the diaphragm for splits, distortion or hardening
of the material. If it is not in perfect condition it should be
renewed. Check all other components for wear or damage,
renewing parts as necessary. If the valves are defective and
do not operate correctly after carefully cleaning with
petrol, the valve body must be renewed complete as the
valves cannot be renewed separately.

Reassemble the unit in the reverse order of dismantling,
lubricating the control lever and pivot with oil. Use new
gaskets, lightly coated with grease. Before tightening the
screws connecting the upper and lower bodies, operate
the control lever through half its travel so that the
diaphragm is flat. Hold in this position while alternately
and evenly tightening the screws.

Refitting:

This is a reversal of the removal procedure, but
adjustments should be carried out in the following manner
to ensure correct pump pushrod stroke.

Refer to **FIG 2:8**. Fit a new gasket 3 on the engine,
then install insulator 4 with a new 0.3mm (0.012in)
gasket 2. Fit pushrod 5, then turn the engine until projection **A** of pushrod is at a minimum. This ensures that

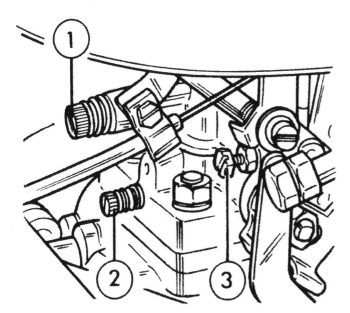

FIG 2 : 9 Typical carburetter idle adjustment screws, European models

Key to Fig 2 : 9   1 Idle speed adjuster   2 Idle mixture adjuster (volume control screw)   3 Throttle stop screw (factory-set)

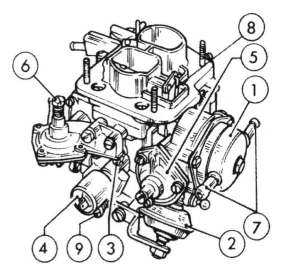

FIG 2 : 10 1300 model USA automatic choke carburetter (32 DATRA)

Key to Fig 2 : 10   1 Automatic choke cover   2 Dashpot 3 Idle speed adjuster   4 Anti run-on solenoid valve 5 Choke diaphragm housing   6 Primary throttle opening adjuster   7 Coolant feed and return hose connectors 8 Choke plate linkage   9 Idle mixture adjuster

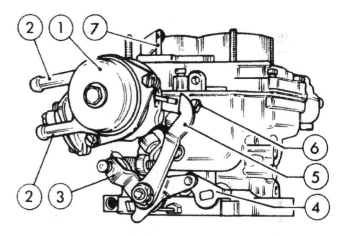

FIG 2 : 11 1500 model carburetter (34 DATR 7/250)

Key to Fig 2 : 11   1 Automatic choke cover   2 Coolant feed and return connectors   3 Primary throttle control lever   4 Secondary throttle control lever   5 Choke control lever   6 Fast-idle adjuster   7 Choke plate linkage

the pushrod is operating on the back of the cam in the engine. Under these conditions, dimension **A** should be 15.0 to 15.5mm (0.59 to 0.61in). If necessary, install a thicker or thinner gasket 3 to bring pushrod projection to within the limits stated. This done, refit the fuel pump, making sure that the pushrod correctly engages the pump operating lever. Tighten the retaining nuts alternately and evenly to avoid distortion of the flange. Reconnect the fuel pipes, then start the engine and check for fuel leaks.

Electrically-operated fuel pump :

The electrically-operated pump is not standard equipment but may be fitted to certain USA models.

The pump operates whenever the ignition is switched on. Except initially, it is controlled by the engine's oil pressure electrical system via its own relay. This arrangement ensures that if the engine stops (possibly due to it being installed), but the ignition is not switched off, the pump is deactivated.

If the pump fails to operate, suspect the electrical supply to it before suspecting a pump failure and check that there is voltage at the pump. If there is not, check the relevant fuse, relay and continuity. Remove the pump by disconnecting the wiring, uncoupling the hoses and removing the retaining bolts. Carry out the checks described earlier for the mechanical pump. Access to the filter, etc., requires the pump to be separated into two parts. No repair procedures are prescribed and if the diaphragm or valves are defective, a new pump should be fitted.

2:7 Carburetter tuning and adjustment

Adjusting carburetter controls :

Remove the air cleaner assembly for access, as described in **Section 2:3**. Have an assistant operate the accelerator pedal through a full stroke and hold it to the floor. Check that the linkage at the carburetter opens the throttle fully but without strain. Have the accelerator pedal

released, then check that the linkage moves freely to the closed position. If adjustment is necessary, slacken the locknut and adjust throttle operating rod as necessary then retighten locknut. Lightly lubricate joints in the linkage.

On models fitted with manual choke unit, operate the control in the car fully then check that the cable has moved the choke linkage at the carburetter to the fully closed position. Return the control to the fully off position, then check that the linkage at the carburetter has returned fully. There should be a small amount of slack in the cable when the control is fully home, to ensure that the choke always releases fully. If adjustment is necessary, slacken the cable clamp (see 3 in **FIG 2 : 3**) at carburetter linkage, adjust cable as necessary, then retighten clamp. Lightly lubricate moving parts of linkage.

Limitations on adjustment procedures :

Carburetters fitted to earlier 1300 engines are not tamper-proofed and not only the idling speed adjuster but also the idling mixture adjuster is readily accessible. The carburetters fitted to 1500 engines and later 1300 engines are tamper-proofed. Idling speed adjusters are unsealed, but the idling mixture adjusters are factory-sealed to discourage improper readjustment. Such re-adjustment will not normally be necessary and replacement seals which have to be fitted in the event of a factory seal having been disturbed are only available to authorised agents who are equipped with exhaust content CO meters, etc. Even if adjustment of the idling mixture seems to be necessary, **no adjustment should be attempted by an owner unless an exhaust gas analyser is used.** An owner who cannot comply with this limitation should have the adjustment carried out by an authorised agent.

Incorrect adjustment will result in exhaust gases containing excessive CO (carbon monoxide). This is not only socially offensive but is also a legal offence in countries where emission control limitations are mandatory. In describing the following adjustment procedures, it is assumed that an owner possesses, or has access to, appropriate CO measurement equipment and that this will be used to confirm that the recommended or mandatory CO maximum content will not be disregarded.

Idling speed adjustment :

Idling speed and mixture settings can only be effective if sparking plugs, contact breaker points and ignition timing are in good order, valve clearances correct and the engine at normal operating temperature (thermostat open).

With the engine at temperature, remove the air cleaner (for access reasons) as described in **Section 2:3.** Depending upon the model and carburetter type, refer to **FIG 2:3, 2:4, 2:9** or **2:10.** Start the engine and allow it to idle. Idling speed for European models should be 875 ± 25rev/min. Idling speed for USA models is marked on the tag affixed to the underside of the engine compartment lid.

If necessary, correct the idling speed by turning the idling adjuster in the appropriate direction. Refit the air cleaner assembly. This, normally, is all that will be necessary but, if the idling mixture has to be adjusted, proceed as follows.

Idling mixture adjustment :

Follow the manufacturer's instructions and **connect up an exhaust gas CO content meter.** Adjust the idling speed as described earlier.

Turn the idling mixture screw a little at a time to obtain the highest possible idling speed. Using the idling speed adjuster, bring the idling speed back to the specified rev/min. Repeat the idling mixture adjustment and again correct the idling speed. When no further increase in idling results from adjustment of the mixture screw, check the CO meter reading. Final adjustment should now be made, if necessary, to bring the CO content meter reading within the range specified in **Technical Data** or, in the case of USA models, within the range marked on the tag affixed to the underside of the engine compartment lid.

In the case of a carburetter which has been factory tamper-proofed, the mixture adjuster seal will have to be prised out or otherwise removed. After adjustment, have

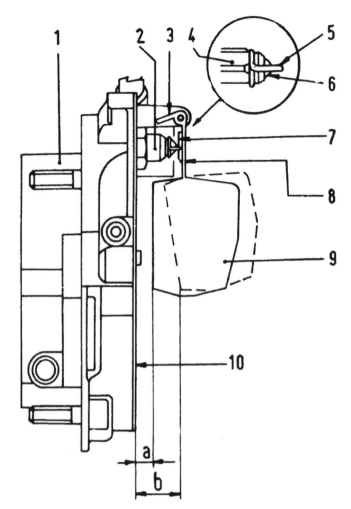

FIG 2:12 Checking float level

Key to Fig 2:12   1 Carburetter cover   2 Needle valve assembly   3 Tang   4 Needle   5 Return hook   6 Moveable ball   7 Tang   8 Float arm   9 Float   10 Gasket

the CO content checked by an authorised agent and a new seal fitted to the adjuster point.

Checking float and needle valve :

Checking of float and needle valve assemblies will be necessary if carburetter flooding is encountered, or if fuel starvation problems are traced to the carburetter. Flooding can be caused by incorrect float level, a damaged or punctured float, or by a needle valve which is worn or sticking in the open position. Fuel starvation can be caused by incorrect float level or by a needle valve which sticks in the closed position.

Remove the air cleaner assembly as described in **Section 2:3.** Disconnect fuel feed pipe and, on models with automatic choke units, the water pipes from the choke unit. Plug water pipes to prevent leakage. Disconnect carburetter linkages as necessary, noting their positions for correct reassembly, then remove the screws securing carburetter top cover to carburetter body. Lift off the cover, taking care not to damage the floats, then remove and discard the gasket. Carefully remove the pivot pin, then remove the float assembly, carefully unhooking the tang from the wire hook on the needle valve. Unscrew the needle valve housing from the top cover, collecting the sealing washer. Remove the cover plug and extract the

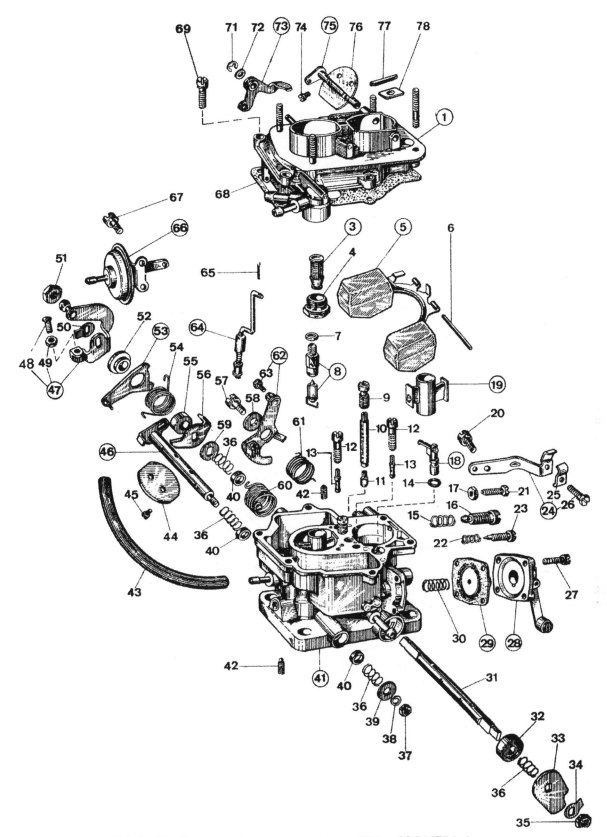

FIG 2 : 13   Typical carburetter components, Weber 32 DMTRA shown

Key to Fig 2 : 13   1 Carburetter cover   3 Filter   4 Filter plug   5 Float   6 Float pivot pin   7 Gasket   8 Needle valve   9 Air metering jet   10 Emulsion tube   11 Main jet   12 Idle jet holders   13 Idle jets   14 Gasket   15 Spring   16 Idle bypass screw   17 Nut   18 Accelerator pump cover   19 Venturi   20, 21 Screws   22 Spring   23 Idle mixture screw   24 to 26 Choke cable support bracket   27 Screw   28 Accelerator pump cover   29 Diaphragm   30 Spring   31 Throttle shaft, primary   32 Oil vapour distributor   33 Lever   34 Lockwasher   35 Nut   36 Spring   37 Nut   38 Spring washer   39 Washer   40 Bushing   41 Carburetter body   42 Secondary throttle stop screw   43 Hose   44 Throttle plate   45 Screw   46 Throttle shaft, secondary   47 to 49 Throttle lever assembly   50 Lockwasher   51 Nut   52 Bushing   53 Lever   54 Spring   55 Bushing   56 Primary shaft lever   57 Screw   58, 59 Washers   60, 61 Springs   62 Lever   63 Screw   64 Choke rod   65 Cotter pin   66 Choke override   67 Screw   68 Cover gasket   69 Screw   71 Circlip   72 Washer   73 Choke override control   74 Screw   75 Choke plate shaft   76 Choke plate   77 Clip   78 Dust cover

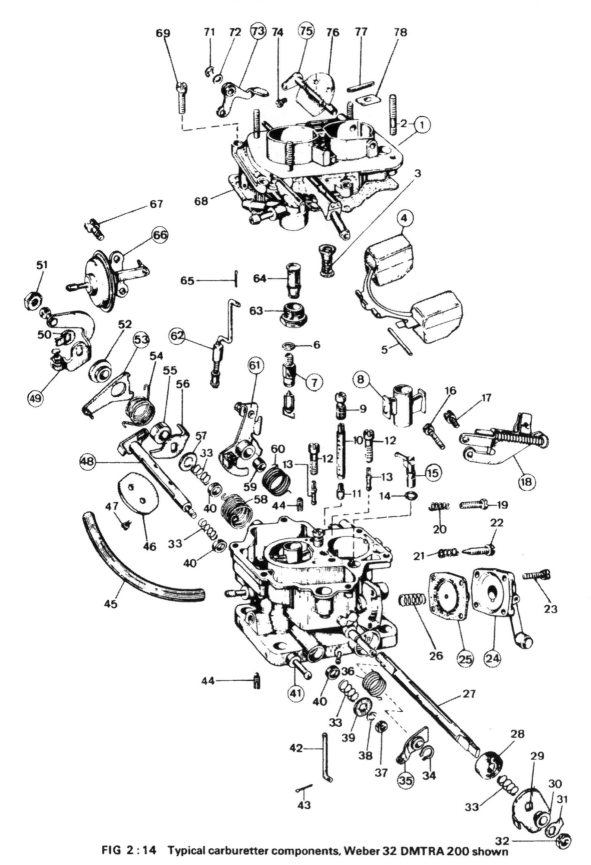

FIG 2:14 Typical carburetter components, Weber 32 DMTRA 200 shown

Key to Fig 2:14   1 Carburetter cover   2 Stud   3 Bowl vent valve   4 Float   5 Pin   6 Gasket   7 Needle valve
8 Venturi   9 Air metering jet   10 Emulsion tube   11 Main jet   12 Idle jet holders   13 Idle jets   14 Gasket   15 Accelerator
pump nozzle   16, 17 Screws   18 Support   19 Idle screw   20, 21 Springs   22 Idle mixture control   23 Screw
24 Accelerator pump cover   25 Diaphragm   26 Spring   27 Throttle shaft, primary   28 Oil vapour distributor   29 Lever
30 Bushing   31 Lockwasher   32 Nut   33 Spring   34 Ring   35 Choke rod   36 Spring   37 Nut   38 Spring washer
39 Washer   40 Bushing   41 Carburetter body   42 Lever   43 Cotter pin   44 Secondary throttle stop screw   45 Hose
46 Throttle plate   47 Screw   48 Throttle shaft, secondary   49 Lever   50 Lockwasher   51 Nut   52 Bushing   53 Lever
54 Spring   55 Bushing   56 Primary shaft lever   57 Washer   58 Spring   59 Bushing   60 Spring   61 Lever   62 Rod
63 Filter plug   64 Filter   65 Cotter pin   66 Choke override   67 Screw   68 Cover gasket   69 Screw   71 Circlip
72 Washer   73 Choke override control   74 Screw   75 Choke plate shaft   76 Choke plate   77 Clip   78 Dust cover

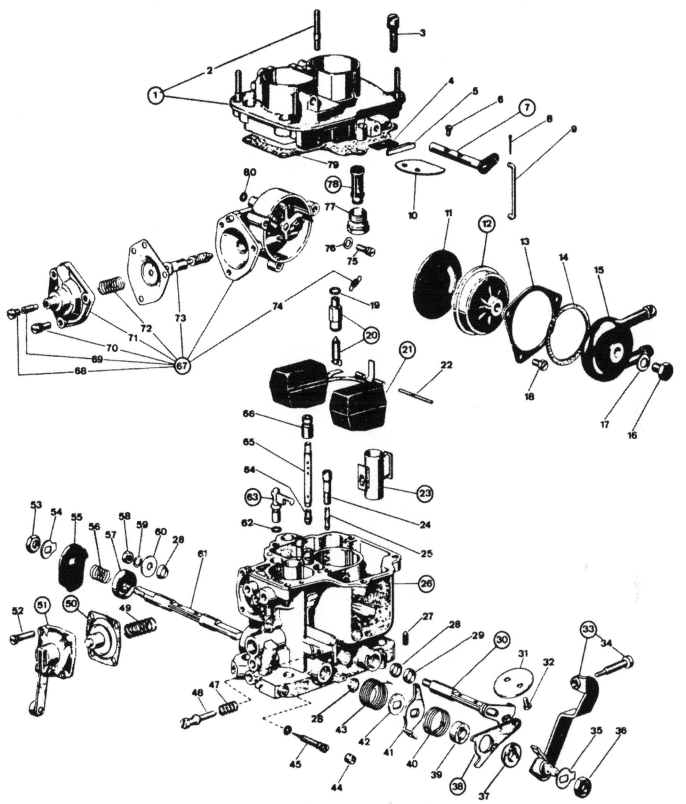

FIG 2:15   Components of a Weber 34 DATR 7/250 carburetter

Key to Fig 2:15   1 Carburetter cover   2 Stud   3 Screw   4 Dust cover   5 Clip   6 Screw   7 Spindle
8 Splitpin   9 Linkage   10 Choke plate   11 Heat shield   12 Automatic choke bi-metal housing   13 Retaining plate
14 Seal   15 Choke cover   16 Screw   17 Washer   18 Screw   19 Gasket   20 Needle valve and body   21 Float
assembly   22 Pivot pin   23 Venturi   24 Idle jet holder   25 Idle jet   26 Carburetter body   27 Grub screw
28, 29 Seal   30 Secondary throttle shaft   31 Secondary throttle plate   32 Screw   33 Choke control lever   34 Screw
35 Washer   36 Nut   37 Seal   38 Secondary throttle control lever   39 Seal   40 Spring   41 Primary shaft
lever   42 Washer   43 Spring   44 Tamper-proof cap   45 Mixture adjustment screw   47 Spring   48 Idle speed
adjuster   49 Diaphragm spring   50 Diaphragm assembly   51 Accelerator pump housing   52 Screw   53 Nut
54 Washer   55 Lever   56 Spring   57 Seal   58 Nut   59 Washer   60 Washer   61 Primary throttle shaft
62 Gasket   63 Accelerator pump nozzle   64 Main jet   65 Emulsion tube   66 Air metering jet   67 Bi-metal choke
assembly   68 Plug   69 Adjuster   70 Screw   71 Diaphragm housing   72 Spring   73 Diaphragm and spindle
assembly   74 Spring   75 Screw   76 Washer   77 Filter plug   78 Gauze filter   79 Joint gasket   80 Gasket

filter gauze, then carefully clean the gauze using petrol and a small brush. If the filter is damaged or will not clean up properly, it should be renewed.

Check the floats carefully for signs of damage or leakage. Float leakage can generally be detected by shaking the float and listening for the sound of fuel splash inside, or by immersing the float in warm water and looking for a stream of bubbles which will indicate any point of leakage. Renew the float assembly if any fault is found.

Check the float needle valve assembly carefully, renewing the assembly if there is any sign of a ridge on the tapered valve seat. Check for correct sealing by blowing through from the feed end. The air flow should be cut off completely when the needle is held onto its seat by gentle finger pressure. Renew the assembly if there is any doubt about its condition. Check the needle valve assembly sealing washer and renew if damaged or distorted. Note that the correct sealing washer must always be installed, as this affects control of the fuel level in float chamber.

Refit the fuel filter and sealing plug, then install and tighten the needle valve assembly with sealing washer. Install the float assembly, making sure that the needle valve hook fits correctly over the tang and that the assembly moves freely on the pivot pin. Float level should now be checked in the following manner.

Fit a new gasket to the carburetter top cover, then hold the assembly in a vertical position as shown in FIG 2 : 12 so that the float arm rests against the needle valve under its own weight, without depressing the spring-loaded ball in the valve. Measure distance a between the gasket surface and upper edge of float. This should be as quoted in Technical Data in the Appendix. If necessary, adjust by carefully bending tang 7. Turn the carburetter cover gently to its normal attitude so that the float hangs free. Now check dimension b, which should be 15mm (0.59in) in all cases. If necessary, adjust by carefully bending tang 3.

On completion, refit the carburetter top cover in the reverse order of removal, using the new gasket. Tighten the fixing screws alternately and evenly to avoid distortion. Check and if necessary adjust control linkage and make slow running adjustments, as described previously. On models fitted with automatic choke unit, check and if necessary top up and bleed the cooling system as described in Chapter 4.

2:8 Carburetter removal and refitting

Removal:

Remove the air cleaner as described in Section 2:3. Disconnect the carburetter fuel pipes and the throttle control linkage. On models with manual choke, disconnect the choke cable at carburetter linkage. On models with automatic choke, disconnect and plug the water pipes at the choke unit.

Disconnect wiring from carburetter thermoswitch and disconnect distributor vacuum pipe at carburetter. Disconnect the wiring from the anti run-on solenoid valve (if fitted). Remove the fixing nuts and lift the carburetter from inlet manifold, then remove and discard the flange gasket.

Refitting:

This is a reversal of the removal procedure, using a new flange gasket. On completion, carry out carburetter control adjustments and, if necessary, slow running adjustments, all as described previously. On models with automatic choke, check and if necessary top up and bleed the cooling system as described in Chapter 4.

2:9 Carburetter overhaul

Remove the carburetter as described in Section 2:8. Remove the top cover and service float and needle valve assemblies as described in Section 2:7. Remove the ancillary components and the internal jets from the carburetter body, but do not remove shafts and levers unless worn or damaged components are to be renewed. Note the positions of jets and mark shafts, levers and plate valves if they are to be removed, so that they can be reassembled in their correct relative positions. Use the correct size of screwdriver when removing jets, to avoid damage. Typical carburetter components are shown in FIGS 2:13, 2:14 and 2:15. Specifications and jet sizes for the alternative types of carburetter which may be fitted are given in Technical Data. When removing idle adjustment screws, carefully count the number of turns taken to do so, then they or any replacement units fitted can be installed in the same positions to provide initial settings. This will facilitate later tuning and adjustment procedures.

Clean all parts in petrol or an approved carburetter cleaner, then examine them for wear or damage. Renew any faulty parts. Clean jets and passages thoroughly, using compressed air, clean petrol and a small brush. Do not use cloth for cleaning purposes, as small fibres may remain after cleaning and clog the jets or passages. Never use a wire probe as this will damage or enlarge the jets. If a jet has a blockage which cannot be cleared with compressed air, use a single bristle from a stiff brush for the purpose. If this method is unsuccessful, renew the jet. Carefully examine the tips of idle adjustment screws and renew if the tapered sealing surface is worn or damaged. Make sure that all sediment is cleared from the float chamber.

On completion, reassemble the carburetter in the reverse order of dismantling, using new gaskets throughout. Take care not to overtighten the jets or component fixing screws to avoid stripping the threads in the light alloy castings. Reassemble the carburetter top cover and make float level adjustments as described in Section 2:7. Refit the carburetter as described in Section 2:8 and carry out linkage and slow running adjustments as described in Section 2:7.

2:10 Emission control systems

CO (carbon monoxide) in exhaust gases:

Carbon monoxide is poisonous. It cannot be completely eliminated from the exhaust gases but correct adjustment of the carburetter will ensure that atmospheric pollution by CO is restricted to the minimum at which a particular type of carburetter operates. It is not possible to judge the CO content of exhaust gases and the use of an analyser is essential. It is important that an owner does not disregard this aspect of tuning. It is important also that devices which are designed to improve carburetter emission control are kept serviceable. An example is the dashpot fitted to 32 DATRA carburetters which, by limiting the

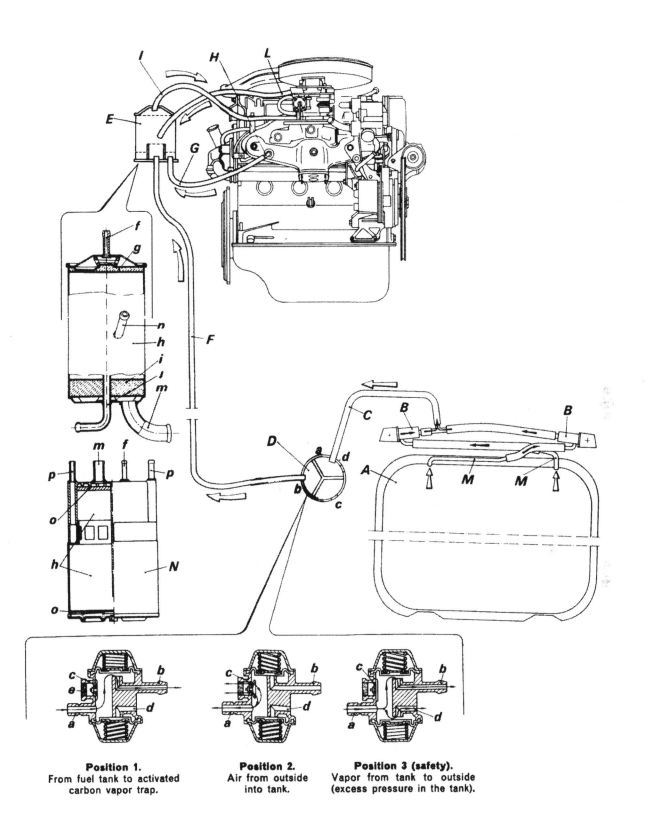

FIG 2 : 16 An evaporative loss control system

Key to Fig 2 : 16   **A** Fuel tank   **B** Liquid vapour separator   **C** Line from separator to 3-way valve   **D** 3-way control valve   **E** Activated carbon trap   **F** Line from 3-way valve to carbon trap   **G** Hot air purge tube   **H** Exhaust manifold **I** Line from carbon trap to carburetter (downstream of throttle)   **L** From carburetter bowl   **M** Lines between separator and fuel tank   **N** Activated carbon trap alternate type   **a** From fuel tank   **b** To activated carbon trap   **c** Fuel tank air inlet   **d** Safety outlet   **e** Air filter   **f** To carburetter (downstream of throttle)   **g** Synthetic filter   **h** Activated carbon **i** Air purge paper filter   **l** Fuel vapour inlet from tank   **m** Hot air purge inlet   **n** Fuel vapour inlet from carburetter **o** Synthetic fibre filter   **p** Fuel vapours inlet throttle rate of closure, prevents excessive richness (and consequential excess CO) during deceleration.

Evaporative loss control :

The evaporative loss control arrangement which is shown diagrammatically in **FIG 2 : 16** is only fitted to cars which are exported to countries in which this anti-pollution system is mandatory such as the USA.

The system is designed to eliminate contamination of the atmosphere by evaporated fuel. Renewal of the activated carbon trap at the intervals specified in **Section 2 : 2** and checks on the security of pipes, hoses and their joints is the only servicing which an owner should undertake. Functional checks on the three-way valve, separators, etc., should be entrusted to an authorised agent.

2:11 Fault diagnosis

(a) Leakage or insufficient fuel delivered

1 Air vent to tank restricted
2 Fuel pipe blocked
3 Air leaks at pipe connections
4 Fuel filter blocked
5 Pump gaskets faulty
6 Pump diaphragm defective
7 Pump valves sticking or seating badly

(b) Excessive fuel consumption

1 Carburetter requires adjustment
2 Fuel leakage
3 Sticking choke control
4 Float level too high
5 Dirty air cleaner
6 Worn jets in carburetter
7 Excessive engine temperature
8 Idling speed too high

(c) Idling speed too high

1 Rich fuel mixture
2 Throttle control sticking
3 Choke control sticking
4 Worn throttle valve

(d) Noisy fuel pump

1 Loose pump mountings
2 Air leaks on suction side of diaphragm
3 Obstruction in fuel pipeline
4 Clogged fuel filter

(e) No fuel delivery

1 Float needle valve stuck
2 Tank vent system blocked
3 Defective pump diaphragm
4 Pump valve stuck
5 Pipeline obstructed
6 Bad air leak on suction side of pump

CHAPTER 3

THE IGNITION SYSTEM

3:1 Description

The ignition system is conventional, comprising an ignition coil, distributor and contact breaker assembly. The distributor incorporates automatic timing control by centrifugal mechanism and, on USA export models, a vacuum operated unit. As engine speed increases, the centrifugal action of rotating weights pivoting against the tension of small springs moves the contact breaker cam relative to the distributor drive shaft and progressively advances the ignition. On USA export models, the vacuum control unit is connected by small bore pipe to a fitting on the carburetter. At high degrees of vacuum the unit advances the ignition, but under load, at reduced vacuum, the unit progressively retards the ignition. On early models, the distributor is mounted in a horizontal position on the cylinder head and driven from the end of the camshaft. On later models, the distributor is mounted in a vertical position on the cylinder block and driven by the engine auxiliary shaft.

The ignition coil is wound as an auto-transformer with the primary and secondary windings connected in series, the common junction being connected to the contact breaker with the positive feed from the battery going to the opposite terminal of the LT windings via the ignition switch. When the contact breaker points are closed, current flows in the coil primary winding, magnetising the core and setting up a fairly strong magnetic field. Each time the contacts open, the battery current is cut off and the magnetic field collapses, inducing a high current in the primary winding and a high voltage in the secondary. The primary current is used to charge the capacitor connected across the contacts and the flow is high and virtually instantaneous. It is this high current peak which induces the surge in the secondary winding to produce the sparking voltage across the plug points. Without the capacitor the current peak would be much smaller and the sparking voltage considerably reduced, in fact to a point where it would be insufficient to fire the mixture in the engine cylinders. The capacitor, therefore, serves the dual purpose of minimising contact breaker points wear and providing the necessary high charging surge to ensure a powerful spark.

3:2 Maintenance

Distributor lubrication:

Every 10,000km (6000 miles), lubricate the distributor as follows. Remove the distributor cap and pull off the rotor. Refer to **FIG 3 : 1**. If a felt pad is fitted as shown at 1, apply just sufficient engine oil to the pad to saturate it. Apply a thin smear of grease to the faces of the cam. Ensure that no oil or grease contaminates the contact breaker points 2. Thoroughly clean the rotor and cap before refitting them.

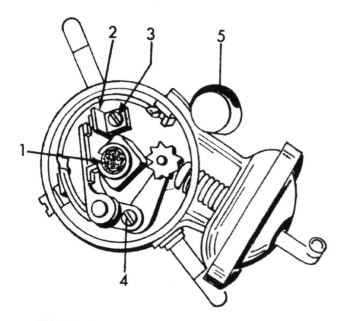

FIG 3:1 Upper components of typical distributor

Key to Fig 3:1   1 Felt pad   2 Contact breaker points
3, 4 Screw   5 Capacitor

Contact breaker points :

Every 10,000km (6000 miles), check and, if necessary, adjust the points gap to that quoted in **Technical Data** in the **Appendix**. The procedure is as follows.

Turn the engine until one of the cams has opened the points fully as shown in **FIG 3:1**. Using feeler gauges measure the points gap. If adjustment is required, loosen screw 3 and move the fixed contact point until the gap is correct. Tighten the screw and recheck the gap.

If the points faces are dirty or pitted, use a fine carborundum stone or a contact point file to polish the faces. Keep the faces flat and square and, on completion, clean the points with a petrol moistened lint-free rag. Points which will not clean up must be renewed.

Every 20,000km (12,000 miles), renew the contact breaker points as follows. Refer to **FIG 3:1**. Remove screws 3 and 4, disconnect the LT wire and remove the points. Clean the faces of the new points, connect the LT wire and install the points and their retaining screws. Set the gap as described earlier.

Ignition timing :

Every 10,000km (6000 miles), stroboscopically check and, if necessary, adjust the timing as described in **Section 3:5**.

Sparking plugs :

Every 10,000km (6000 miles), refer to **Section 3:6** and clean and regap the sparking plugs.

Every 20,000km (12,000 miles), fit a new set of sparking plugs of an approved type (see **Technical Data** in the **Appendix**).

Vacuum hoses :

At least every 20,000km (12,000 miles), check the condition and the security of the vacuum hoses.

Distributor rotor, cap and HT cables :

Every 40,000km (24,000 miles), to preclude ignition faults due to 'tracking', renew the rotor and cap. Check the condition of the HT cables and, if there are any indications of cracking or perishing, renew them.

Emission control system :

Every 40,000km (24,000 miles), on relevant models, have the spark control modulation device serviced by a fully equipped agent and have the diaphragm unit, valves, etc., renewed as necessary.

3:3 Ignition faults

If the engine runs unevenly, set it to idle at approximately 1000rev/min and, taking care not to touch any conducting part of the sparking plug leads, remove and replace each lead from its plug in turn. To avoid shocks during this operation it is necessary to wear a thick glove or to use insulated pliers. Doing this to a plug which is firing correctly will accentuate uneven running but will make no difference if the plug is not firing.

Having by this means located the faulty cylinder, stop the engine and remove the plug lead. Pull back the insulation or remove the connectors so that the end of the lead is exposed. Alternatively, use an extension piece, such as a small bar or drill, pushed into the plug connector. Hold the lead carefully to avoid shocks, so that the end is about $\frac{1}{8}$in away from the cylinder head. Crank the engine with the starter. A strong, regular spark confirms that the fault lies with the sparking plug which should be removed and cleaned as described in **Section 3:6**, or renewed if defective.

If the spark is weak and irregular, check the condition of the lead and, if it is perished or cracked, renew it and repeat the test. If no improvement results, check that the inside of the distributor cap is clean and dry and that there is no sign of tracking, which can be seen as a thin black line between the electrodes or to some metal part in contact with the cap. Tracking can only be cured by fitting a new cap. Check that the carbon brush in the cap is in good condition and free to move in and out against its internal spring. Check the brass segments inside the cap for wear or burning. Renew the cap if any fault is found.

If these checks do not cure a weak HT spark, or if no spark can be obtained at the plug or lead, check the LT circuit as described next.

Testing the low tension circuit :

Check that the contact breaker points are clean and correctly set, then proceed as follows :

Remove the sparking plugs. Disconnect the thin wire from the coil that leads to the distributor. Connect a 12 volt test lamp between these terminals, switch on the ignition and turn the engine slowly by pulling on the alternator drive belt or by using a spanner on the crankshaft pulley nut. If the lamp lights and goes out as the points close and open, the circuit is in order. If the lamp fails to light, there is a fault in the LT circuit.

Remove the lamp and connect the wire to the coil and distributor. If the fault lies in the LT circuit, use the lamp to carry out the following tests with the ignition switched on. Remove the wire from the ignition switch side of the coil and connect the lamp between the end of this wire and

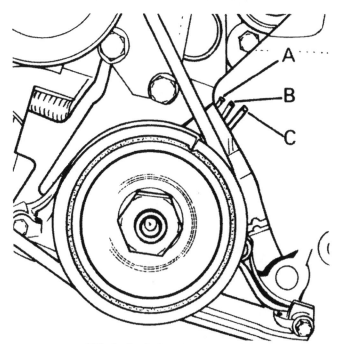

FIG 3 : 2   Pulley timing marks

Key to Fig 3 : 2   A 10° BTDC   B 5° BTDC   C 0° (TDC)

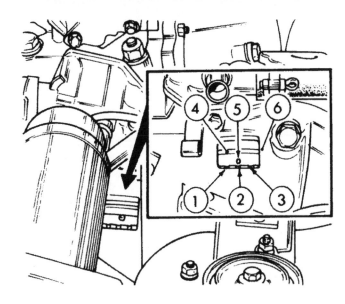

FIG 3 : 3   The flywheel timing marks

Key to Fig 3 : 3   1 0° (TDC)   2 5° BTDC   3 10° BTDC
4 Flywheel   5 Mark on flywheel   6 Transmission casing

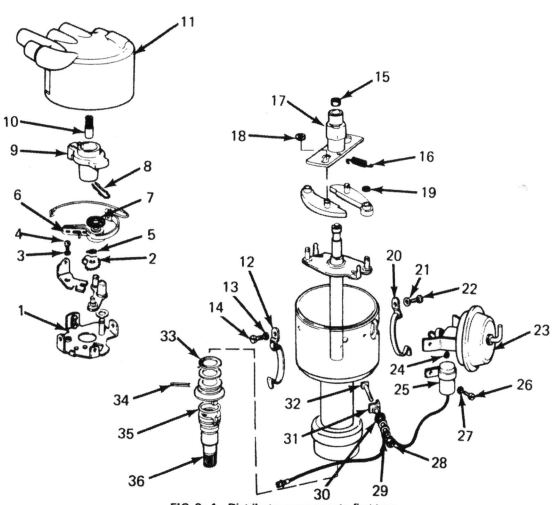

FIG 3 : 4   Distributor components, first type

Key to Fig 3 : 4   1 Contact breaker plate   2 Star gear   3 Washer   4 Screw   5 Clip   6 Contact breaker points
7 Washer   8 Clip   9 Rotor arm   10 Spring contact   11 Cap   12 Clip   13 Washer   14 Screw   15 Rubber ring
16 Spring   17 Cam   18 Circlip   19 Washer   20 Clip   21 Washer   22 Screw   23 Vacuum unit   24 Washer
25 Capacitor   26 Screw   27 Washer   28 Nut   29 Lockwasher   30 Fibre washer   31 Terminal   32 Bolt
33 Washer   34 Pin   35 Seal   36 Gear

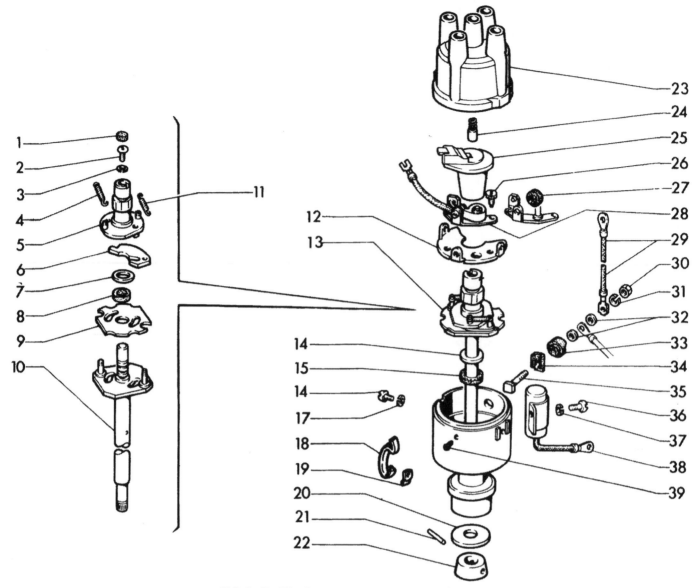

FIG 3 : 5 Distributor components, second type

Key to Fig 3 : 5   1 Felt pad   2 Screw   3 Washer   4 Spring   5 Cam assembly   6 Advance weight   7 Washer
8 Insulator   9 Advance mechanism plate   10 Shaft assembly   11 Spring   12 Contact breaker plate   13 Centrifugal
advance mechanism   14 Washer   15 Insulator   16 Screw   17 Washer   18 Spring clip   19 Hinge   20 Washer
21 Pin   22 Collar   23 Distributor cap   24 Carbon brush   25 Rotor arm   26 Lockscrew   27 Insulator   28 Contact
breaker   29 LT lead   30 Terminal nut   31, 32 Washers   33, 34 Insulators   35 Terminal bolt   36 Screw
37 Washer   38 Capacitor   39 Screw

earth. If the lamp fails to light, it indicates a fault in the wiring between the battery and the coil or in the ignition switch. Reconnect the wire if the lamp lights.

Disconnect the wire from the coil that connects to the distributor. Connect the lamp between the coil terminal and earth. If the lamp fails to light it indicates a fault in the coil primary winding and a new coil must be fitted. Reconnect the wire if the lamp lights and disconnect its other end from the distributor. If the lamp does not light when connected between the end of this wire and earth, it indicates a fault in the section of wire.

Capacitor :

The best method of testing a capacitor (condenser) is by substitution. Disconnect the original capacitor and connect a new one between the LT terminal on the distributor and earth for test purposes. The capacitor is shown at 5 in **FIG**

3 : 1. If a new capacitor is proved to be required, it can then be properly fitted. The capacitor is of 0.22 to 0.23 or 0.20 to 0.22 microfarad capacity (see **Technical Data**).

3 : 4 Removing and dismantling distributor

Removal :

Timing marks are shown in **FIGS 3 : 2** and **3 : 3**.

Turn the engine until No 1 cylinder is at TDC on the firing stroke. No 1 is the cylinder nearest the timing gear end of the engine. To do this, remove the distributor cap and turn the engine until the rotor points towards the cap segment for No 1 cylinder, or turn the engine until both valves in No 1 cylinder are closed, removing the camshaft cover to view the cam lobes (see **Chapter 1**). This done, turn the engine a little more as necessary until the timing notch in the crankshaft pulley or the flywheel aligns with the static advance mark on the front of the timing gear cover or on the transmission casing which corresponds to the static ignition timing quoted in **Technical Data** for the relevant engine.

With the distributor cap removed, disconnect the LT wiring from the distributor. Note the position of the rotor relative to the distributor body and mark the position of the distributor body relative to the engine block or, on early engines, the cylinder head. Release the clamp securing distributor in position, then pull the distributor from its mounting. Distributor installation will be facilitated if the engine is not turned while the distributor is removed.

Refitting:

With the timing marks aligned correctly as previously described, offer the distributor into position with the mark on the body aligned with the mark on block or, on early engines, the head. Turn the rotor to the position noted during removal and push the distributor fully into place, noting that the rotor may have to be turned a fraction to allow the drive mechanism to engage correctly. When the distributor seats the rotor most be pointing towards the cap segment for firing No 1 cylinder. Temporarily tighten the clamp to secure the distributor, then check the ignition timing as described in **Section 3:5**.

Dismantling:

Pull the rotor from the distributor shaft, then remove the contact breaker points as described in **Section 3:2**. Refer to **FIG 3:4** or **3:5** according to the type of distributor fitted.

If a vacuum unit is installed, remove the fixing screws and detach the unit from the contact breaker plate. Use a suitable punch to remove the retaining pin, then remove the drive gear and washers. Pull the distributor shaft with upper components from the distributor body and dismantle into the order shown in the illustration if necessary.

Thoroughly clean all parts in petrol or other suitable solvent and dry them. Examine for wear or damage and renew parts as necessary. Service the contact breaker points as described in **Section 3:2**.

After inspection and servicing, reassemble the distributor in the reverse order of dismantling. Lightly lubricate the shaft bearings with engine oil and the centrifugal advance mechanism with grease. Lubricate upper distributor components and set contact points gap as described in **Section 3:2**. Check that the centrifugal advance mechanism operates by holding the shaft while turning the rotor to the limit of its travel. When released, the rotor should snap back to its original position.

3:5 Timing the ignition

The piston for No 1 cylinder must be at TDC on the compression stroke. To check this, either remove the rocker cover and check that both cam lobes are pointing away from tappets for No 1 cylinder (see **Chapter 1**), or by removing No 1 sparking plug and turning the engine forwards until compression can be felt by a thumb placed over the plughole. This done, turn the engine a little more as necessary to correctly align the timing marks as described in **Section 3:4**. **Do not turn the engine backwards.**

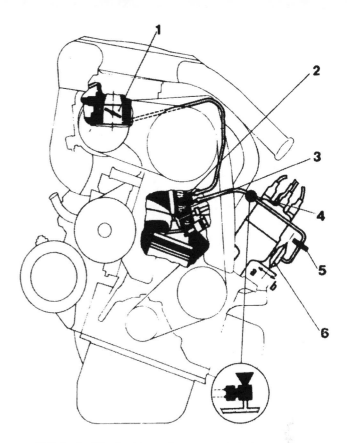

FIG 3:6   The ignition advance modulation system

Key to Fig 3:6   1 Carburetter   2 Thermovalve 3 Coolant   4 Electrovalve   5 Delay valve   6 Distributor vacuum capsule   a Advance   b Retard

Electrical setting:

With the engine correctly set as previously described, connect a 12 volt test lamp in parallel with the contact breaker points. One lead will go to the terminal on the side of the distributor and one to earth. Slacken the distributor clamp bolt just enough to allow the distributor body to be turned by hand. Switch on the ignition and ensure that the contact points are fully closed, turning the distributor body to ensure this. Now turn the distributor body very slowly until the lamp just lights, which indicates that the points are beginning to open. Tighten the clamp bolt at this point and confirm the accuracy of the setting by turning the engine and checking that the test lamp lights up again exactly as the notch in the crankshaft pulley or the flywheel lines up with the appropriate timing mark on the front cover or the transmission casing. It is recommended that the setting be checked for accuracy using stroboscopic equipment as described next.

Stroboscopic timing:

If a stroboscopic timing lamp is available a more accurate setting can be obtained with the engine running at idling speed. Note that the engine must be at normal operating temperature and idling at a speed of 850rev/min. Adjust idle speed if necessary as described in **Chapter 2**. The procedure will be facilitated if the timing marks are marked with white paint.

Connect the stroboscopic lamp equipment according to the manufacturer's instructions, into the ignition circuit for No 1 cylinder. Start the engine and allow it to idle at the correct speed, then aim the stroboscopic lamp at the timing marks. If the marks do not appear correctly in alignment, slacken the distributor clamp bolt slightly and rotate the distributor body until timing is correct, then retighten the bolt. Switch off the ignition and remove the stroboscopic equipment, then check engine idle speed as described in **Chapter 2**.

3 : 6 Sparking plugs

Sparking plugs should be of the recommended type, details of which are given in **Technical Data**. The gaps should be set by bending the outer electrode only. Have sparking plugs cleaned on an abrasive-blasting machine and tested under pressure with the electrode gaps correctly set. Any plug which fails the test should be renewed. As a general rule, plugs should be cleaned, regapped and tested at about 10,000km (6000 mile) intervals and renewed at about 20,000km (12,000 mile) intervals.

Sparking plug leads:

Renew HT leads if they are defective in any way. Inspect for broken, swollen or deteriorated insulation which can be the cause of current leakage, especially in wet weather conditions. Also check the condition of the plug connectors at the ends of the leads.

Sparking plugs as a tuning guide :

Inspection of the deposits on electrodes can be helpful as a tuning guide. Normally, from mixed periods of high and low speed driving, the deposits will be powdery and range in colour from brown to greyish tan. There will also be some slight wear of the electrodes. Long periods of fairly constant speed driving or low speed city driving will produce white or yellowish deposits. Dry, black fluffy deposits are due to incomplete combustion and indicate running with a rich mixture, excessive idling and, possibly, defective ignition. Overheated plugs have a white or light grey look round the centre electrode and the electrodes themselves will appear bluish and burnt. This may be due to weak mixture, poor cooling, incorrect ignition timing or sustained high speed running with a heavily loaded car. Black, wet deposits result from oil in the combustion chambers caused by worn pistons, rings, valve stems or guides or by worn and scored cylinder bores. Sparking plugs which run hotter may alleviate this problem temporarily but the cure is in an engine overhaul.

3 : 7 Emission control

Ignition advance modulation system :

The system is designed to reduce the CO content of the exhaust gases during acceleration and is only fitted to relevant USA models. At idling speed and at partial loads, the distributor centrifugal advance curve is delayed by a pneumatic mechanism which is operated by vacuum from the carburetter. The control signal is, in turn, controlled by a delay valve which slows down the time taken to reach the advance of the normal centrifugal curve when the intake manifold depression drops during engine accelerations.

The system is shown diagrammatically in **FIG 3 : 6**. Every 40,000km (24,000 miles), have the system serviced by an authorised agent.

3 : 8 Fault diagnosis

(a) Engine will not fire

1 Battery discharged
2 Contact breaker points dirty, pitted or maladjusted
3 Distributor cap dirty, cracked or tracking
4 Brush inside distributor cap not touching rotor
5 Faulty cable or loose connection in LT circuit
6 Distributor rotor arm cracked
7 Faulty coil
8 Broken contact breaker spring
9 Contact points stuck open

(b) Engine misfires

1 Check 2, 3, 5 and 7 in (a)
2 Weak contact breaker spring
3 HT plug or coil lead cracked or perished
4 Loose sparking plug
5 Sparking plug insulation cracked
6 Sparking plug gap incorrect
7 Ignition timing too far advanced

(c) Poor acceleration

1 Ignition retarded
2 Centrifugal advance weights seized
3 Centrifugal advance springs weak, broken or disconnected
4 Loose distributor mounting
5 Excessive contact points gap
6 Worn sparking plugs
7 Faulty vacuum unit or leaking pipe

CHAPTER 4
THE COOLING SYSTEM

4 : 1 Description

The cooling system is pressurised and thermostatically controlled, using a corrugated fin type radiator located at the front of the car. The radiator is connected to the engine cooling system by means of pipes and hoses routed beneath the car. Water circulation is assisted by a centrifugal pump which is mounted on the engine cylinder block. The cooling fan, powered by an electric motor, is mounted in a shroud attached to the radiator and controlled by a thermoswitch.

The water pump, together with the alternator, is driven by means of a belt from the crankshaft pulley. The water pump takes coolant from the bottom of the radiator and delivers it to the cylinder block from which it rises to the cylinder head. At normal operating temperatures the thermostat is open and the coolant returns to the top of the radiator. At lower temperatures, the thermostat is closed and the coolant bypasses the radiator and returns directly to the pump inlet. This provides a rapid warm up and good heater performance.

A metal or plastic expansion tank containing a quantity of coolant is connected to the main system by means of a hose. At high operating temperatures, when the coolant in the system expands, excess coolant passes through a valve into the expansion tank. When the system cools, the valve allows coolant from the tank to flow back into the system. With this system, no coolant loss should occur during normal operation.

4 : 2 Maintenance

Coolant level :

Every 500km (300 miles) or weekly, check the level of the coolant in the expansion tank and top up as required. The tank level should be approximately 75mm (3in) above the 'MIN' mark but will be higher if the system is hot. To avoid diluting the coolant, use the correct antifreeze solution (see **Section 4 : 8**).

If frequent topping up is required, suspect a leaking hose or joint. Trace and correct the leak without delay.

Hoses and joints :

Every 20,000km (12,000 miles), check the condition of hoses and the security of the joints. Renew any hose(s) which show signs of cracking or perishing. Include the heater hoses in this inspection.

Drain, flush and refill :

Every 60,000km (36,000 miles) or every two years (whichever comes first), drain, flush and refill the system with new antifreeze solution. If draining is being carried out for access reasons and not because the coolant is aged, serviceable solution should be collected for re-use.

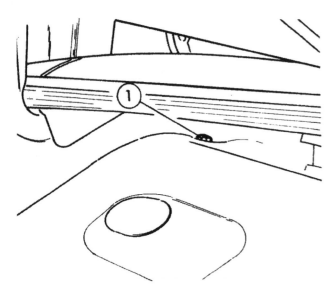

FIG 4:1   Radiator bleed screw 1

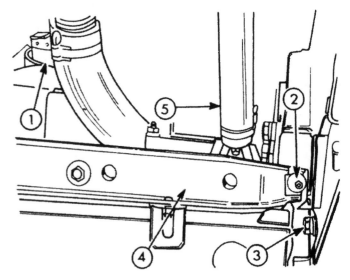

FIG 4:2   Radiator removal

Key to Fig 4:2   1 Fan unit   2 Nut   3 Bolt
4 Crossmember   5 Hose

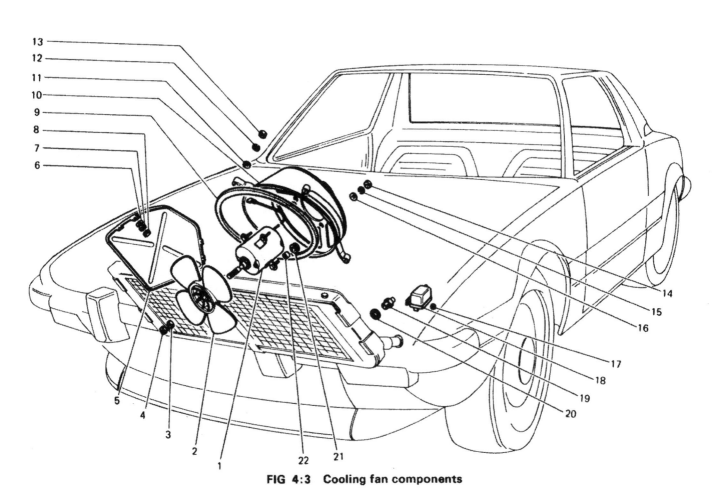

FIG 4:3   Cooling fan components

Key to Fig 4:3   1 Fan motor   2 Fan   3 Washer   4 Nut   5 Plate   6 Washer   7 Lockwasher   8 Nut   9 Gasket   10 Shroud
11 Washer   12 Lockwasher   13 Nut   14 Nut   15 Lockwasher   16 Washer   17 Nut   18 Relay   19 Thermoswitch   20 Gasket
21 Lockring   22 Spacer

Draining:

Allow the system to cool before draining. Set the heater temperature control in the 'HOT' position and remove the expansion tank cap. Open the front luggage compartment. Refer to **FIG 4:1**. Remove the rubber access plug and remove the radiator bleed screw 1. Open the cylinder block drain tap/plug from beneath the engine manifolds (23 in **Chapter 1, FIG 1:2**). Remove the two coolant drain plugs from the radiator feed and return pipes beneath the front of the car. If, on the particular model, no drain plugs are provided, unclamp and detach the radiator bottom hose.

Flushing:

Use a hose to run clean water into the expansion tank filler orifice. When the outflows run clean, close all the drain points and fill the system via the expansion tank. Run the engine up to normal operating temperature (thermostat open) without refitting the filler cap. Drain as before. If necessary, repeat this operation but **allow the engine to cool before flushing**.

Filling:

Close all drain points. Set the heater control in the 'HOT' position. Prepare the requisite quantity of antifreeze solution (see 'Capacities' in **Technical Data** in the **Appendix**) of the correct proportions (see **Section 4:8**). Fill the system until coolant issues from the radiator bleed. Fit the bleed screw and continue filling until the level is approximately 75mm (3in) above the 'MIN' mark in the expansion tank. Fit the tank cap. Run the engine to circulate the coolant throughout the system. Stop the engine and bleed the system via the bleed screw. When no further air issues from the bleed, tighten it fully. Top up the coolant to the specified level as described earlier.

4:3 The radiator
Removal:

Drain the radiator as described in **Section 4:2**, there being no need to drain the cylinder block. Refer to **FIG 4:2** and remove the three lower screws holding grille to crossmember 4. Loosen the four nuts holding plate to body, then remove the plate. Disconnect hoses 5 from radiator. Disconnect the wiring for fan unit 1 and disconnect wiring from thermoswitch at radiator. Raise and safely support the front of the car, then carefully lower the radiator from the car, taking care not to damage the fan unit.

Refitting:

This is a reversal of the removal procedure. Make sure that all hose connections are secure, then refill and bleed the cooling system as described in **Section 4:2**.

4:4 The cooling fan

The cooling fan is electrically operated and switched on and off, according to coolant temperature, by a thermoswitch attached to the radiator. The layout of the system is shown in **FIG 4:3**.

If the fan operates when the cooling system is cold, the thermoswitch is faulty or there is a shortcircuit in the fan wiring. If the fan does not operate at all, check the relevant fuse (see **Chapter 11, Section 11:5**), then check that the motor is in order by connecting jumper leads from the battery to the motor terminals. If the motor is in order, check the thermoswitch by removing the two leads from the switch and connecting them together then turning on the ignition. If the fan then operates, the thermoswitch is faulty. If the switch is in order, disconnect wires from terminals 30/51 and 87 on the relay and connect these wires together. If the fan then runs, it indicates either a faulty fan relay or no current supply to the relay. Check current supply to relay by disconnecting the wire from terminal 86 on the relay and connecting a 12 volt test lamp between the end of this wire and earth with the ignition switched on. If the lamp lights, the wiring is in order and the relay must be at fault.

If the fan motor or any operating components in the circuit are faulty, the component in question must be renewed complete. Note that the thermoswitch should switch on and cause the fan to cut in and switch off at the temperatures quoted in **Technical Data**. The thermoswitch can be removed from the radiator after disconnecting the wiring, then a new unit fitted complete with new gasket. As a small amount of coolant will be lost during this operation, top up and bleed the system afterwards as described in **Section 4:2**. Removal of the cooling fan, motor and shroud are straightforward operations, but disconnect the battery earth cable before disconnecting fan circuit wiring.

4:5 Drive belt tensioning

It is important to maintain the correct tension of the alternator and water pump drive belt as a tight belt will cause undue wear on the pulleys and component bearings. Conversely, a slack belt will slip and, possibly, cause decreased output from the driven components. If the belt is worn, damaged or oil contaminated it must be renewed.

Tension is correct when the belt can be deflected by 10 to 15mm (0.4 to 0.6in) when firm hand pressure is applied at the points arrowed at **A** in **FIG 4:4**. If adjustment is necessary, slacken the alternator mounting bolts **B** and **C** then pivot the alternator away from the engine until belt tension is correct. If a lever is used to move the alternator, it must be applied to the mounting bracket only, never to the alternator body. Hold the alternator in position while tightening the mounting bolts. The belt can be removed by slackening the bolts, swinging the alternator towards the engine then removing the belt over the pulleys. Fit the new belt over the pulleys then set to the correct tension. The tension of a new belt should be checked after driving for a few miles, then readjusted if necessary to take up the initial stretch.

4:6 The water pump
Removal:

Drain the cooling system as described in **Section 4:2**. Remove the protective panels from bottom righthand side of engine. Remove the drive belt as described in **Section 4:5**, then refer to **FIG 4:5**.

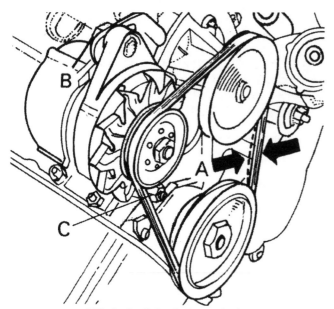

FIG 4 : 4   Drive belt tensioning

Key to Fig 4 : 4   A 15mm (0.4 to 0.6in)   B, C Mounting bolts

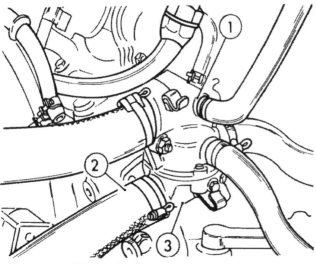

FIG 4 : 5   Water pump removal

Key to Fig 4 : 5   1 Air pump support   2 Coolant pump   3 Alternator   4 Three nuts and washers   5 Pipe   6 Bolts

FIG 4 : 6   Thermostat removal

Key to Fig 4 : 6   1 Union   2 Hose   3 Cover

Disconnect the wiring from the rear of alternator 3, then remove the mounting bolts and detach the alternator. Disconnect hoses from water pump 2. Remove the three nuts and washers 4 securing pipe 5 to pump. On models with emission control system, remove bolt securing air pump support 1 to water pump. Remove the four bolts 6 securing water pump to engine, then remove the pump. Remove and discard the gasket.

If the water pump is internally defective it is possible for repairs to be carried out, but as the work requires the use of special tools and press equipment it should be carried out by a fully equipped service station.

Refitting:

This is a reversal of the removal procedure, using a new gasket. On completion, set drive belt tension as described in **Section 4:5** then fill and bleed cooling system as described in **Section 4:2**.

4:7 The thermostat

Removal:

Drain sufficient coolant as described in **Section 4:2** to bring the level below that of the thermostat housing. Remove the air cleaner assembly as described in **Chapter 2**. Refer to **FIG 4:6** and disconnect hose 2. Remove the three bolts and washers securing cover 3 to union 1, then remove the thermostat and gaskets.

Testing :

Clean the thermostat and immerse it in a container of cold water together with a zero to 100°C thermometer. Heat the water, keeping it stirred, and check that the valve opens at and is fully open within the temperature ranges quoted in **Technical Data**. The valve should close tightly when the thermostat is removed from the hot water and placed in cold water. If the thermostat operates correctly it may be refitted, but if not it must be renewed.

Refitting:

This is a reversal of the removal procedure, using new gaskets. On completion, fill and bleed the cooling system as described in **Section 4:2**.

4:8 Frost precautions

With the correct coolant solution in use as described in **Section 4:2**, no additional frost precautions should be necessary. However, it is advisable to have the solution tested at intervals during the winter to make certain that it has not weakened. A hydrometer calibrated to read both specific gravity and temperature for the type of coolant in the system must be used, most garages having such equipment. Always ensure that the antifreeze mixture used for filling the system is of sufficient strength to provide protection against freezing, according to the manufacturer's instructions.

Fiat recommend that their Paraflu II antifreeze is mixed half-and-half with water which will give protection down to −35°C.

4:9 Fault diagnosis

(a) Internal coolant leakage

1 Cracked cylinder wall
2 Loose cylinder head bolts or nuts
3 Cracked cylinder head
4 Faulty head gasket

(b) Poor circulation

1 Radiator blocked
2 Engine water passages restricted
3 Low coolant level
4 Slack pump drive belt
5 Defective thermostat
6 Perished or collapsed radiator hoses
7 Faulty water pump

(c) Corrosion

1 Impurities in the coolant
2 Infrequent draining and flushing

(d) Overheating

1 Check (b)
2 Sludge in crankcase
3 Faulty ignition timing
4 Low oil level in engine sump
5 Tight engine
6 Choked exhaust system
7 Binding brakes
8 Slipping clutch
9 Incorrect valve timing
10 Mixture too weak
11 Faulty fan motor, relay or thermoswitch

Inches		Decimals	Milli-metres	Inches to Millimetres		Millimetres to Inches	
				Inches	mm	mm	Inches
	1/64	.015625	.3969	.001	.0254	.01	.00039
1/32		.03125	.7937	.002	.0508	.02	.00079
	3/64	.046875	1.1906	.003	.0762	.03	.00118
1/16		.0625	1.5875	.004	.1016	.04	.00157
	5/64	.078125	1.9844	.005	.1270	.05	.00197
3/32		.09375	2.3812	.006	.1524	.06	.00236
	7/64	.109375	2.7781	.007	.1778	.07	.00276
1/8		.125	3.1750	.008	.2032	.08	.00315
	9/64	.140625	3.5719	.009	.2286	.09	.00354
5/32		.15625	3.9687	.01	.254	.1	.00394
	11/64	.171875	4.3656	.02	.508	.2	.00787
3/16		.1875	4.7625	.03	.762	.3	.01181
	13/64	.203125	5·1594	.04	1.016	.4	.01575
7/32		.21875	5.5562	.05	1.270	.5	.01969
	15/64	.234375	5.9531	.06	1.524	.6	.02362
1/4		.25	6.3500	.07	1.778	.7	.02756
	17/64	.265625	6.7469	.08	2.032	.8	.03150
9/32		.28125	7.1437	.09	2.286	.9	.03543
	19/64	.296875	7.5406	.1	2.54	1	.03937
5/16		.3125	7.9375	.2	5.08	2	.07874
	21/64	.328125	8.3344	.3	7.62	3	.11811
11/32		.34375	8.7312	.4	10.16	4	.15748
	23/64	.359375	9.1281	.5	12.70	5	.19685
3/8		.375	9.5250	.6	15.24	6	.23622
	25/64	.390625	9.9219	.7	17.78	7	.27559
13/32		.40625	10.3187	.8	20.32	8	.31496
	27/64	.421875	10.7156	.9	22.86	9	.35433
7/16		.4375	11.1125	1	25.4	10	.39370
	29/64	.453125	11.5094	2	50.8	11	.43307
15/32		.46875	11.9062	3	76.2	12	.47244
	31/64	.484375	12.3031	4	101.6	13	.51181
1/2		.5	12.7000	5	127.0	14	.55118
	33/64	.515625	13.0969	6	152.4	15	.59055
17/32		.53125	13.4937	7	177.8	16	.62992
	35/64	.546875	13.8906	8	203.2	17	.66929
9/16		.5625	14.2875	9	228.6	18	.70866
	37/64	.578125	14.6844	10	254.0	19	.74803
19/32		.59375	15.0812	11	279.4	20	.78740
	39/64	.609375	15.4781	12	304.8	21	.82677
5/8		.625	15.8750	13	330.2	22	.86614
	41/64	.640625	16.2719	14	355.6	23	.90551
21/32		.65625	16.6687	15	381.0	24	.94488
	43/64	.671875	17.0656	16	406.4	25	.98425
11/16		.6875	17.4625	17	431.8	26	1.02362
	45/64	.703125	17.8594	18	457.2	27	1.06299
23/32		.71875	18.2562	19	482.6	28	1.10236
	47/64	.734375	18.6531	20	508.0	29	1.14173
3/4		.75	19.0500	21	533.4	30	1.18110
	49/64	.765625	19.4469	22	558.8	31	1.22047
25/32		.78125	19.8437	23	584.2	32	1.25984
	51/64	.796875	20.2406	24	609.6	33	1.29921
13/16		.8125	20.6375	25	635.0	34	1.33858
	53/64	.828125	21.0344	26	660.4	35	1.37795
27/32		.84375	21.4312	27	685.8	36	1.41732
	55/64	.859375	21.8281	28	711.2	37	1.4567
7/8		.875	22.2250	29	736.6	38	1.4961
	57/64	.890625	22.6219	30	762.0	39	1.5354
29/32		.90625	23.0187	31	787.4	40	1.5748
	59/64	.921875	23.4156	32	812.8	41	1.6142
15/16		.9375	23.8125	33	838.2	42	1.6535
	61/64	.953125	24.2094	34	863.6	43	1.6929
31/32		.96875	24.6062	35	889.0	44	1.7323
	63/64	.984375	25.0031	36	914.4	45	1.7717

UNITS	Pints to Litres	Gallons to Litres	Litres to Pints	Litres to Gallons	Miles to Kilometres	Kilometres to Miles	Lbs. per sq. In. to Kg. per sq. Cm.	Kg. per sq. Cm. to Lbs. per sq. In.
1	.57	4.55	1.76	.22	1.61	.62	.07	14.22
2	1.14	9.09	3.52	.44	3.22	1.24	.14	28.50
3	1.70	13.64	5.28	.66	4.83	1.86	.21	42.67
4	2.27	18.18	7.04	.88	6.44	2.49	.28	56.89
5	2.84	22.73	8.80	1.10	8.05	3.11	.35	71.12
6	3.41	27.28	10.56	1.32	9.66	3.73	.42	85.34
7	3.98	31.82	12.32	1.54	11.27	4.35	.49	99.56
8	4.55	36.37	14.08	1.76	12.88	4.97	.56	113.79
9		40.91	15.84	1.98	14.48	5.59	.63	128.00
10		45.46	17.60	2.20	16.09	6.21	.70	142.23
20				4.40	32.19	12.43	1.41	284.47
30				6.60	48.28	18.64	2.11	426.70
40				8.80	64.37	24.85		
50					80.47	31.07		
60					96.56	37.28		
70					112.65	43.50		
80					128.75	49.71		
90					144.84	55.92		
100					160.93	62.14		

UNITS	Lb ft to kgm	Kgm to lb ft	UNITS	Lb ft to kgm	Kgm to lb ft
1	.138	7.233	7	.967	50.631
2	.276	14.466	8	1.106	57.864
3	.414	21.699	9	1.244	65.097
4	.553	28.932	10	1.382	72.330
5	.691	36.165	20	2.765	144.660
6	.829	43.398	30	4.147	216.990

CHAPTER 5

THE CLUTCH

5:1 Description

A single dry plate clutch of diaphragm spring type is fitted, the main components being the driven plate, pressure plate assembly and release bearing.

The driven plate consists of a resilient steel disc attached to a hub which slides on the splined gearbox input shaft. The pressure plate assembly consists of the pressure plate, diaphragm spring and cover, this cover being attached to the outer face of the engine flywheel. The release bearing is a ballbearing of special construction with an elongated outer ring that presses directly against the diaphragm spring when the clutch pedal is operated.

The clutch operating mechanism is hydraulic, the clutch pedal actuating a master cylinder where pressure on the fluid is generated, this pressure being transmitted through a hose to a clutch slave cylinder mounted on the clutch housing. Slave cylinder action is transmitted to the release bearing by a lever.

The 181.5mm (7.1in) diameter clutch fitted to the 1300 model 4-speed transmission requires routine adjustment as described in **Section 5 : 2**. The 190mm (7.4in) diameter clutch fitted to the 1500 model 5-speed transmission is self-adjusting and requires no routine attention.

5 : 2 Maintenance

Hydraulic fluid level :

Every 500km (300 miles) or weekly, check the fluid level and top up as necessary. Investigate the cause of any rapid drop in level. This may be caused by a defective master or slave cylinder seal, a leaking connection or a defective hose.

Adjustment :

Every 10,000km (6000 miles), check the clutch pedal travel and free play and, if necessary, adjust as follows.

4-speed transmission clutch adjustment :

Total travel of the clutch pedal from the stop on the pedal bracket to the floor should be 170mm (6.7in) on early models and 160mm (6.3in) on models produced in 1977 and onwards. To adjust, refer to **FIG 5 : 1**, loosen locknut 1 and turn the adjuster screw 2 until the travel of the pedal 3 is as specified. Tighten the locknut.

Operate the pedal by hand to determine the amount of free play before pressure can be felt. This should be 30mm (1.2in). If adjustment is required, refer to **FIG 5 : 2**. Loosen locknut 9 and adjust the effective length of the pushrod by turning the adjuster nut 8. Tighten the locknut. Adjust and recheck as necessary. Recheck after road testing the car.

5-speed transmission clutch adjustment :

The total clutch travel should be 120mm (4.7in). There is no free play as the pedal is tensioned to give instant response when depressed. No routine attention is required as the release mechanism is self-adjusting. The initial setting of the pushrod after the release mechanism has been removed and refitted is covered in **Section 5 : 5**.

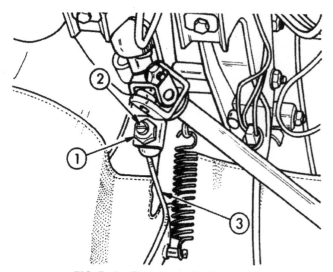

FIG 5:1 Pedal travel adjustment

Key to Fig 5:1   1 Locknut   2 Adjuster screw   3 Pedal arm

Hydraulic system overhaul:

Every 60,000km (36,000 miles) or every three years (whichever comes first), drain off the hydraulic fluid, overhaul the slave and master cylinders, fit a new hydraulic hose and refill the system with fresh fluid.

5:3 Removing and dismantling clutch

Remove the gearbox as described in **Chapter 6**. Refer to **FIG 5:3**. Mark the clutch cover and engine flywheel as shown at 1, so that the clutch cover can be refitted in its original position to preserve the balance of the assembly. Slacken the bolts securing clutch cover to flywheel alternately and evenly until all spring pressure is released. Remove the bolts and lift off the clutch pressure plate assembly and driven disc, taking care not to get grease or oil on the friction linings.

If the release bearing is to be removed from the clutch housing, refer to **FIG 5:4**. Remove spring clips 5 securing release bearing carrier to operating lever and remove the

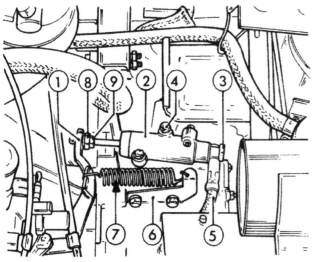

FIG 5:2 Slave cylinder installation

Key to Fig 5:2   1 Engagement lever   2 Slave cylinder
3 Union   4 Bolt   5 Hose   6 Bracket   7 Return spring
8, 9 Adjustment nuts

bearing assembly. If the lever assembly is to be removed, remove bolt 11 and washer 12, then pull lever 1 out of the fork and clutch housing.

Servicing:

The clutch cover, pressure plate and diaphragm spring assembly must not be dismantled. If any part is faulty the assembly must be renewed complete.

Inspect the surfaces of the flywheel where the driven plate makes contact. Small scratches on the surface are unimportant, but if there are deep scratches the flywheel must be machined smooth or renewed. Check the pressure plate for scoring or damage and check that the working surface is flat and true, using a metal straightedge. Make the check at several points. Check the diaphragm spring for cracks or other damage and the clutch cover for damage or distortion.

Check the release bearing for roughness when it is pressed and turned by hand. Clean the bearing by wiping with a cloth only. Do not use solvents for cleaning purposes as they would wash the internal lubricant from the bearing. If the engagement lever has been removed from the clutch housing, check the components for wear or damage, paying particular attention to bearing bush 9 and 'O' ring 8. It is recommended that the latter be renewed whenever the components are dismantled. Note that the bush and the bore in the bearing carrier should be lightly greased during reassembly.

Check the driven plate for loose rivets and broken or very loose torsional springs. Check the plate for distortion. Slight distortion can often be cured by installing the plate on the gearbox input shaft splines and twisting the plate by hand. If not, the plate should be renewed, as distortion can cause rapid wear and operational faults. Friction linings should be well proud of the rivets and have a polished glaze through which the grain of the material is clearly visible. A dark, glazed deposit indicates oil on the facings and, as this condition cannot be rectified, a new or relined plate will be required. Any sign of oil in the clutch indicates leakage from the engine or gearbox and the cause must be traced and rectified. Check the splines in the driven plate hub and on the gearbox input shaft, removing any burrs or, if there are signs of heavy wear, renewing parts as necessary.

It is not recommended that owners attempt to reline the clutch driven plate themselves, as the linings must be fitted and trued on the disc and the whole checked under a press. For this reason, the driven plate should be relined at a service station or an exchange unit obtained and fitted.

5:4 Assembling and refitting clutch

When the clutch assembly is refitted to the engine flywheel, it must be centralised before tightening down, using tool A.70210, a universal clutch alignment tool or a spare gearbox input shaft, as shown at 3 in **FIG 5:3**.

Fit the tool through the pressure plate and driven plate then offer the assembly to the flywheel, engaging the ends of the tool in the pilot bearing at the end of the crankshaft. Note that the protruding side of driven plate hub must face away from the engine flywheel. Index the alignment marks on cover and flywheel which were made previously, then fit the retaining bolts finger tight. Tighten the bolts alternately and evenly to the torque quoted in **Technical Data**.

Refit the release bearing and engagement lever mechanism in the reverse order of removal. Make sure that the 'O' ring is installed on the shaft, then press the shaft down into transmission and through operating fork. Continue pressing down until the shaft engages in the transmission boss, then align the fork and fit and tighten the locking bolt and washer.

Remove the alignment tool from the clutch assembly, then refit the gearbox as described in **Chapter 6**.

5:5 Servicing hydraulic system

At regular intervals the level of fluid in the clutch master cylinder reservoir, shown at 1 in **FIG 5:5**, should be checked. If necessary, fluid must be added to bring the level up to the neck of the reservoir. Wipe dirt from around the cap before removing it and make sure that the vent hole is clear before refitting. The same fluid should be used as recommended for the braking system in **Chapter 10**.

Master cylinder:

Removal:

Refer to **Chapter 9** and remove the steering column. Refer to **FIG 5:5**. Place suitable rags beneath the master cylinder assembly to catch any fluid spillage, noting that fluid is poisonous and that it can damage paintwork. Release clip 4 and release hose 2 from master cylinder connection, immediately plugging the hose to prevent leakage. Disconnect and plug pipe 3. Remove the two bolts and washers 6 securing master cylinder to bracket 5, then remove cylinder by pulling away from pushrod 8.

Dismantling:

Refer to **FIG 5:6**. Remove dust boot 3, then remove circlip 1. Remove the remaining components from cylinder bore, using a compressed air nozzle or tyre pump at the fluid outlet hole if removal proves difficult. Remove lockplate 6 and connector 5 with seal 4.

Discard all rubber seals and the rubber boot and obtain new parts to replace them. Wash all remaining parts in the correct grade of brake fluid or methylated spirits only. Examine the parts and renew any found to be worn or damaged. Check the piston and cylinder bore for scoring, damage or corrosion and renew if any fault is found. Ensure that the inlet port from the reservoir and the outlet port to the pipe union are clear.

Reassembly:

Observe absolute cleanliness during assembly to prevent oil or dirt from contacting the parts. Dip all internal components in clean approved brake fluid and assemble them wet. Use the fingers only to enter the seals in the bore to prevent damage. Press the piston assembly down the cylinder bore against the spring and hold in position while installing the circlip. Fit the new rubber boot.

Installation:

This is a reversal of the removal procedure, using a new clip to secure fluid supply hose to connector on master cylinder. Refit steering column as described in **Chapter 9**. On completion, bleed the system as described later then carry out adjustment procedures described in **Section 5:2**.

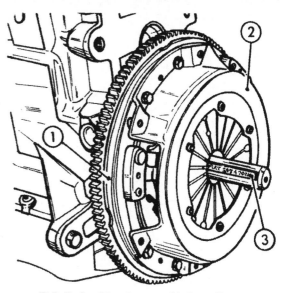

FIG 5:3   Clutch assembly installation

Key to Fig 5:3   1 Mark clutch cover and flywheel
2 Clutch cover assembly   3 Alignment tool A.70210
(or equivalent)

Slave cylinder:

Removal:

Refer to **FIG 5:2**. If the cylinder is to be removed for overhaul, unscrew union 3 and remove fluid hose 5, plugging or taping the ends to prevent leakage. If the cylinder is to be removed for access to other components only, leave the hose connected and support the cylinder by

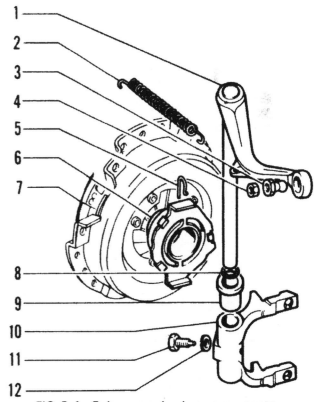

FIG 5:4   Release mechanism components

Key to Fig 5:4   1 Engagement lever and shaft   2 Return spring   3 Adjustment nut   4 Locknut   5 Spring clip
6 Carrier   7 Clutch assembly   8 'O' ring   9 Bush
10 Fork   11 Lock bolt   12 Washer

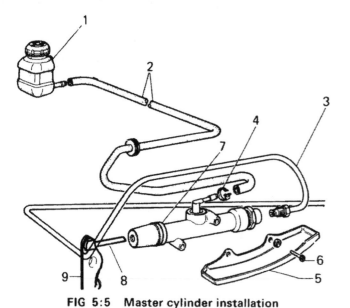

FIG 5:5 Master cylinder installation

Key to Fig 5:5 1 Fluid reservoir   2 Supply hose   3 Pipe
4 Clip   5 Bracket   6 Bolt   7 Master cylinder   8 Pushrod
9 Clutch pedal

suitable means after removal to prevent strain on the hose.
In this case, the system will not require bleeding when the
cylinder is refitted, but note that the clutch pedal must not
be touched while the cylinder is removed.

Remove the splitpin retaining pushrod to engagement
lever 1. Open the bleed screw to allow the pushrod to
retract, then disconnect spring 7 and close the bleed
screw. Push the engagement lever away from the cylinder,
then remove the two bolts and washers 4 securing cylinder

to support plate 6. Pull the cylinder away from the support
plate.

Dismantling:

Refer to **FIG 5:7**. Remove pushrod and boot 7, then
remove internal components from cylinder using
compressed air or a tyre pump at the fluid outlet hole if
removal proves difficult. Remove bleed screw 5. Service
the internal components in the manner described
previously for the master cylinder assembly.

Installation:

This is a reversal of the removal procedure, holding the
engagement lever against spring pressure while installing
and tightening the retaining bolts. If the fluid hose was disconnected from the slave cylinder, reconnect using new
gaskets, then bleed the system as described later. In all
cases, finally adjust clutch mechanism as described in
Section 5:2.

In the case of a 5-speed transmission, it is important to
check the initial setting of the slave cylinder pushrod after
any dismantling of the release mechanism. Proceed as
follows.

Measure the distance between the centre line of the
slave cylinder retaining bolt nearest the rubber boot and
the washer on the end of the pushrod. This should be
95mm (3.74in). Adjustment, should it be necessary, is
similar to that described for the 4-speed transmission and
shown in **FIG 5:2**. Operate the clutch pedal a number of
times and check the measurement. Readjust and recheck
if necessary.

Bleeding the system:

This operation is necessary to remove any air which may
have entered the system, due to the removal of

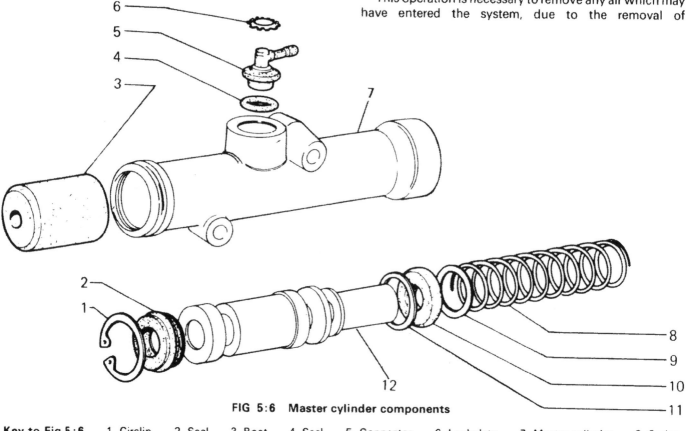

FIG 5:6 Master cylinder components

Key to Fig 5:6   1 Circlip   2 Seal   3 Boot   4 Seal   5 Connector   6 Lockplate   7 Master cylinder   8 Spring
9, 10 Seals   11 Gasket   12 Piston

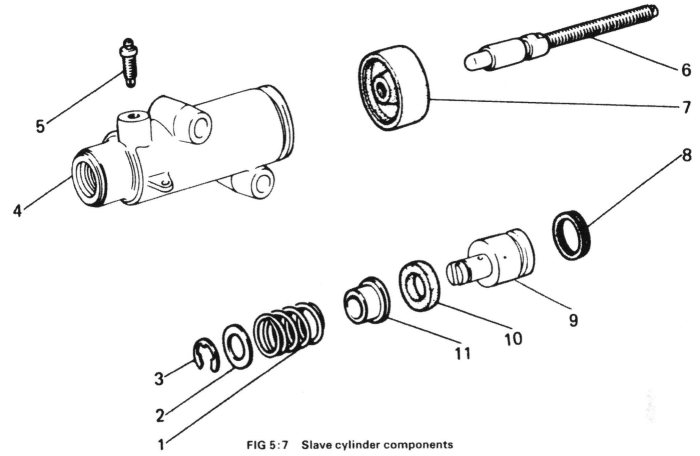

FIG 5:7 Slave cylinder components

Key to Fig 5:7 1 Spring 2 Washer 3 Retaining clip 4 Slave cylinder 5 Bleed screw 6 Pushrod 7 Boot
8 Seal 9 Piston 10 Seal 11 Bush

components, or if the fluid level in the reservoir has been allowed to drop too low and air has entered through the fluid supply passage.

A need for bleeding can be indicated if the clutch drags and cannot be fully released with the pedal pushed to the floor.

Make sure that the fluid level in the reservoir is correct, topping up if necessary. Locate the bleed screw on the slave cylinder, then remove the rubber dust cap if fitted. Attach a length of rubber or plastic tubing to the bleed screw and lead the free end of the tube into a clean glass jar, into which sufficient fluid of the correct type has been added to cover the end of the tube.

Unscrew the bleed screw by about three-quarters of a turn. Have an assistant depress the clutch pedal fully to the floor, then pause for a moment before allowing the pedal to return gently. Continue this action and watch the stream of fluid being pumped into the jar. When no air bubbles can be seen, hold the pedal at the end of a downstroke and tighten the bleed screw. Replenish the fluid in the reservoir frequently during this operation. If the level falls too low, air may be drawn into the system and the operation will have to be restarted.

On completion, top up the fluid to the correct level and check clutch mechanism adjustment as described in **Section 5:2**. It is not advisable to re-use fluid drained from the system unless it is new and perfectly clean. If so, allow it to stand for at least 24 hours before re-use to ensure that it is free from air bubbles. Always store the fluid in sealed containers to prevent dirt or moisture contamination.

5:6 Fault diagnosis

(a) Drag or spin

1 Oil or grease on driven plate linings
2 Misalignment between engine and splined shaft
3 Driven plate hub binding on splined shaft
4 Distorted driven plate
5 Warped or damaged pressure plate or clutch cover
6 Broken driven plate linings
7 Dirt or foreign matter in clutch
8 Air in hydraulic system
9 Clutch adjustment incorrect

(b) Fierceness or snatch

1 Check 1, 2, 3 and 9 in (a)
2 Worn driven plate linings

(c) Slip

1 Check 1, 2 and 9 in (a)
2 Worn driven plate linings
3 Weak diaphragm spring
4 Seized piston in master or slave cylinder

(d) Judder

1 Check 1 and 2 in (a)
2 Pressure plate not parallel with flywheel face
3 Contact area of driven plate linings unevenly worn
4 Bent or worn splined shaft

5 Badly worn splines in driven plate hub
6 Distorted driven plate
7 Faulty engine or gearbox mountings

5 Excessive backlash in transmission
6 Wear in transmission bearings
7 Release bearing loose on mounting

(e) Rattles

1 Check 4 and 5 in (d)
2 Weak diaphragm spring
3 Broken or loose spring in driven plate
4 Worn release mechanism

(f) Tick or knock

1 Check 4 and 5 in (d)
2 Release bearing incorrectly installed
3 Loose flywheel

CHAPTER 6
THE TRANSMISSION

6 : 1 Description

The location of the rear wheel drive transmission in relation to the engine is described in **Chapter 1, Section 1 : 1**. The transmission can be removed from the car leaving the engine in position.

The transmission comprises the clutch bellhousing which is bolted to the engine, the gearbox and final drive casing which is bolted to the bellhousing and an end cover together with, in the case of the 5-speed transmission, an intermediate plate. The gearbox input shaft is splined to the clutch driven plate which operates directly on the flywheel face. The clutch and its release mechanism are covered in **Chapter 5**. 1300 models have a 4-speed and reverse gearbox ; 1500 models have a 5-speed and reverse gearbox. Synchromesh engagement is provided on all forward speeds. Gear ratios are listed in **Technical Data**. First, second, third, reverse and the final drive ratios are the same for both gearboxes. The fifth ratio gears of the 1500 model transmission are, in effect, added to the 4-speed box and are accommodated by an intermediate plate which is located between the gearbox casing and a modified end cover. Gear selection is by linkage from the centrally mounted remote gearchange lever.

Final drive is by helical gearing with a conventional differential. The drive shafts (see **Chapter 8**) engage with the differential side gears, but the design of drive shaft differs between the 4-speed and the 5-speed trans-

mission. The differential casing is made up of two half casings in the 4-speed transmission and is a single piece casing in the 5-speed transmission. In both instances the speedometer drive is by skew gearing from the differential casing.

The number of special tools required for dismantling and reassembling the transmission is not great, but an owner who does not have experience of gearboxes should entrust overhaul work to an authorised agent.

Note, however, that certain special tools are necessary in order to carry out some of the overhaul procedures described in this chapter. If these factory tools or suitable substitutes are not available, the work should be carried out by a fully equipped service station.

6 : 2 Maintenance

Oil level :

Every 20,000km (12,000 miles), check the oil level and top up if necessary. The correct level is up to the bottom of the filler plug orifice. Clean off round the plug thoroughly before removing it. Use a short length of wire bent at a right angle as a dipstick. On completion, ensure that the plug is tightened securely.

Oil renewal :

Every 40,000km (24,000 miles), drain off the old oil, refit the drain plug securely and fill with approved oil up to

FIG 6 : 1 Gearchange linkage adjustment

Key to Fig 6 : 1   1 Flexible coupling   2 Bolt   3 Coupling
bolts   4 Gearchange rod

the bottom of the filler plug orifice as described earlier.
Refer to **Technical Data** in the **Appendix** for the capacity
of the transmission.

Gearchange linkage :

Every 20,000km (12,000 miles), refer to **Section 6 : 3**
and lubricate the gearchange linkage. Adjustment, should
it be necessary, is also covered in **Section 6 : 3**.

6:3 Gearchange linkage

Adjustment :

Check gearchange linkage adjustment by selecting
neutral then detaching the rubber boot from the base of the
gearlever. In the neutral position, the gearlever should be
centralised in the guide plate mounted on the car floor and
should be vertical when viewed from the side. If not, raise
and safely support the rear of the car, then locate the gearchange linkage flexible coupling beneath the car, as shown
in **FIG 6 : 1**.

Scribe a line across the coupling and clamp plate
assembly (arrowed) so that the original position can be
regained if necessary, then slacken the two bolts 3 to
release flexible coupling 1 from gearchange rod 4. Move
the flexible coupling within the limits allowed by the
oversize mounting holes until the gearlever is in the centre

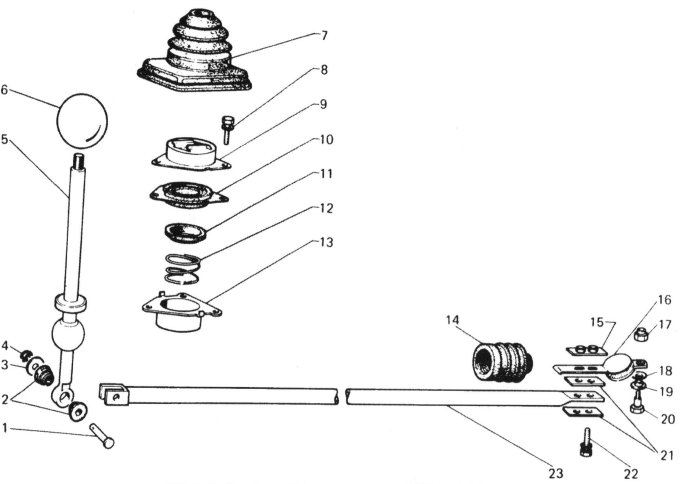

FIG 6 : 2 Gearchange linkage components (1300 model shown)

Key to Fig 6 : 2   1 Pin   2 Rubber bush   3 Washer   4 Retaining clip   5 Gearlever   6 Knob   7 Boot   8 Bolt
9 Guide plate   10 Cap   11 Ball socket   12 Spring   13 Support   14 Boot   15 Plate   16 Flexible coupling
17 Nut   18 Lockwasher   19 Bush   20 Bolt   21 Plates   22 Bolt   23 Rod

of the guide plate and vertical when viewed from the side. Firmly tighten the two bolts then recheck the adjustment. Refit the gearlever boot.

Gearchange linkage removal :

Refer to **FIG 6 : 2**. Remove rubber boot 7 from base of gearlever, then remove the three bolts 8 securing guide plate 9 to body panel. Lift the gearlever, guide plate and support assembly from the mounting, then remove retaining clip 4 and pin 1 to release gearlever, bushes and washer from gearchange rod. Remove bolt 20 securing flexible coupling to transmission selector shaft, then remove gearchange rod rearwards to remove. Do not disturb bolts 22 securing flexible coupling to rod.

Refit the gearchange linkage in the reverse order of removal. On completion, check linkage adjustment as described previously and correct if necessary.

6:4 Transmission removal and refitting

Removal :

Refer to **Chapter 2** and remove the air cleaner and duct for carburetter cooling. Disconnect the battery. Refer to **Chapter 5** and remove clutch slave cylinder without disconnecting fluid hose.

Remove nuts and bolts holding transmission to engine crankcase which are accessible from above, then raise and safely support the rear of the car and remove the rear wheels. Fit suitable lifting equipment and tension sufficiently to take the weight of the engine.

Working from beneath the car, remove the three splash guard panels shown in **FIG 6 : 3**. Scribe or paint mark the gearchange linkage coupling and plates as shown in **FIG 6 : 1**, then remove both bolts 3 and collect the plates. Slacken bolt 2 and swing coupling 1 away from the work area.

Refer to **FIG 6 : 4**. Disconnect the connector 1 for reversing lights, then remove the clamp holding wires to body. If seat belt interlock system is incorporated, disconnect the system wiring connector which is located inboard and forward of transmission near engine water hoses. Remove three bolts 2, disconnect wiring and remove starter motor. Disconnect speedometer cable from transmission.

Refer to **FIG 6 : 5** and disconnect earth strap 1. Remove exhaust system 2 by detaching from exhaust manifold, removing two bolts and washers holding bracket to top of exhaust pipe then removing two bolts and washers securing pipe to crossmember 3. Refer to **Chapter 8** and remove the hub nuts securing drive shafts to wheel hubs. Remove two bolts and nuts securing suspension control arm to supports. Pull wheel hub from drive shafts then prevent shafts from coming out of transmission by suitably tying in place.

Remove the flywheel cover then remove the crossmember supporting engine. Remove remaining bolts and nuts securing transmission to engine. Using a suitable support and jack, or with the help of an assistant, support the weight of the gearbox while moving it away from the engine until the splined shaft is clear of the clutch. Lower the transmission assembly and remove from beneath the

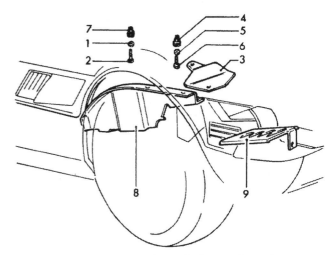

FIG 6 : 3   Removing splash guard panels

Key to Fig 6 : 3   1 Washer   2 Bolt   3 Splash guard 4 Fastener   5 Washer   6 Bolt   7 Fastener   8, 9 Splash guards

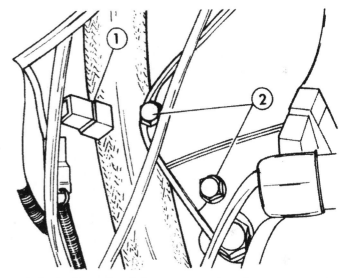

FIG 6 : 4   Reversing light connector 1 and starter mounting bolts 2

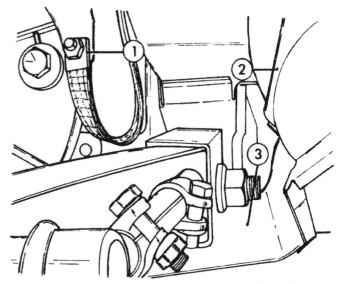

FIG 6 : 5   Earth strap 1, exhaust system 2 and crossmember 3

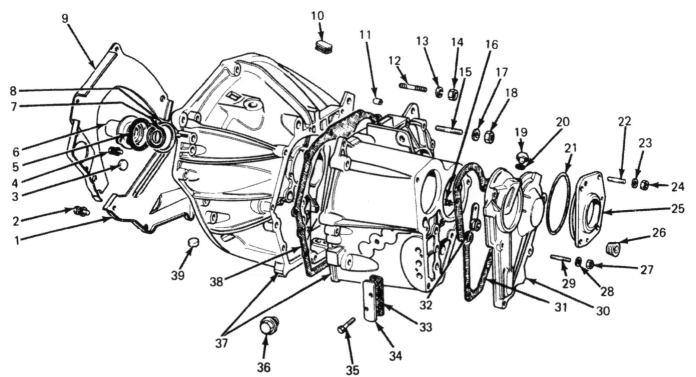

FIG 6:6 Transmission case and cover components (4-speed transmission)

Key to Fig 6:6   1 Cover   2 Bolt and washer   3 Plug   4 Bolt and washer   5 Gasket   6 Cover   7 Seal   8 Plug
9 Cover   10 Plug   11 Dowel   12 Stud   13 Lockwasher   14 Nut   15 Stud   16 Bolt and washer   17 Lockwasher
18 Nut   19 Vent   20 Gasket   21 Seal   22 Stud   23 Lockwasher   24 Nut   25 Flange   26 Plug   27 Nut
28 Lockwasher   29 Stud   30 Cover   31 Gasket   32 Magnet   33 Gasket   34 Cover   35 Bolt   36 Plug
37 Castings   38 Gasket   39 Plug

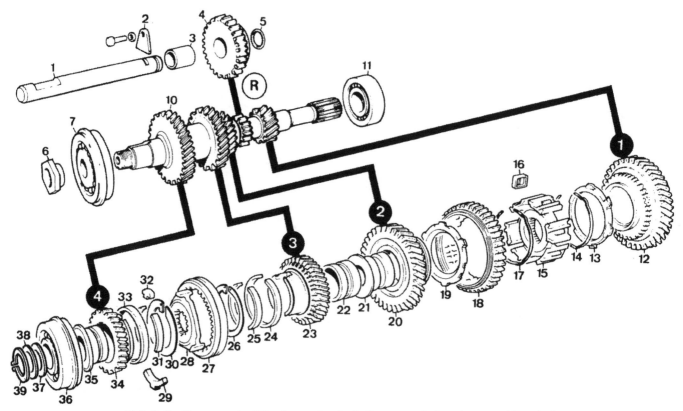

FIG 6:7 Components of the 4-speed mainshaft, countershaft and reverse idler shaft

Key to Fig 6:7   1 Reverse idler shaft   2 Plate   3 Bush   4 Idler gear   5 Seal   6 Nut (circlip on earlier models)
7 Bearing   10 Mainshaft   11 Bearing   12 Driven first speed gear   13 Synchroniser   14 Spring   15 Hub
16 Pad   17 Spring   18 Sleeve and reverse driven gear   19 Synchroniser   20 Driven second speed gear   21, 22 Bush
23 Driven third speed gear   24 Synchroniser ring   25 Spring   26 Circlip   27 Sleeve   28 Hub   29 Pad
30 Circlip   31 Spring   32 Pad   33 Synchroniser ring   34 Driven fourth speed gear   35 Bush   36 Bearing
37, 38 Spring washer   39 Circlip

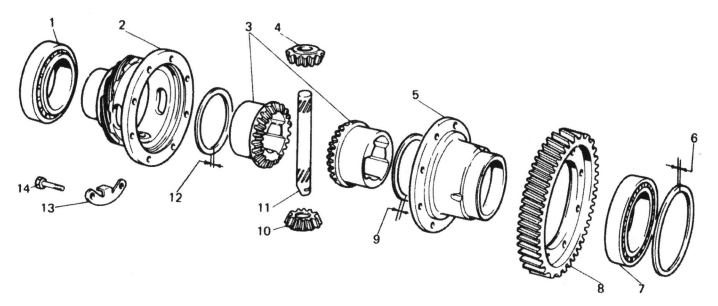

FIG 6:8   Differential assembly components

Key to Fig 6:8   1 Bearing   2 Half case   3 Side gears   4 Pinion gear   5 Half case   6 Ring   7 Bearing
8 Ring gear   9 Thrust washer   10 Pinion gear   11 Pinion shaft   12 Thrust ring   13 Lockplate   14 Bolt

car. **Do not allow the weight of the transmission to hang on the splined shaft while it is in the clutch unit, otherwise serious damage to clutch components may occur.**

Refitting:

This is a reversal of the removal procedure, observing the correct tightening torques for component fixings. Note that suspension components must be finally tightened with the car properly laden as described in **Chapter 8**. Take care to avoid clutch damage when entering splined shaft through clutch assembly. On completion, check transmission oil level as described in **Section 6:2** and gearchange linkage adjustment as described in **Section 6:3**.

6:5 Transmission dismantling

Attach the transmission assembly to a suitable support stand, if available. If not, use suitable blocks of wood to hold the transmission in the required attitudes when dismantling.

4-speed and 5-speed transmissions:

Refer to **Section 6:2** and drain the transmission. Refer to **Chapter 8, Section 8:6** and withdraw the drive shafts from the transmission. Remove the clutch release bearing, lever and fork as described in **Chapter 5, Section 5:3**.

4-speed transmission:

The components of the casings and end cover are shown in **FIG 6:6**. The components of the mainshaft, reverse idler shaft and the countershaft are shown in **FIG**

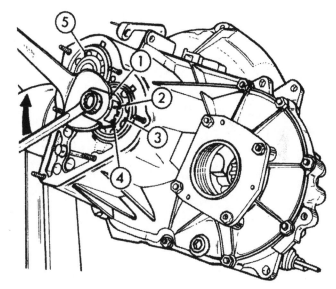

FIG 6:9   Compressing   countershaft   bearing   spring washer

Key to Fig 6:9   1 Tool A.70284   2 Circlip   3 Bearing
4 Countershaft   5 Bearing

6:7. The first/second synchronisers are spring ring type. The third/fourth synchronisers are slip ring type. The components of the final drive and differential gearing are shown in **FIG 6:8**.

Refer to **FIG 6:6**. Remove cover 30 and joint gasket 31. Using tool A.70284 or a suitable bolt, washer and piece of tube (profiled for circlip clearance), compress the spring washers 37 and 38 in **FIG 6:7** as shown in **FIG 6:9**. Tighten the bolt so that tool 1 compresses the washer, then remove circlip 2 (this is 39 in **FIG 6:7**) from

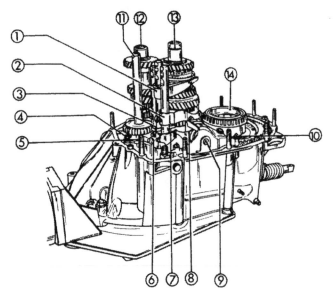

FIG 6 : 10 Removing selectors, gears and differential

Key to Fig 6 : 10 1 3rd and 4th gear selector fork 2 1st and 2nd gear selector fork 3 3rd and 4th gear dog 4 Nut 5 Plate 6 Reverse selector fork 7 1st and 2nd gear dog 8 Gear selector and engagement lever 9 Support 10 Nut 11 Reverse gearshaft 12 Mainshaft assembly 13 Countershaft assembly 14 Differential assembly

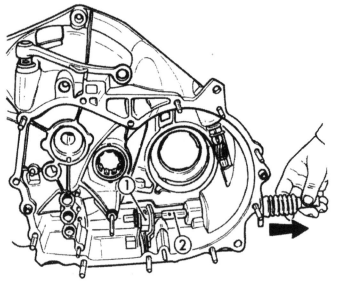

FIG 6 : 11 Selector rod removal

Key to Fig 6 : 11 1 Lever 2 Selector rod

countershaft 4. Remove circlip from mainshaft bearing 5. Remove cover 34 shown in **FIG 6 : 6**, then remove the three detent springs and balls from the bores in the case. Remove bearings 3 and 5 from shafts (see **FIG 6 : 9**).

Refer to **FIG 6 : 6**. Remove the fixing nuts, then separate transmission case halves 37 and detach gasket 38. Refer to **FIG 6 : 10**. Remove screws retaining selector forks and dogs 1, 2, 3, 6 and 7, then remove rods, forks and dogs from their seats in housing. Remove nut 10 and detach selector lever support 9. Remove nut 4 and detach plate 3 retaining reverse shaft 11. Remove the reverse idler shaft. Remove mainshaft assembly 12 and countershaft assembly 13 with gears, then remove differential assembly 14.

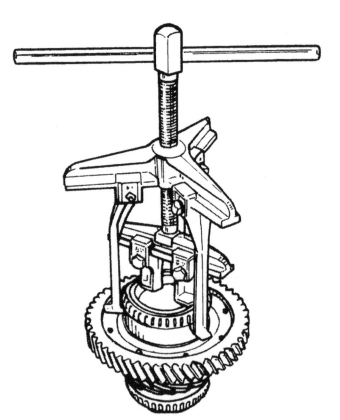

FIG 6 : 12 Removing bearing inner race from differential

Refer to **FIG 6 : 11**. Remove screw retaining lever 1, then remove selector rod 2 as indicated by the arrow.

If the countershaft assembly is to be dismantled, refer to **FIG 6 : 7** and, as the components are withdrawn from the shaft, note which way round they were fitted. The final drive gear is integral with the shaft.

Note that the mainshaft may either be retained in bearing 7 by a nut (item 6 in **FIG 6 : 7**) or, in the case of earlier models, by a circlip. Should a new mainshaft be required, ensure that the replacement is the same type as that originally fitted.

The plate 2 in **FIG 6 : 7** which retains the reverse idler shaft may itself be retained by a bolt and washer as shown or, in the case of earlier versions, by a stud, washer and nut.

If the differential bearings are worn or damaged, remove the inner races from differential carrier using a suitable puller tool as shown in **FIG 6 : 12**. Use a suitable puller tool to remove the outer bearing races from the case. Collect the shims fitted between bearing outer race and the sealing cover. To dismantle the differential assembly, refer to **FIG 6 : 8**. Make a reference mark on half cases 2 and 5, so that they can be reassembled in their original relative positions. Remove the eight fixing bolts and separate the half cases, then remove lockplate from pinion shaft and drive the shaft from the case. Remove the side gears, pinion gears and thrust washers.

5-speed transmission :

The components of the casings, intermediate plate and end cover are shown in **FIG 6 : 13**. The components of the mainshaft, reverse idler shaft and the countershaft are shown in **FIG 6 : 14**. The first/second synchronisers are spring ring type. The third/fourth and fifth synchronisers are slip ring type. The components of the final drive driven

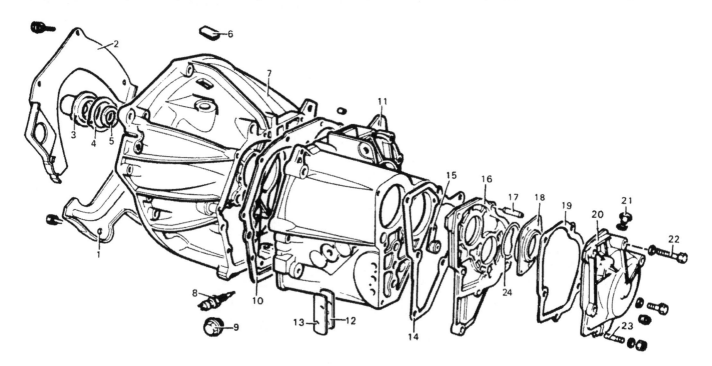

FIG 6:13   Transmission case and cover components (5-speed transmission)

Key to Fig 6:13   1, 2, 3 Cover   4 Gasket   5 Seal   6 Plug   7 Clutch bellhousing   8 Reversing light switch
9 Plug   10 Gasket   11 Casing   12 Gasket   13 Cover   14 Gasket   15 Magnet   16 Intermediate plate   17 Stud
18 Bearing retainer   19 Gasket   20 End cover   21 Vent   22 Bolt   23 Stud   24 Shim

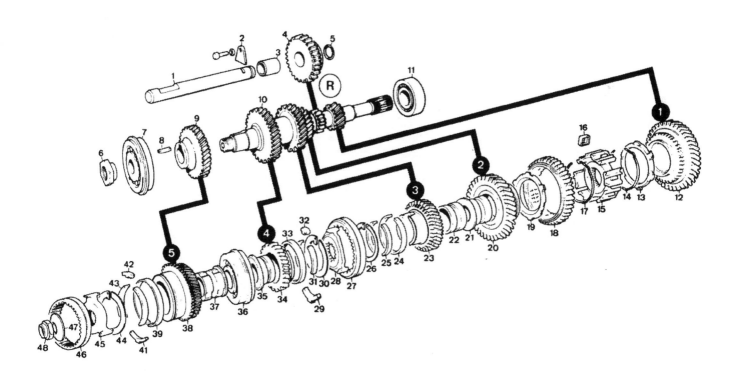

FIG 6:14   Components of the 5-speed mainshaft, countershaft and reverse idler shaft

Key to Fig 6:14   1 Reverse idler shaft   2 Plate   3 Bush   4 Idler gear   5 Seal   6 Nut   7 Bearing   8 Key
9 Fifth speed driving gear   10 Mainshaft   11 Bearing   12 Driven first speed gear   13 Synchroniser   14 Spring
15 Hub   16 Pad   17 Spring   18 Sleeve and reverse driven gear   19 Synchroniser   20 Driven second speed gear
21, 22 Bush   23 Driven third speed gear   24 Synchroniser ring   25 Spring   26 Circlip   27 Sleeve   28 Hub
29 Pad   30 Circlip   31 Spring   32 Pad   33 Synchroniser ring   34 Driven fourth speed gear   35 Bush   36 Bearing
37 Bush   38 Driven fifth speed gear   39 Synchroniser ring   41, 42 Pad   43 Spring   44 Circlip   45 Hub
46 Sleeve   47 Spring washer   48 Nut

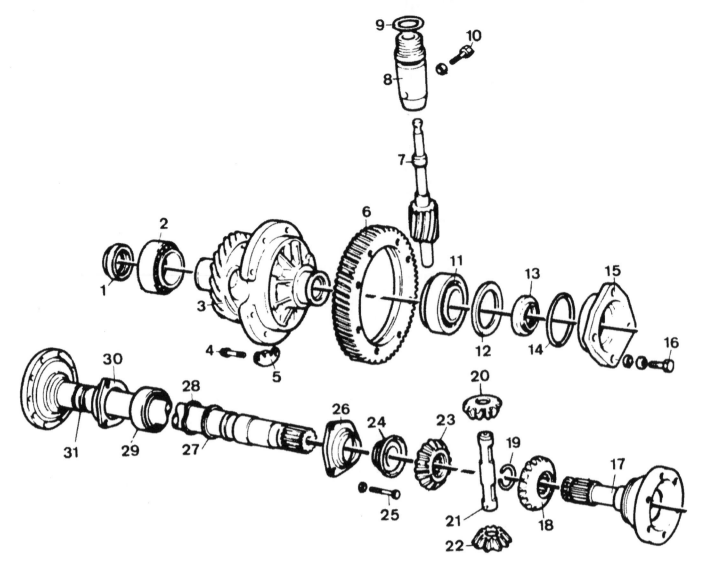

FIG 6 : 15 Five-speed differential and final drive gearing and drive shafts

Key to Fig 6 : 15   1 Seal   2 Bearing   3 Differential casing   4 Bolt   5 Lockplate   6 Driven final drive gear
7 Speedometer driven gear unit   8 Housing   9 Washer   10 Retaining bolt   11 Bearing   12 Thrust ring   13 Seal
14 Ring   15 Retaining flange   16 Bolt   17 Drive shaft   18 Side gear   19 Snap ring   20 Pinion   21 Shaft
22 Pinion   23 Side gear   24 Seal   25 to 31 Drive shaft components

gear and the differential gearing are shown in **FIG 6 : 15**. The final drive driving gear is integral with the countershaft. The drive shafts are also shown in **FIG 6 : 15**.

Refer to **FIG 6 : 13**. Remove the end cover 20 and joint gasket 19. Remove the bearing retainer 18 and shim 24. Refer to **FIG 6 : 14**. Remove nut 48 and washer 47. Remove the intermediate plate 16 and joint gasket 14 as shown in **FIG 6 : 13**.

Proceed substantially as described earlier for the 4-speed transmission, but refer to **FIGS 6 : 13, 6 : 14** and **6 : 15**. Note that the fifth speed mainshaft driving gear 9 in **FIG 6 : 14** is keyed to the mainshaft. Do not lose the key 8.

Inspection, 4-speed and 5-speed transmissions :

Clean all parts and examine them for excessive wear or for damage. Pay particular attention to the bearings and the synchroniser components. Check the sliding sleeve hubs for nicks and damage to the sliding surfaces. If the splined parts of the synchroniser assemblies do not slide

smoothly, examine them for burrs which should be removed using an oilstone. Do not attempt, however, to salvage seriously worn or damaged components. Examine the condition of the gearteeth. If an owner does not have experience of gearbox overhauls, he should seek professional inspection assistance. If a differential side gear or pinion is unserviceable, renew the set of gears and ensure that the correct parts are obtained. The side gear bores differ between models.

6 : 6 Transmission reassembly

Reassemble by reversing the dismantling sequence. Fit new gaskets and seals and lubricate all internal moving parts with clean approved transmission oil. Remove any burrs or blemishes from the joint faces of the casings and the end cover.

Reassembly of synchroniser assemblies will be facilitated by the use of the special tool as shown in **FIG 6 : 16**. If this tool is not available, a length of suitably bored out tubing can be used to push the circlip into position. Ensure that circlips are correctly seated in their grooves.

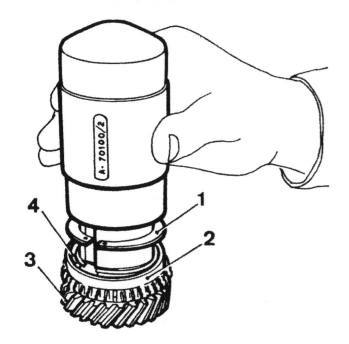

FIG 6 : 16   Reassembling synchroniser components

Key to Fig 6 : 16   1 Circlip   2 Synchroniser ring
3 Gear   4 Spring

Check the backlash between the side gears and the pinion gear in the reassembled differential gearing. This should not exceed 0.10mm (0.004in). Provided that it is not due to excessive gear wear, backlash may be corrected by fitting thicker thrust washers. Excessive backlash which is due to worn parts can only be corrected by fitting new components. If the original parts are refitted, the original differential bearing shims should be refitted. If new casings, new bearings or new differential case halves have been required, the differential bearing preloading will need to be adjusted. No special tools are required and the procedure is as follows.

Refer to **FIG 6 : 17**. Position the outer ring 4 of the carrier bearing in its seat and place the shims which were originally fitted on top of the bearing as shown at 1. Position the flange 2 on the shims and, using feeler gauges, measure the clearance **X** between the flange and the transmission casing. This should be 0.08 to 0.12mm (0.003 to 0.005in). Add or remove shims until the thickness of the shim pack 1 gives a clearance **X** within the specified range. Tighten down the retaining flange 2. Rotate the differential assembly through a number of turns to settle the bearings, remove the retaining flange and recheck the clearance **X**. Modify the shim pack thickness if necessary, refit the flange and torque tighten the retaining nuts.

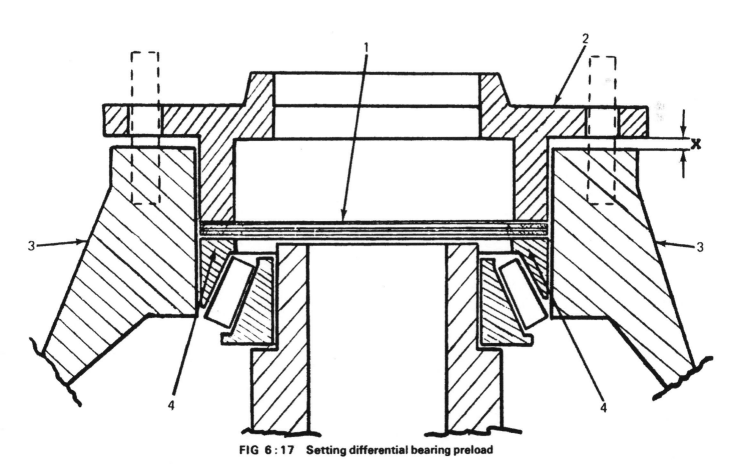

FIG 6 : 17   Setting differential bearing preload

Key to Fig 6 : 17   1 Shims   2 Retaining flange   3 Transmission housing   4 Bearing   **X** Clearance (see text)

6:7 Fault diagnosis

(a) Jumping out of gear

1 Excessively worn selector shafts
2 Worn synchromesh assemblies
3 Loose or worn selector fork or dog

(b) Noisy transmission

1 Insufficient oil
2 Bearings worn or damaged
3 Worn drive shaft joints
4 Worn gears or shafts
5 Worn synchromesh units

(c) Difficulty in engaging gear

1 Incorrect clutch adjustment
2 Faulty clutch components
3 Worn synchromesh assemblies
4 Worn selector shafts or forks
5 Gearchange linkage adjustment incorrect

(d) Oil leaks

1 Damaged joint gaskets
2 Worn or damaged oil seals
3 Faulty joint faces·on transmission casings

CHAPTER 7

FRONT SUSPENSION AND HUBS

7:1 Description

Independent front suspension is by means of McPherson struts. These suspension struts incorporate telescopic hydraulic dampers and coil springs mounted between pressed steel cups. The damper units also act as pivots for the front wheel hub carriers, to accommodate steering movement. A section through a front suspension and hub assembly is shown in **FIG 7:1**, the inset showing details of suspension strut upper mounting.

The front wheel hub carrier assembly is located at the upper point by the damper unit attachment and at the lower point by a control arm and reaction strut. To accommodate suspension movement, control arm to carrier attachment is by means of a ball joint. The front wheel hubs are supported in wide twin-row ballbearings. All joints and pivots in the front suspension are lubricated for life. There are geometrical differences between the front suspensions of the 1300 and 1500 models. For information on both models refer to **Technical Data**.

7:2 Maintenance

Tyres and wheels:

Every 500km (300 miles), check the tyre pressures and reinflate as necessary. Recommended tyre pressures are quoted in **Technical Data** in the **Appendix**.

Every 10,000km (6000 miles) (if the car is operating on rough roads, halve this interval), interchange the wheels to even out tyre wear. An interchange scheme is as follows.

Fit the spare wheel to the front lefthand position ; move the front lefthand wheel to the rear righthand position, the rear righthand wheel to the front righthand position, the front righthand to the rear lefthand and the rear lefthand to the spare position. At this same interval, have the wheels rebalanced.

At this same interval, the depth of the tyre tread should be checked to ensure that it is not below the legal minimum. If uneven wear of the front wheel treads is apparent, check the wheel alignment as described in **Chapter 9, Section 9 : 7**.

General :

Every 5000km (3000 miles), visually check the condition of the ball joints, pivots, dampers and springs. If indications of unserviceability, excessive wear or damage due to road stones is evident, refer to the relevant section in this chapter and renew the defective parts or unit.

7:3 Control arms and reaction struts

Reaction struts mounting bushes and control arm inner mounting bush assembly can be renewed separately if worn or damaged, but if the ball joint is worn or damaged

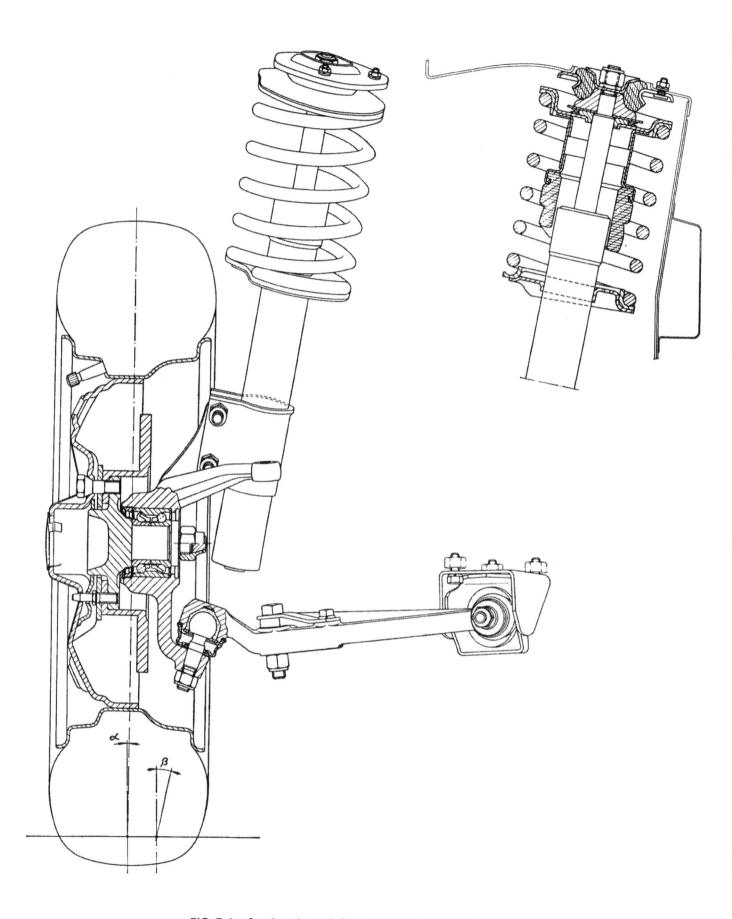

FIG 7:1   Section through front suspension and hub assembly

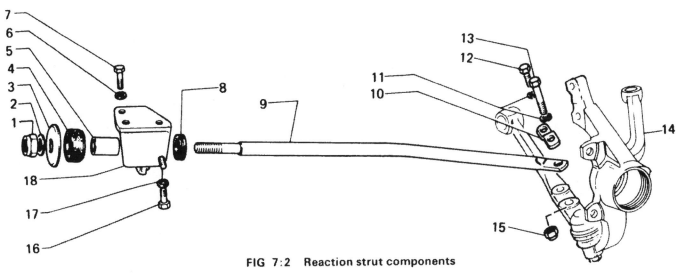

FIG 7:2   Reaction strut components

Key to Fig 7:2   1 Nut   2 Washer   3 Cup washer   4 Rubber bush   5 Spacer   6 Lock washer   7 Bolt   8 Rubber bush
9 Reaction strut   10 Lock plate   11 Lock washer   12, 13 Bolts   14 Hub carrier   15 Nut   16 Bolt   17 Washer
18 Mounting bracket

the control arm must be renewed complete. Always renew the control arm assembly if the ball joint rubber boot is damaged, as the ingress of road dirt will cause rapid wear of the joint.

Reaction strut removal:

Refer to **FIG 7:2**. Remove self-locking nut 1 and washer 2, then remove bolts 12 and 13 securing reaction strut to control arm. Remove the strut, collecting and carefully noting the position of any shims fitted at the mounting bracket end.

Examine all parts for wear or damage and renew as necessary. Slight distortion of the reaction strut can be rectified at a service station, but major distortion will dictate renewal. Refit in the reverse order of removal, making sure that any shims are refitted in their original positions. Renew all self-locking nuts. On completion, it is recommended that suspension geometry be checked as described in **Section 7 : 6**.

Control arm removal:

Raise and safely support the front of the car, and remove the road wheel. Detach the reaction strut from control arm as described previously. **FIG 7:3** shows control arm components. Remove nut 10, then use a suitable puller tool to disconnect ball joint from hub carrier 11. Remove nut 1 and bolt 9 to detach control arm.

Examine all components for wear or damage. If the ball joint or the control arm is faulty, the assembly must be renewed complete, but if the inner bushing is worn or damaged this can be renewed. However, as special tools and press equipment are needed to install the bushes and flare the ends of the inner spacer, the work should be carried out by a fully equipped service station.

Refit the components in the reverse order of removal, using new self-locking nuts. On completion, it is recommended that suspension geometry be checked as described in **Section 7 : 6**.

7 : 4   Wheel hubs and carriers

Hub carrier removal:

Raise and safely support the front of the car, then remove the road wheel. If the hub assembly is to be dismantled after removal, have an assistant depress the brake pedal to lock the hub and disc against rotation, then slacken the hub retaining nut located on the inboard side. Remove brake caliper 5 and mounting 6 (see **FIG 7:4**) then support caliper so that hose is not strained, referring to **Chapter 10** for detailed instructions concerning brake system components. Remove bolt 1 and centring stud 2 securing disc 3 and plate 4.

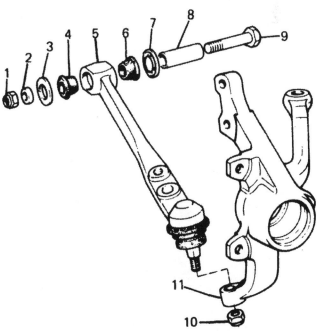

FIG 7:3   Control arm components

Key to Fig 7:3   1 Nut   2, 3 Washers   4 Rubber bush
5 Control arm   6 Rubber bush   7 Washer   8 Spacer
9 Bolt   10 Nut   11 Hub carrier

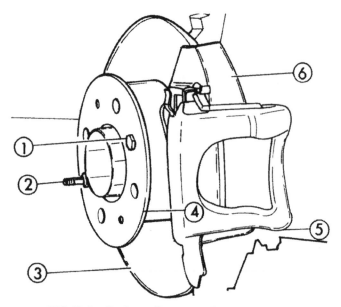

FIG 7:4   Brake caliper and disc mountings

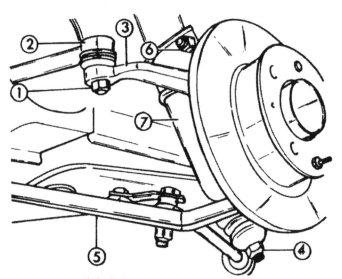

FIG 7:5   Hub carrier removal

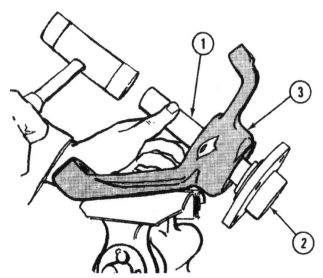

FIG 7:6   Removing hub from carrier

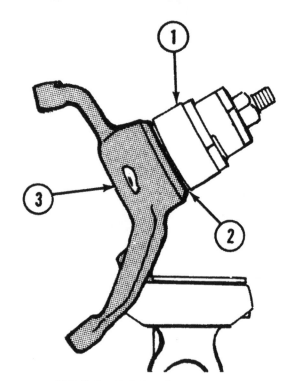

FIG 7:7   Hub bearing removal

Refer to **FIG 7:5** and remove nut 1 securing tie rod ball joint 2 to hub carrier 3. Use a suitable puller to disconnect ball joint from carrier. Remove nut 4 and disconnect control arm ball joint in a similar manner. Remove two nuts and bolts 6 securing hub carrier to suspension strut, then remove the carrier.

Hub bearing renewal:

Refer to **FIG 7:6**. Remove and discard the hub securing nut. Clamp hub carrier 3 in a vice having padded jaws, then use tool 8015 or other suitable drift 1 to drive hub 2 from carrier. Use tool A.57123 or similar to remove ring nut securing bearing in carrier. Discard the nut as a new one must be used when reassembling. Refer to **FIG 7:7** and use tool 8015 or other suitable tool (1) to pull bearing 2 from carrier 3.

Make sure that the bore in the hub carrier is clean, then install a new hub bearing using tool 8015 or similar, as shown at 1 in **FIG 7:8**, to pull new bearing 2 into carrier 3. Refer to **FIG 7:9** and screw a new ring nut 2 into place. Use tool A.57123 or similar, in conjunction with a torque wrench, to tighten the ring nut to 5.9daNm (44lbf ft). Use a suitable punch to stake the ring nut in position as shown by the arrow in **FIG 7:10**.

Refit the hub bearing in carrier, preferably using press equipment. Install the two washers and a new nut, then tighten nut to 13.5daNm (100lbf ft) if it has an M18 thread or 21.6daNm (160lbf ft) for an M20 thread. Stake the nut against rotation. If the hub cannot be held securely against rotation, screw the nut on as tightly as possible, then fully tighten to the correct torque after refitting the assembly, with the brake applied to lock the hub and disc assembly.

Refitting:

This is a reversal of the removal procedure. Reconnect all fixings shown in **FIG 7:5**, but do not fully tighten at this

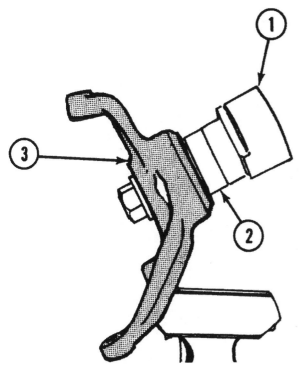

FIG 7:8   Hub bearing installation

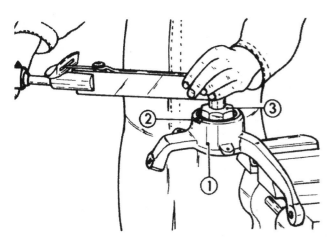

FIG 7:9   Tightening ring nut

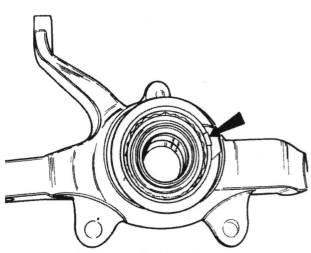

FIG 7:10   Staking ring nut

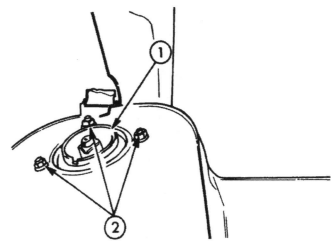

FIG 7:11   Suspension strut upper mounting

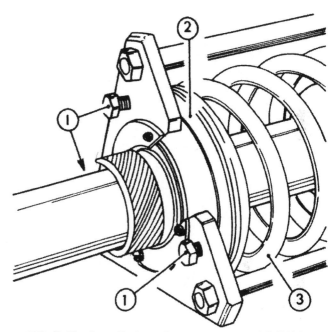

FIG 7:12   Installation of compressor tool A.74241

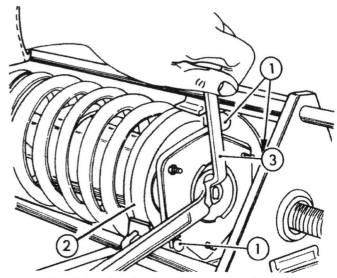

FIG 7:13   Slackening damper retaining nut

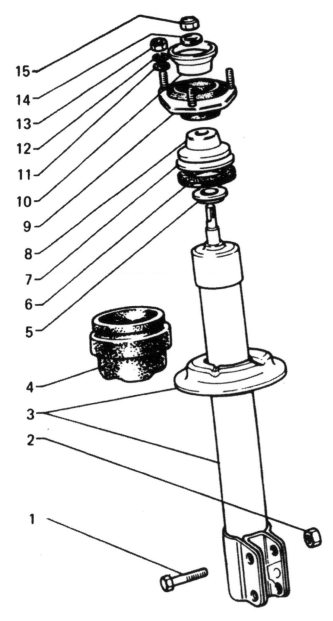

FIG 7:14 Damper mounting components

Key to Fig 7:14 1 Bolt 2 Nut 3 Damper and spring seat 4 Rubber pad 5 Thrust plate 6 Rubber ring 7 Washer 8 Spacer 9 Pad 10 Cup 11 Washer 12 Lock washer 13 Nut 14 Washer 15 Nut

stage. Refit caliper and disc, fully tightening the attachments. Refit the road wheel and lower the car, then finally tighten the remaining fixings to recommended torque with the car in a laden condition. For these purposes, this is with two persons plus 20kg (44lb) of luggage, with tyres correctly inflated. On completion, it is recommended that suspension geometry be checked as described in **Section 7 : 6**.

7 : 5 Suspension struts
Removal :

Raise and safely support the front of the car, then remove the road wheel. Use a suitable jack or stand placed beneath the hub carrier to support the weight of the assembly. Refer to **FIG 7:11** and detach suspension strut

1 from upper mounting by removing the three nuts and washers 2. Remove the two nuts and bolts shown at 6 in **FIG 7:5**, then remove suspension strut from car.

Dismantling :

In order to remove coil springs from suspension strut it is essential to use a spring compressor tool, such as A.74241 or similar, as shown in **FIG 7:12**. If the factory tool is used, make sure that screws 1 are touching seat 2 for spring 3, and note that one screw at each end must be in the recess in the seat.

Refer to **FIG 7:13**. Make sure that screws 1 are properly located, then tighten the tool to compress the spring until it is clear of seat 2. Use a suitable spanner to slacken the damper retaining nut, using tool A.57020 or other suitable tool (3) to hold the damper stud against rotation. Remove the nut, then detach the damper from coil spring. If the spring is not to be renewed, leave it compressed ready for installation.

If a damper unit is faulty it can be overhauled, but as this work requires the use of special tools and equipment it should be carried out by a fully equipped service station.

Refit the coil spring to damper in the reverse order of removal, making sure that the mounting components are correctly located as shown in **FIG 7:14**. When nut 15 has been fully tightened, remove the spring compressor.

Refitting :

This is a reversal of the removal procedure, renewing self-locking nuts and tightening all fixings to the recommended torque figures.

7 : 6 Suspension geometry

Due to the need for special optical measuring equipment for accurate results, the checking and adjusting of front wheel caster and camber angles should be carried out by a fully equipped service station. Checks must be carried out with the tyres inflated correctly and with the car unladen.

The correct caster and camber angles are given in **Technical Data**. Caster is adjusted by adding or removing shims between reaction struts and their front mounting brackets. Camber angles cannot be adjusted so if found to be incorrect all front suspension components should be examined for damage or distortion and parts renewed as necessary.

The method for setting the alignment of front wheels is described in **Chapter 9, Section 9 : 7**.

7 : 7 Fault diagnosis
(a) Wheel wobble

1 Worn hub bearings
2 Broken or weak front spring
3 Uneven tyre wear
4 Worn suspension linkage
5 Loose wheel fixings
6 Incorrect front wheel alignment

(b) Car pulls to one side

1 Unequal tyre pressures

2 Incorrect suspension geometry
3 Defective suspension bushes or damaged parts
4 Weak spring on one side
5 Fault in steering system

(c) Bottoming of suspension

1 Broken or weak coil spring
2 Defective damper

(d) Excessive body roll

1 Defective spring or damper

(e) Rattles

1 Check 2 and 4 in (a) and check (c)
2 Defective suspension strut mountings
3 Defective suspension arm bushes

(f) Suspension hard

1 Tyre pressures too high
2 Suspension arm ball joints stiff
3 Dampers faulty

Inches	Decimals	Milli-metres	Inches to Millimetres — Inches	Inches to Millimetres — mm	Millimetres to Inches — mm	Millimetres to Inches — Inches
1/64	.015625	.3969	.001	.0254	.01	.00039
1/32	.03125	.7937	.002	.0508	.02	.00079
3/64	.046875	1.1906	.003	.0762	.03	.00118
1/16	.0625	1.5875	.004	.1016	.04	.00157
5/64	.078125	1.9844	.005	.1270	.05	.00197
3/32	.09375	2.3812	.006	.1524	.06	.00236
7/64	.109375	2.7781	.007	.1778	.07	.00276
1/8	.125	3.1750	.008	.2032	.08	.00315
9/64	.140625	3.5719	.009	.2286	.09	.00354
5/32	.15625	3.9687	.01	.254	.1	.00394
11/64	.171875	4.3656	.02	.508	.2	.00787
3/16	.1875	4.7625	.03	.762	.3	.01181
13/64	.203125	5.1594	.04	1.016	.4	.01575
7/32	.21875	5.5562	.05	1.270	.5	.01969
15/64	.234375	5.9531	.06	1.524	.6	.02362
1/4	.25	6.3500	.07	1.778	.7	.02756
17/64	.265625	6.7469	.08	2.032	.8	.03150
9/32	.28125	7.1437	.09	2.286	.9	.03543
19/64	.296875	7.5406	.1	2.54	1	.03937
5/16	.3125	7.9375	.2	5.08	2	.07874
21/64	.328125	8.3344	.3	7.62	3	.11811
11/32	.34375	8.7312	.4	10.16	4	.15748
23/64	.359375	9.1281	.5	12.70	5	.19685
3/8	.375	9.5250	.6	15.24	6	.23622
25/64	.390625	9.9219	.7	17.78	7	.27559
13/32	.40625	10.3187	.8	20.32	8	.31496
27/64	.421875	10.7156	.9	22.86	9	.35433
7/16	.4375	11.1125	1	25.4	10	.39370
29/64	.453125	11.5094	2	50.8	11	.43307
15/32	.46875	11.9062	3	76.2	12	.47244
31/64	.484375	12.3031	4	101.6	13	.51181
1/2	.5	12.7000	5	127.0	14	.55118
33/64	.515625	13.0969	6	152.4	15	.59055
17/32	.53125	13.4937	7	177.8	16	.62992
35/64	.546875	13.8906	8	203.2	17	.66929
9/16	.5625	14.2875	9	228.6	18	.70866
37/64	.578125	14.6844	10	254.0	19	.74803
19/32	.59375	15.0812	11	279.4	20	.78740
39/64	.609375	15.4781	12	304.8	21	.82677
5/8	.625	15.8750	13	330.2	22	.86614
41/64	.640625	16.2719	14	355.6	23	.90551
21/32	.65625	16.6687	15	381.0	24	.94488
43/64	.671875	17.0656	16	406.4	25	.98425
11/16	.6875	17.4625	17	431.8	26	1.02362
45/64	.703125	17.8594	18	457.2	27	1.06299
23/32	.71875	18.2562	19	482.6	28	1.10236
47/64	.734375	18.6531	20	508.0	29	1.14173
3/4	.75	19.0500	21	533.4	30	1.18110
49/64	.765625	19.4469	22	558.8	31	1.22047
25/32	.78125	19.8437	23	584.2	32	1.25984
51/64	.796875	20.2406	24	609.6	33	1.29921
13/16	.8125	20.6375	25	635.0	34	1.33858
53/64	.828125	21.0344	26	660.4	35	1.37795
27/32	.84375	21.4312	27	685.8	36	1.41732
55/64	.859375	21.8281	28	711.2	37	1.4567
7/8	.875	22.2250	29	736.6	38	1.4961
57/64	.890625	22.6219	30	762.0	39	1.5354
29/32	.90625	23.0187	31	787.4	40	1.5748
59/64	.921875	23.4156	32	812.8	41	1.6142
15/16	.9375	23.8125	33	838.2	42	1.6535
61/64	.953125	24.2094	34	863.6	43	1.6929
31/32	.96875	24.6062	35	889.0	44	1.7323
63/64	.984375	25.0031	36	914.4	45	1.7717

UNITS	Pints to Litres	Gallons to Litres	Litres to Pints	Litres to Gallons	Miles to Kilometres	Kilometres to Miles	Lbs. per sq. In. to Kg. per sq. Cm.	Kg. per sq. Cm. to Lbs. per sq. In.
1	.57	4.55	1.76	.22	1.61	.62	.07	14.22
2	1.14	9.09	3.52	.44	3.22	1.24	.14	28.50
3	1.70	13.64	5.28	.66	4.83	1.86	.21	42.67
4	2.27	18.18	7.04	.88	6.44	2.49	.28	56.89
5	2.84	22.73	8.80	1.10	8.05	3.11	.35	71.12
6	3.41	27.28	10.56	1.32	9.66	3.73	.42	85.34
7	3.98	31.82	12.32	1.54	11.27	4.35	.49	99.56
8	4.55	36.37	14.08	1.76	12.88	4.97	.56	113.79
9		40.91	15.84	1.98	14.48	5.59	.63	128.00
10		45.46	17.60	2.20	16.09	6.21	.70	142.23
20				4.40	32.19	12.43	1.41	284.47
30				6.60	48.28	18.64	2.11	426.70
40				8.80	64.37	24.85		
50					80.47	31.07		
60					96.56	37.28		
70					112.65	43.50		
80					128.75	49.71		
90					144.84	55.92		
100					160.93	62.14		

UNITS	Lb ft to kgm	Kgm to lb ft	UNITS	Lb ft to kgm	Kgm to lb ft
1	.138	7.233	7	.967	50.631
2	.276	14.466	8	1.106	57.864
3	.414	21.699	9	1.244	65.097
4	.553	28.932	10	1.382	72.330
5	.691	36.165	20	2.765	144.660
6	.829	43.398	30	4.147	216.990

CHAPTER 8

REAR SUSPENSION AND DRIVE SHAFTS

8 : 1 Description

8 : 2 Maintenance

8 : 3 Control arms and reaction struts

8 : 4 Wheel hubs and carriers

8 : 5 Suspension struts

8 : 6 Drive shafts

8 : 7 Suspension geometry

8 : 8 Fault diagnosis

8 : 1 Description

Independent rear suspension is by means of McPherson struts. The suspension struts consist of telescopic hydraulic dampers with coil springs mounted between two pressed steel support cups. Each rear wheel hub carrier is located at the upper point by the damper unit attachment and at the lower point by a control arm and reaction strut. The control arm inner mountings have provision for shim adjustment to set rear wheel geometry correctly. **FIG 8:1** shows a section through the rear suspension and hub assembly, control arm front (1) and rear (2) adjustment shim locations being shown inset. Ball joints are used at the control arm to hub carrier attachments in order to accommodate suspension movement.

The wheel hubs are carried on wide twin-row ball-bearings. Drive shafts differ between 1300 and 1500 models. Each type is provided with two constant velocity joints but, in the case of 1300 models, the inner joint and the shaft drive from the differential side gear is combined as a tripode joint and the second is incorporated in the shaft. In the case of 1500 models, the drive from the side gears is by conventional splines and two constant velocity joints are incorporated in each drive shaft.

All joints and pivots for rear suspension and drive shafts are sealed assemblies, so no routine maintenance is required between overhauls. However, an occasional check should be made on the condition of components and security of fixings, carefully examining the rubber sealing boots on control arm ball joints and drive shaft constant-velocity joints. A damaged boot must be renewed without delay, otherwise rapid wear will result from the ingress of dirt.

8 : 2 Maintenance

Tyres and wheels :

Every 500km (300 miles), check the tyre pressures and reinflate as necessary. Recommended tyre pressures are quoted in **Technical Data** in the **Appendix**.

Every 10,000km (6000 miles) (if the car is operating on rough roads, halve this interval), interchange the wheels to even out tyre wear. An interchange scheme is described in **Chapter 7, Section 7 : 2**.

General :

Every 5000km (3000 miles), visually check the condition of the drive shaft inner and outer boots. If a boot shows signs of cracking or deterioration, renew as soon as possible. A boot which is split or torn should be renewed without delay. Check the condition of the ball joints, pivots, dampers and springs. If indications of unserviceability, excessive wear or damage by road stones is evident, refer to the relevant section in this chapter and renew the defective part or unit.

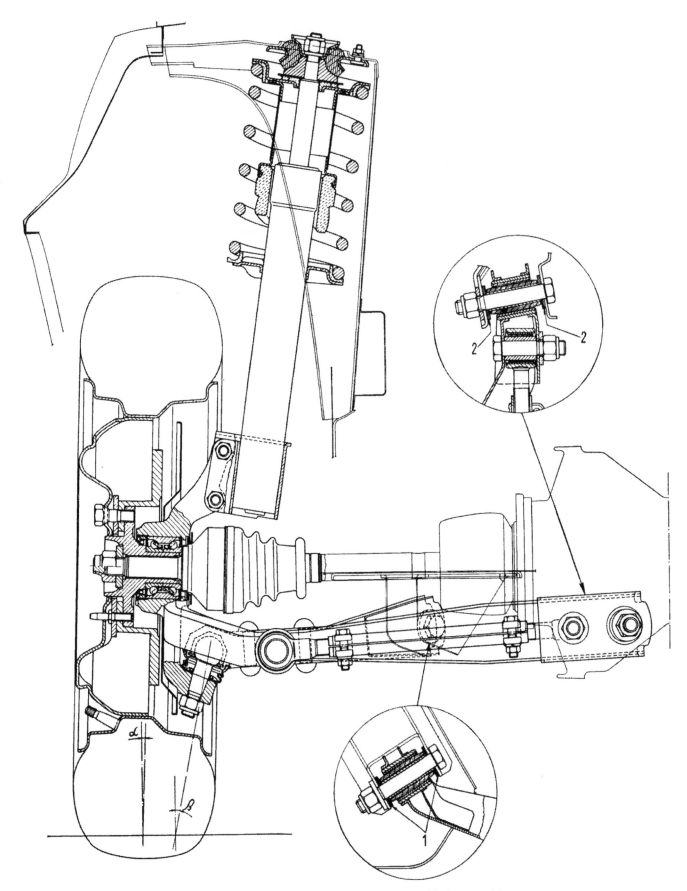

FIG 8 : 1   Section through rear suspension and hub assembly

Key to Fig 8 : 1   1 Control arm front shims   2 Control arm rear shims

80

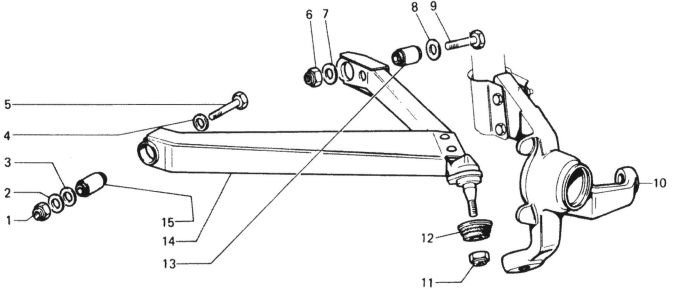

FIG 8:2   Control arm components

Key to Fig 8:2   1 Nut   2, 3, 4 Washers   5 Bolt   6 Nut   7, 8 Washers   9 Bolt   10 Hub carrier   11 Nut   12 Boot
13 Bush   14 Control arm   15 Bush

Constant velocity joint lubrication :

Every 20,000km (12,000 miles), refer to **Section 8 : 6**, pull back the outer boot at each side and lubricate the joints.

8 : 3   Control arms and reaction struts

Control arm inner mounting bushes can be renewed after control arm removal and the rubber boot for outer ball joint can be renewed after disconnecting ball joint from hub carrier, but if the ball joint is worn or damaged the control arm must be renewed complete.

For some operations, it will be necessary first to detach the exhaust system after removing nuts securing pipe flange to manifold and bolts securing silencer to mounting bracket.

Control arm removal :

Raise and safely support the rear of the car, then remove the road wheel. **FIG 8:2** shows control arm components. Remove nut 11, then use a suitable puller tool to disconnect control arm ball joint from hub carrier 10. Remove the inner mounting nuts and washers, then remove the bolts and detach control arm from mountings. Carefully note positions of shims fitted at mounting points so that they can be refitted in their original positions. This is important to retain correct suspension geometry.

Check all parts for wear or damage and renew as necessary.

Refitting :

This is a reversal of the removal procedure, making sure that shims removed previously are refitted in their original positions. Use new self-locking nuts for control arm inner mountings, but do not fully tighten yet. When the road wheel has been refitted and the car lowered to the ground, load the car with two persons plus 20kg (44lb) of luggage and check that tyres are correctly inflated, then fully tighten control arm inner mountings to the recommended torque. On completion, it is recommended that suspension geometry be checked as described in **Section 8 : 7**.

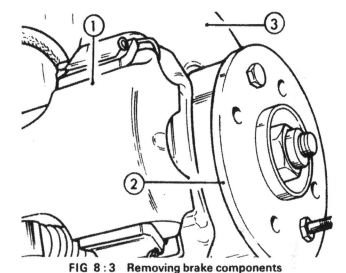

FIG 8 : 3   Removing brake components

Key to Fig 8 : 3   1 Brake caliper   2 Plate   3 Disc

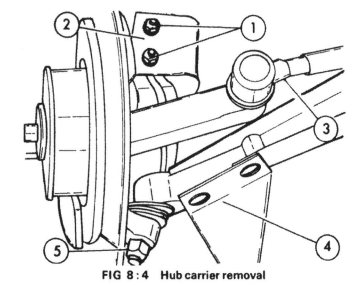

FIG 8 : 4   Hub carrier removal

Key to Fig 8 : 4   1 Hub carrier/strut nuts   2 Hub carrier
3 Reaction strut   4 Control arm   5 Nut

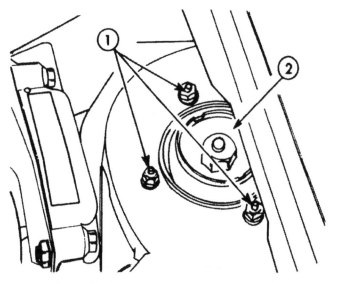

FIG 8:5 Suspension strut upper mounting

Key to Fig 8:5   1 Nuts and washers   2 Suspension strut

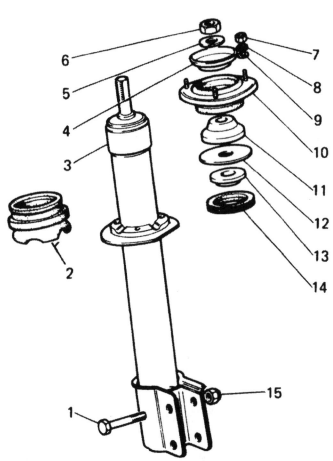

FIG 8:6 Damper mounting components

Key to Fig 8:6 1 Bolt   2 Rubber pad   3 Damper   4 Cup
5 Washer   6, 7 Nuts   8 Lock washer   9 Washer
10 Pad   11 Spacer   12 Washer   13 Thrust plate
14 Rubber ring   15 Nut

Reaction strut removal:

Raise and safely support the rear of the car, then remove the road wheel. Disconnect the reaction strut ball joint from the hub carrier, then remove the control arm rear attachment bolt as described previously, noting the positions of shims. Do not slacken clamps for the reaction strut sleeve, unless parts are to be renewed.

Refitting:

This is a reversal of the removal procedure, making sure that adjustment shims are refitted in their original positions. Use new self-locking nuts, left loose until the car is properly laden as described previously, when final tightening to the recommended torque must be carried out. On completion, it is recommended that suspension geometry be checked as described in **Section 8 : 7**, this being essential if the sleeve clamps have been loosened.

8 : 4 Wheel hubs and carriers

Hub carrier removal:

With the brakes applied by an assistant, slacken the hub nut. Raise and safely support the rear of the car, then remove the road wheel and the hub nut. Refer to **FIG 8 : 3**. Remove brake caliper 1 and mounting bracket without disconnecting fluid hose, as described in **Chapter 10**. Support caliper with length of wire so that hose is not strained. Remove bolts securing plate 2 and disc 3 to hub, then remove plate and disc.

Refer to **FIG 8:4**. Remove the two nuts and bolts 1 securing hub carrier to suspension strut. Remove nut 5 securing ball joint for control arm 4 and the nut securing ball joint for reaction strut 3, then separate ball joints from hub carrier using a suitable puller tool. Remove the hub carrier, supporting the drive shaft by wiring to suspension strut to avoid strain on the shaft joints.

Hub bearing renewal:

This work is carried out in the same manner as that described for front wheel bearings in **Chapter 7, Section 7 : 4**.

Refitting:

This is a reversal of the removal procedure, renewing all self-locking nuts. Tighten component fixings to the recommended torques. When the hub carrier and brake caliper assembly have been refitted, fit a new hub nut to the drive shaft and, with an assistant applying the brake pedal firmly, tighten to 13.5daNm (100lbf ft) if it has M18 thread or 21.6daNm (160lbf ft) for M20 thread. Stake the nut to lock against rotation, using a suitable punch to drive lock collar into the groove provided.

8 : 5 Suspension struts

Removal:

Raise and safely support the rear of the car, then remove the road wheel. Place a suitable stand or jack beneath the hub carrier to support the weight of the assembly. Refer to **FIG 8 : 5** and remove the three nuts and washers 1 securing suspension strut 2 in upper mounting. Remove the two nuts and bolts 1 (see **FIG 8:4**) securing suspension strut to hub carrier, then remove the unit from the car.

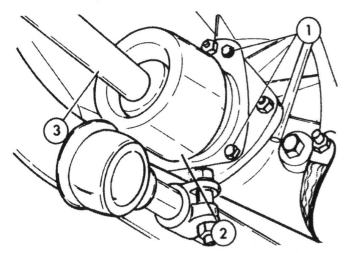

FIG 8:7   Drive shaft inner mounting (1300 model)

Key to Fig 8:7   1 Boot to flange bolts and washers
2 Boot   3 Drive shaft

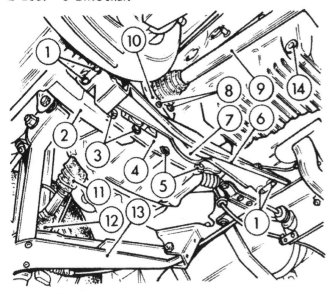

FIG 8:8   The drive shafts (1500 model)

Key to Fig 8:8   1 Bolts   2 Exhaust pipe lower bracket
3 Bolts   4 Rubber mount bracket   5 Bolts   6 Engine/
transmission unit centre bracket   7 Rubber mount   8 Bolts
9 Righthand drive shaft   10 Righthand inner constant
velocity joint   11 Lefthand inner constant velocity joint
12 Lefthand outer constant velocity joint   13 Suspension
control arm   14 Sump drain plug

Dismantling :

Dismantling and servicing of suspension strut assemblies is carried out in a similar manner to that described for front suspension units described in **Chapter 7, Section 7:5**. Refer to **FIG 8:6** for identification of damper unit components.

Refitting :

This is a reversal of the removal procedure, using new self-locking nuts. Tighten upper and lower fixings to the recommended torques.

8:6 Drive shafts

Drive shaft removal :

Raise the rear of the car and support safely on floor stands, then remove the road wheel. Refer to **Chapter 6** and drain sufficient oil from the transmission to avoid leakage when the drive shaft is removed.

Refer, in the case of a **1300 model**, to **FIG 8:7**. Remove three bolts and washers 1 which retain the boot 2 to the transmission. Pull the drive shaft from the transmission and then from the hub. Refer, in the case of a **1500 model**, to **FIG 8:8**. Remove the bolts 8 which retain the joint to the transmission. Pull the shaft from the transmission and then from the hub. Withdraw the shaft from beneath the car.

Dismantling :

In the case of a **1300 model**, refer to **FIG 8:9**. Remove the clamp 12, pull back the boot 6, remove the circlip 7 and withdraw the joint 8 from the shaft. Remove the clamp 9 and pull off the boot 6. The tripode joint 1 may be withdrawn from the shaft splines after removing the circlip 2. The inner boot 5 and the flange 4 may now be removed.

In the case of a **1500 model**, refer to **FIG 8:10**. Remove the clamp 9. Remove the snap ring 8. Withdraw the joint assembly 7 from the shaft and remove the washer 5. Remove the bolts 6 and separate the flanged sleeve 10 from the joint. The boot 4 may be withdrawn from the shaft 3 after releasing the clamp 11. Follow this same sequence to deal with the joint at the other end of the shaft.

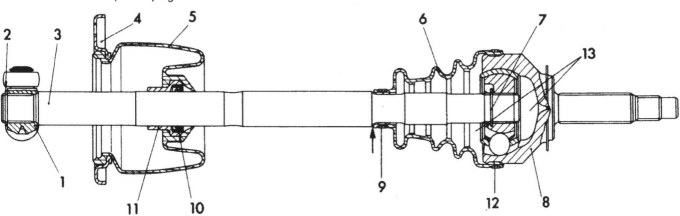

FIG 8:9   Drive shaft components (1300 model)

Key to Fig 8:9   1 Tripode joint   2 Circlip   3 Drive shaft   4 Flange   5 Inner sealing boot   6 Outer joint boot
7 Circlip   8 Constant velocity joint   9 Clamp   10 Sealing ring   11 Bush   12 Clamp   13 Lubricate with MRM2 grease

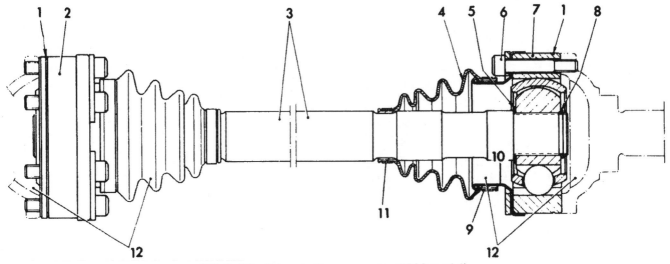

FIG 8 : 10   Drive shaft components (1500 model)

Key to Fig 8 : 10   1 Reference splines   2 Inner constant velocity joint   3 Drive shaft   4 Boot   5 Spring washer
6 Bolt   7 Outer constant velocity joint   8 Snap ring   9 Clamp   10 Flanged sleeve   11 Clamp   12 Lubricate
with MRM2 grease

FIG 8 : 11   The wheel alignment adjusting sleeve

Key to Fig 8 : 11   1 Reaction strut   2 Clamps

Reassembly :

Remove all old grease. Thoroughly clean and inspect the components and renew parts or assemblies as necessary.

Follow the reverse of the dismantling sequence in each case. If there is any doubt regarding the serviceability of a boot, renew it. Use new snap rings and circlips. Apply about 100 grams (3.5oz) of Grassofiat MRM2 grease to each constant velocity joint, working it well into the joint sockets and the spaces 13 in **FIG 8 : 9** and 12 in **FIG 8 : 10**. Ensure that boot 6 in **FIG 8 : 9** abuts the arrowed shoulder on the shaft.

Refitting :

This is a reversal of the removal procedure. On completion, refill the transmission with oil to the correct level as described in **Chapter 6**. Tighten the hub nut as described in **Section 8 : 4**.

8 : 7 Suspension geometry

Due to the need for special optical measuring equipment for accurate results, the checking and adjusting of rear wheel camber angles and wheel alignment should be carried out at a fully equipped service station.

Camber angle is adjusted by adding or removing shims at the control arm inner mounting positions (see **FIG 8 : 1**).

Wheel alignment adjustment is carried out by slackening the securing clamps, then rotating the reaction strut sleeve shown at 1 in **FIG 8 : 11**. The clamps 2 must be securely tightened on completion.

Camber and alignment information is listed in **Technical Data**.

8 : 8 Fault diagnosis

(a) Wheel wobble

1 Worn hub bearings
2 Weak rear springs
3 Uneven tyre wear
4 Worn suspension bushes
5 Loose wheel fixings

(b) Car pulls to one side

1 Unequal tyre pressures
2 Incorrect suspension geometry
3 Defective suspension bushes or damaged parts
4 Weak spring on one side
5 Fault in steering system

(c) Bottoming of suspension

1 Broken or weak coil spring
2 Defective damper
3 Car overloaded

(d) Excessive body roll

1 Faulty spring or damper unit

(e) Rattles

1 Check 2 and 4 in (a)
2 Defective suspension strut or control arm bush

(f) Suspension hard

1 Tyre pressures too high
2 Control arm ball joints stiff
3 Dampers faulty

CHAPTER 9

THE STEERING GEAR

9 : 1 Description

Rack and pinion steering is employed. This is shown in **FIG 9 : 1** together with its mounting brackets, the steering wheel, column and shafts. The pinion shaft is turned by the lower end of the steering column shaft and moves the rack to the left or right, transmitting the steering motion to the front wheels by means of the tie rods and the steering arms on hub carriers. The rack and pinion are held in mesh by a spring loaded adjustable yoke assembly. The steering gear housing is held to the car underbody by means of rubber bushed clamps. The steering column shaft is in two parts, the lower part being fitted with universal joints. The tie rod ends are connected to the steering arms by means of ball joint assemblies, the tie rods being threaded to the rack ends to allow for adjustment of front wheel alignment.

A cross-section through an earlier unmodified steering unit is shown in **FIG 9 : 2**. Earlier 1300 models are fitted with this type of steering unit. A cross-section through the later modified type of unit is shown in **FIG 9 : 3**. This type of unit is fitted to later 1300 models and to 1500 models.

The steering column has fixed mountings as shown in **FIG 9 : 4** and is not adjustable for position or angle. The column carries the ignition switch (with which a steering lock is combined) and multi-function switches which are enclosed in detachable covers.

9 : 2 Maintenance

General :

Every 5000km (3000 miles), visually check the condition of the steering rack bellows, the steering linkage and the ball joints. If a bellows shows signs of cracking or deterioration it should be renewed as soon as possible. A bellows which is split or torn should be renewed without delay. Damaged linkage or excessively worn ball joints should be renewed without delay.

Wheel alignment :

Every 10,000km (6000 miles), refer to **Section 9 : 7**, check the wheel alignment and adjust if necessary.

Lubrication :

The steering linkage and suspension ball joints are sealed assemblies and no lubrication is required.

9 : 3 Steering wheel removal

Disconnect the battery, then carefully remove horn button from centre of steering wheel. Remove the retaining nut, then pull the steering wheel from steering shaft. Refit in the reverse order of removal, making sure that the front wheels are in the straightahead position and the steering wheel centralised. Tighten retaining nut to 4.9daNm (36lbf ft).

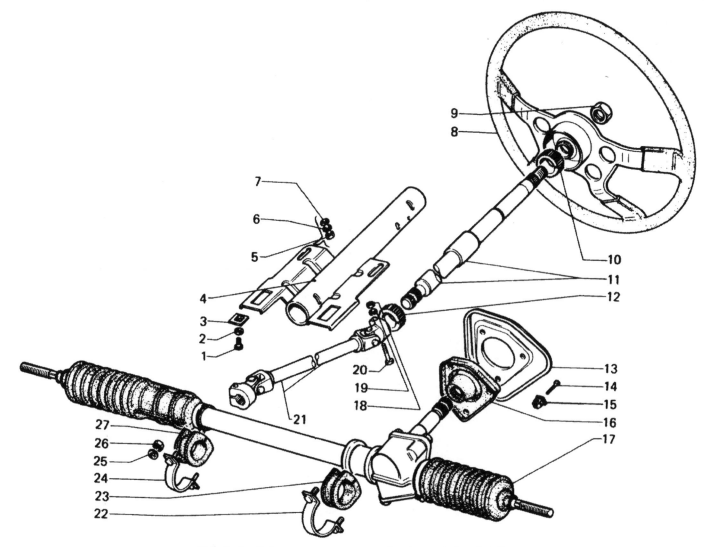

FIG 9 : 1   Column components and rack mounting details

Key to Fig 9 : 1   1 Bolt   2 Washer   3 Retainer   4 Support   5 Nut   6 Lockwasher   7 Washer   8 Steering wheel
9 Nut   10 Bushing   11 Steering column shaft   12 Bushing   13 Cover   14 Screw   15 Pad   16 Seal
17 Steering gear   18 Nut   19 Lockwasher   20 Bolt   21 Lower shaft   22 Clamp   23 Mounting rubber   24 Clamp
25 Lockwasher   26 Nut   27 Mounting rubber

9 : 4 Steering column

Removal :

Disconnect the battery. Remove the five screws securing steering column covers, then remove the covers. Disconnect three electrical connectors and one wire. Remove steering wheel as described previously.

Refer to **FIG 9 : 4**. Remove two nuts and washers 1 and two bolts and washers 2 securing column assembly 3 to body panel. Refer to **FIG 9 : 5**. Remove bolt 1 and nut, then slide the turn indicator switch from shaft. Remove clamp bolt 4 securing universal joint on lower shaft 3 to upper shaft, then pull steering column shaft from joint. If lower shaft removal is necessary, remove the clamp bolt securing lower universal joint to pinion shaft and remove lower steering shaft.

Steering column components are shown in **FIG 9 : 1**. Examine all components carefully and renew any found worn or damaged. Column bushes 10 and 12 should be removed if worn and new bushes pressed into place. If either universal joint is worn or damaged, renew the lower steering shaft 21 complete.

Refitting :

This is a reversal of the removal procedure. Make sure that the splines on upper column shaft and pinion shaft and in universal joint connections are clean, then reconnect joints and align bolt holes with grooves in shafts before installing and tightening clamp bolts and nuts.

9 : 5 Tie rods

Each tie rod and outer ball joint is manufactured as an assembly, which must be renewed complete if the ball joint is defective or the tie rod damaged.

Removal :

Raise and safely support the front of the car, then remove the road wheel. Refer to **FIG 9 : 6** and remove nut 1 securing ball joint to steering arm 3 on hub carrier. Use a suitable puller to separate ball joint from arm. Refer to **FIG 9 : 7**. Loosen locknut 1, while holding rack inner ball joint against rotation with a spanner on hexagon 2. Continue holding the inner ball joint against rotation while unscrew-

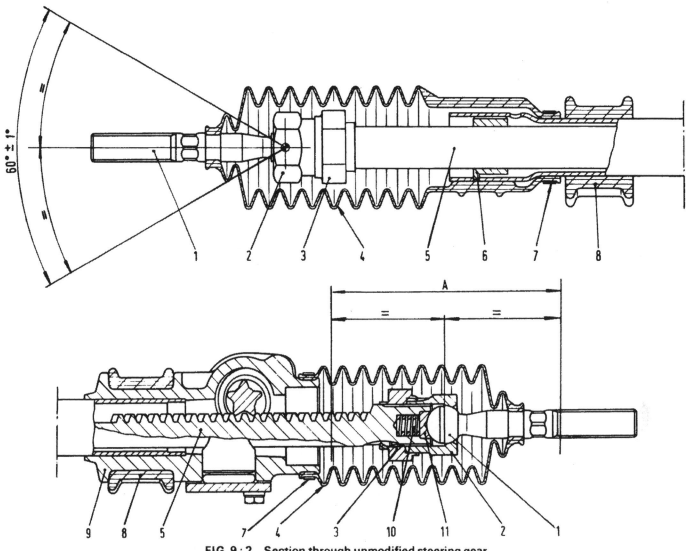

FIG 9 : 2 Section through unmodified steering gear

Key to Fig 9 : 2   1 Ball joint   2 Adjuster   3 Locknut   4 Rubber gaiter   5 Rod and rack   6 Bush   7 Clamp
8 Rubber pad   9 Steering gear housing   10 Spring   11 Ballpin cup   **A** = rack travel 117 ± 1.5mm (4.606 ± 0.059in)

ing tie rod and outer ball joint assembly, carefully counting the number of turns needed for removal.

Refitting :

Hold the rack ball joint against rotation and screw the tie rod into place by the same number of turns as counted during removal. Tighten the locknut to secure. Refit outer ball joint to steering arm, using a new self-locking nut. Refit the road wheel and lower the car, then check front wheel alignment as described in **Section 9 : 7**.

9 : 6 Steering gear
Removal :

Refer to **FIG 9 : 1**. From inside the car, remove clamp bolt from universal joints, then remove cover 13 and seal 16. Disconnect tie rod outer ball joint from steering arm on each side, as decribed in **Section 9 : 5**. Remove the four bolts securing steering gear clamps to bodywork, then remove steering gear complete with tie rods.

Refitting :

Check mounting rubbers for steering gear clamps and renew if damaged or perished. Refit the steering gear in the reverse order of removal, using new self-locking nuts. On completion, check front wheel alignment as described in **Section 9 : 7**.

Overhaul :

Note that certain special tools will be necessary in order to carry out overhaul procedures. If these tools or suitable substitutes are not available, the work should be carried out by a fully equipped service station. Note that two alternative types of steering gear have been fitted in production, the earlier standard type and the later modified type (see **FIGS 9 : 2** and **9 : 3**). Instructions given in this section are for both types, unless otherwise stated.

Disconnect the tie rods from rack end ball joints as described in **Section 9 : 5**. Refer to **FIG 9 : 8** and loosen clamps 2. Drain the oil from the steering gear into a suitable waste container. Remove rubber bellows 1 and the rubber insulators for steering gear mounting clamps. Remove the securing bolts, then detach plate 4 and remove gasket, spring, shims and yoke. Remove the fixing bolts and detach cover plate 3, then remove gasket, shims and pinion with bearing. Note that earth wire 5 attaches to a bolt at cover 4.

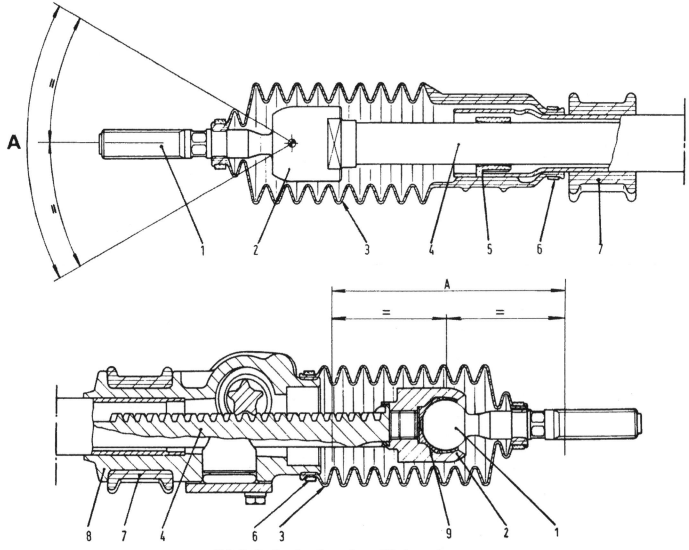

FIG 9:3   Section through modified steering gear

Key to Fig 9:3   1 Ball joint   2 Ball joint head   3 Rubber bellows   4 Rod and rack   5 Bush   6 Clamp   7 Rubber pad   8 Steering gear housing   9 Ball joint socket   **A** = rack travel 117 ± 1.5mm (4.606 ± 0.059in)   Angle **A** = 63° ± 3°

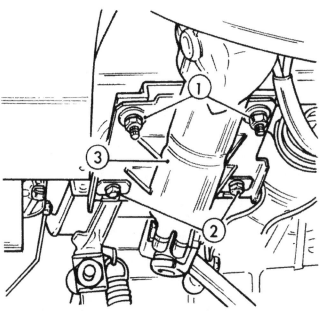

FIG 9:4   Steering column attachment points

Key to Fig 9:4   1 Nuts and washers   2 Bolts and washers   3 Column assembly

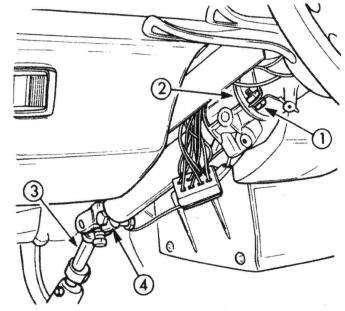

FIG 9:5   Indicator switch and upper universal joint

Key to Fig 9:5   1 Nut and bolt   2 Turn indicator switch   3 Lower shaft   4 Clamp bolt

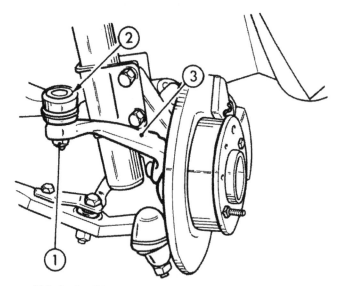

FIG 9:6 Disconnecting ball joint from hub carrier

Key to Fig 9:6   1 Nut   2 Ball joint   3 Steering arm

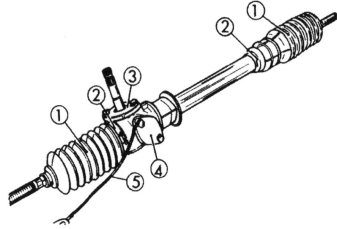

FIG 9:8 Steering gear bellows and cover plates

Key to Fig 9:8   1 Bellows   2 Clamps   3 Cover plate
(pinion)   4 Cover plate (rack yoke)   5 Earth wire

FIG 9:7 Tie rod inner connection

Key to Fig 9:7   1 Locknut   2 Inner ball joint hexagon

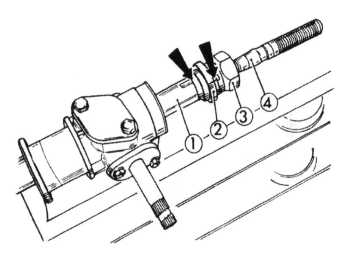

FIG 9:9 Rack ball joint removal. Arrows indicate staking points

Key to Fig 9:9   1 Steering unit   2 Ring locknut
3 Adjuster   4 Ball joint and rack assembly

Note that, on modified steering gear, rack ball joints have a threaded collar and if the joint is removed this must be renewed. For this reason, remove only one joint in order to remove the rack, leaving the other joint in place.

Carefully clamp the steering gear in a vice having padded jaws. On modified steering gear, release the staking on the collar and ball joint then unscrew the ball joint. This must be discarded and a new joint used during reassembly. On unmodified steering gear, refer to FIG 9:9 and release the staking on ring nuts 2. Unscrew the nuts, then slide off ball joints with sockets and springs.

Slide the rack from the steering gear, then remove the lower pinion bearing.

Servicing:

Thoroughly clean all parts and examine them for wear or damage. Check the rubber bellows for splits, holes or perished conditions and check that their fixing clamps are in good order. Check the bearings for wear by pressing and turning them by hand. Check the bushes in the housing for wear or scored surfaces and ensure that the rack moves smoothly in the bushes without excessive play. If necessary, remove the old bushes and install new ones as shown in FIG 9:10. Use tool A.74347 or other suitable driver (1) to install bushes 2 until the tabs 3 on bushes engage in slots 4 provided in housing 5. Check the rack for wear, damage or chipped teeth. Check the rack yoke for wear or scoring and the pinion for chipped teeth or other damage. Renew all worn or damaged parts. Always use new gaskets and seals during reassembly.

Reassembly and adjustment:

Support the steering gear horizontally in a vice having padded jaws, with the cover face upwards. Fit the pinion lower bearing in the housing, using tool A.74219 or other suitable driver. Engage the smooth end of the rack into the supporting bush, turning the rack as necessary to facilitate this operation. Turn the rack to bring the teeth towards the centre line of the pinion seat. Fit the pinion and upper

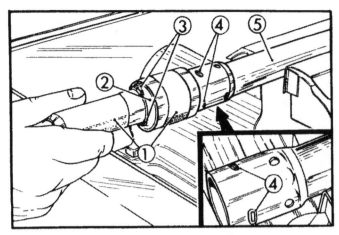

FIG 9:10   Rack bush installation

Key to Fig 9:10   1 Tool A.74347   2 Bushes   3 Tabs
4 Slots   5 Housing

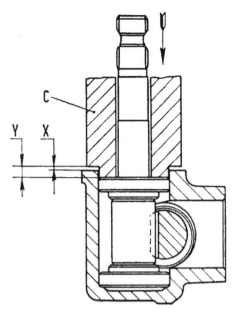

FIG 9:12   Adjusting pinion bearings

Key to Fig 9:12   C Gauge (bearing installer A.74219)
X, Y See text

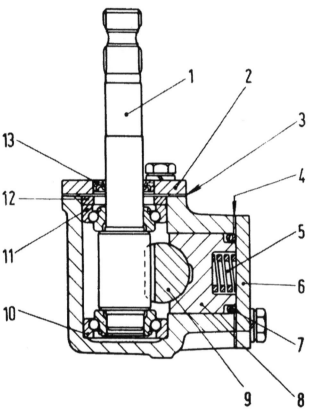

FIG 9:11   Steering gear section across pinion

Key to Fig 9:11   1 Pinion shaft   2 Cover plate   3 Gasket
4 Rack yoke shims   5 Spring   6 Yoke cover plate
7 Sealing ring   8 Rack yoke   9 Rack   10 Pinion lower
bearing   11 Pinion upper bearing   12 Pinion shims   13 Seal

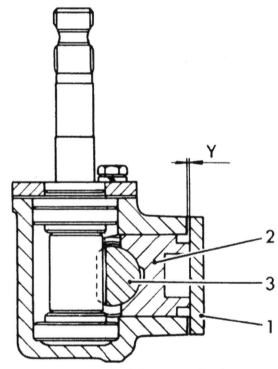

FIG 9:13   Adjusting rack yoke

Key to Fig 9:13   1 Rack yoke cover   2 Rack yoke
3 Rack   **Y** See text

bearing, engaging pinion with rack teeth. **FIG 9:11** shows a section through the assembly. The pinion must now be adjusted by selecting appropriate shims, in the following manner.

Refer to **FIG 9:12**. Using the special gauge **C**, apply sufficient load on the outer race of upper bearing to take up all end play, as shown by the arrow. Use feeler gauges to measure dimension **X**. A suitable shim **S** (12 in **FIG 9:11**) must be selected so that $S = Y - (X + 0.05$ to $+ 0.13mm)$. Note that shims are available in 0.12, 0.20, 0.25 and 2.5mm thicknesses.

Coat the gasket and threads of retaining bolts with a suitable sealing compound, then install gasket, plate, washers and bolts. Tighten bolts alternately and evenly, then install the pinion seal. Check that the pinion turns freely without sticking, even without the yoke installed. The rack must move smoothly and freely over its entire travel. Move the rack to the centre position, then adjust the yoke in the following manner.

Refer to **FIG 9:13**. Install rack yoke and cover plate as shown, then turn pinion 180° in both directions to settle the assembly and return the rack to the centre position.

Use feeler gauges to measure distance **Y** between steering gear and cover plate. Suitable shims **S** (4 in **FIG 9 : 11**) must be selected so that $S = Y + 0.05$ to $+ 0.13$mm. Note that yoke shims are available in 0.10 and 0.15mm thicknesses. Assemble the spring and sealing ring on the yoke, coat surfaces of shims with suitable sealing compound, then install shims, cover plate and fixing bolts. Check that rack still moves smoothly over its entire travel.

On modified steering gear, lubricate the new ball joint with oil, then screw collar of joint onto rack up to the end of the threaded section. Tighten collar to 7.5daNm (54.25lbf ft). Stake the inside of the collar over the edge of rack rod.

On unmodified steering gear, refer to **FIG 9 : 9** and screw nuts 2 onto rack to the end of the threaded section. Assemble spring and socket, lubricate ball joint with oil, then install pin and adjustable joint. Tighten joint until a force of 0.2 to 0.5daNm (1.5 to 3.25lbf ft) is needed to move ballpins 4. Check that the pins can describe a rotation cone with an apex angle of $60° \pm 1°$. Lock the heads in position with the locknuts, then stake the heads at the points indicated by the arrows.

Fit the rubber bellows over ball joints and into position on steering gear. Position the clamping screws as shown in **FIG 9 : 14**, according to the type of steering gear fitted. Refit tie rods as described in **Section 9 : 5**.

Refit the steering gear as described previously. On completion, turn the steering fully towards the passenger side of the car, then raise and safely support the front of the car on the driver's side. Release the clamp for rubber bellows on driver's side, then use a suitable syringe to inject 0.14 litre of SAE.90 EP oil into the rubber bellows. On completion, refit the bellows correctly and clamp in place, then lower the car. Carefully road test to check steering gear operation.

9 : 7 Front wheel alignment

When correctly aligned, the front wheels will converge slightly at the front when viewed vertically from above. The convergence, or toe-in, should be as specified under 'Suspension' in the **Technical Data** section of the **Appendix**.

Alignment should, for accuracy, be measured using optical equipment and checking and adjustment should, consequently, be carried out by a fully equipped authorised agent. An acceptable degree of accuracy can, however, be achieved if a suitable track gauge is available and the following procedure is carried out carefully. Toe-in figures are given for a laden and an unladen car. An owner will probably find it more convenient to work on an unladen vehicle.

With the car standing on level ground and with the tyres correctly inflated, set the steering in the straightahead position. Refer to **FIG 9 : 15**. Measure **A**, the dimension between the centre height of the outer wheel rims at the rear of the wheels. Mark these points with chalk. Push the car forwards until the two chalk marks are at the centre height at the front. Measure dimension **B**. **A** must be greater than **B** by the toe-in figure specified.

If adjustment is required, refer to **FIG 9 : 7**, loosen locknut 1 on each side and, using a spanner on the hexagons 2, rotate the rack ball joints by equal amounts on

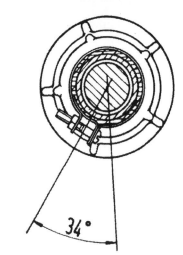

UNMODIFIED STEERING BOX

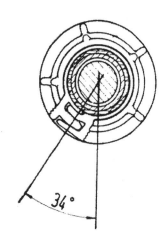

MODIFIED STEERING BOX

FIG 9 : 14 Bellows clamp screw position

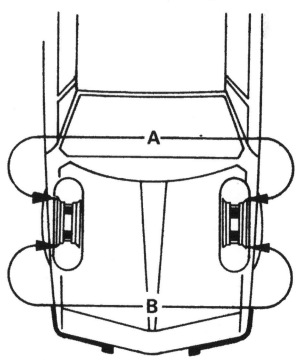

FIG 9 : 15 Checking front wheel toe-in

Key to Fig 9 : 15   A Rear dimension   B Front dimension

each side until the specified toe-in is achieved. Tighten the locknuts and recheck the alignment.

9 : 8 Fault diagnosis

(a) Wheel wobble

1 Unbalanced wheels and tyres
2 Slack steering connections
3 Incorrect steering geometry
4 Excessive play in steering gear
5 Faulty suspension
6 Worn hub bearings

(b) Heavy steering

1 Incorrect steering geometry
2 Very low tyre pressures
3 Lack of lubricant
4 Wheel alignment incorrect

5 Rack adjustment too tight
6 Steering column shaft bent
7 Tight bearings

(c) Wander

1 Check 2, 3 and 4 in (a)
2 Uneven tyre pressures
3 Uneven tyre wear
4 Ineffective dampers

(d) Lost motion

1 Loose steering wheel
2 Worn rack and pinion teeth
3 Worn ball joints
4 Worn suspension strut swivels
5 Worn universal joints
6 Slack pinion bearings

CHAPTER 10

THE BRAKING SYSTEM

10:1 Description

Disc brake units are fitted at all four wheels, operated from the brake pedal through a dual circuit hydraulic system. The master cylinder, which draws fluid from twin reservoirs, is operated from the brake pedal by a short pushrod. Separate outlets from the master cylinder are coupled, via the brake pipes and hoses, to the disc brake caliper at each front wheel. A third outlet feeds the pipelines to the rear brake units. The front and rear brake circuits are operated simultaneously but independently from the two separate fluid chambers of the master cylinder. This dual circuit system is provided as a safety factor as, if one circuit should fail for any reason, the remaining circuit will provide effective braking power. Adjustment to compensate for friction pad wear is automatic.

The handbrake operates on the rear disc brakes only, through a rod and cable linkage. Adjustment is not automatic.

10:2 Maintenance

Hydraulic fluid level :

Every 500km (300 miles) or weekly, check the level of the fluid in the reservoir and top up as necessary. Use only approved fluid (see 'Oils and Fluids' in **Technical Data**). Investigate the cause of any rapid drop in level. This may be due to a defective seal in a caliper or in the master cylinder or to a leaking or defective hose, pipeline or connection.

A low fluid level warning light switch is incorporated in the reservoir filler cap on later models. Periodically check the operation of the facia warning light by depressing the filler cap with the ignition key in the 'MAR' position.

Caliper pads :

At least every 10,000km (6000 miles), inspect the thickness of the front and rear caliper pads. There should always be at least 2mm (0.08in) thickness of friction material. If the thickness is approaching or is less than this, **renew both pads in both front or in both rear calipers as the case may be**. The pad renewal procedure is described in **Section 10 : 3**.

Hydraulic system overhaul :

Every 60,000km (36,000 miles) or every three years (whichever comes first), drain off and discard the hydraulic fluid, overhaul the calipers and the master cylinder, fit new hydraulic hoses and refill the system with fresh approved fluid.

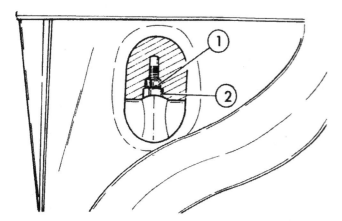

FIG 10:1 Handbrake cable locknut 1 and adjusting nut 2

Handbrake adjustment:

Following renewal of the rear caliper pads or if the hand-brake lever travel becomes excessive, adjust the hand-brake as follows.

Chock the front wheels. Raise and support the rear of the car. Release the handbrake lever. From the fully released position, apply the lever by four notches of the ratchet. Refer to **FIG 10:1** and remove the cover from the access hole. Loosen locknut 1. Tighten the adjuster nut 2 until, when turning the rear wheels by hand, resistance can be felt. Tighten the adjuster further until the rear wheels are just locked against rotation by hand. Release the control lever fully and confirm that the wheels are completely free to turn. Should there be any binding, loosen off the adjuster slightly. On completion, hold the adjuster nut with one spanner while tightening the locknut with another.

10:3 Disc brakes

Front brake caliper components and rear brake caliper components are shown in **FIGS 10:2** and **10:3** respectively.

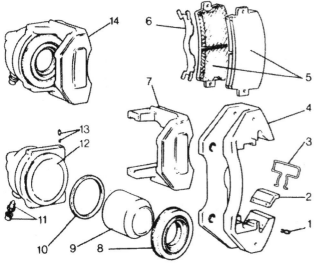

FIG 10:2 Front brake caliper components

Key to Fig 10:2 1 Retaining pin 2 Locking block 3 Spring 4 Mounting bracket 5 Brake pad 6 Pad retaining spring 7 Caliper yoke 8 Rubber boot 9 Piston 10 Seal 11 Bleed screw and dust cap 12 Cylinder 13 Spring and dowel 14 Complete caliper assembly

Brake pad renewal:

When working on front brake units, apply the handbrake, raise and safely support the front of the car, then remove the road wheel. For rear brake units, raise and safely support the rear of the car, chock the front wheels against rotation and fully release the handbrake, then remove the road wheel.

Refer to **FIG 10:4**. Remove retaining pins 1 from locking blocks 2, then carefully tap locking blocks from caliper 3. Refer to **FIG 10:5** and pull caliper 1 from mounting bracket 5, without disconnecting fluid hose 4. Take care to avoid strain on the hose. Collect brake pads 2, the shaped wire spring and the pad retaining spring. Support the caliper by wiring to the suspension so that the hose is not strained. **Do not touch the brake pedal when any caliper is removed.**

If the pads are being removed as part of other servicing operations only and are not to be renewed, mark them so that they will be refitted at the same side of the caliper from which they were removed and take care not to contaminate linings with dirt or grease.

Install the pads in the reverse order of removal, pushing the operating piston in the caliper to the bottom of its bore after pad installation by carefully pulling the pads apart. Take care not to contaminate friction lining material during this operation. Note that this operation will cause the fluid level in the reservoir to rise, so it may be necessary to syphon off a little of the fluid to prevent leakage. Note that brake fluid is poisonous and that it can damage paintwork. Make sure that the pad springs and locking blocks are correctly located and use new retaining pins if the originals are not in good condition. On completion, operate the brake pedal several times to move the brake pads close to the disc, otherwise the brakes may not operate correctly the first time that they are applied. Finally, check and if necessary correct fluid level in supply reservoir.

Caliper removal and refitting:

If the caliper is to be overhauled, remove it from the mounting bracket and detach brake pads as described previously, then disconnect brake hose from caliper and collect the sealing washers. Immediately plug the end of the hose as it is detached, to prevent leakage and ingress of dirt. On rear brake units, refer to **FIG 10:6** and, after removal of hose 1 as previously described, disconnect handbrake cable 3 from caliper 2. If necessary, remove caliper mounting bracket from hub carrier.

If the caliper assembly is to be removed to provide access for other servicing operations, raise and safely support the car then remove the road wheel. Remove the two mounting bolts securing caliper mounting bracket to hub carrier, then carefully detach the assembly and support by wiring to the underbody to prevent strain on the brake hose. Do not touch the brake pedal while the caliper is removed.

Refit the caliper in the reverse order of removal. If the caliper was removed complete without disconnecting the hose, carefully fit the unit into place making sure that the brake pads are positioned correctly at each side of the disc. If necessary, carefully pull the pads apart to provide extra clearance, taking care not to get dirt or oil onto the friction linings.

If the fluid hose was disconnected from the caliper, make sure that it is correctly reconnected with sealing

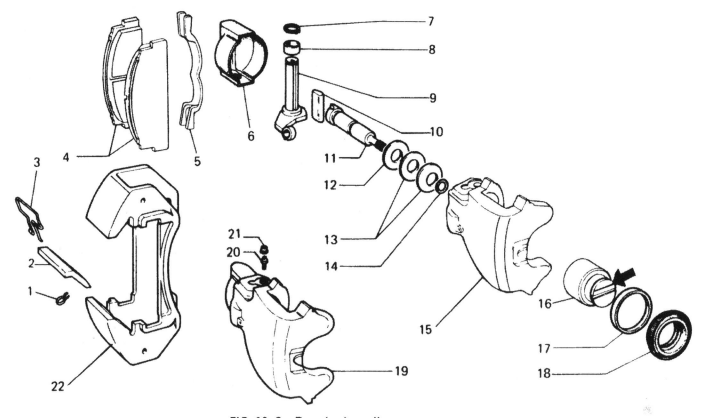

FIG 10:3   Rear brake caliper components

Key to Fig 10:3   1 Retaining pin   2 Locking block   3 Spring   4 Brake pads   5 Pad retaining spring   6 Rubber boot
7 Locking ring   8 Spacer   9 Handbrake shaft   10 Pawl   11 Plunger   12, 13 Spring washers   14 Seal   15 Caliper
cylinder   16 Piston   17 Seal   18 Rubber boot   19 Complete caliper assembly   20 Bleed screw   21 Dust
cover   22 Mounting bracket

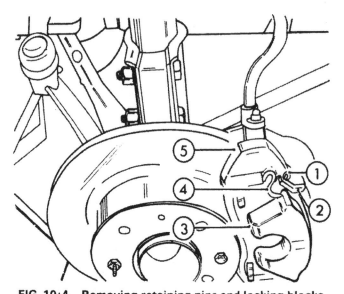

FIG 10:4   Removing retaining pins and locking blocks

Key to Fig 10:4 1 Retaining pin 2 Locking blocks 3 Caliper
4 Spring   5 Mounting bracket

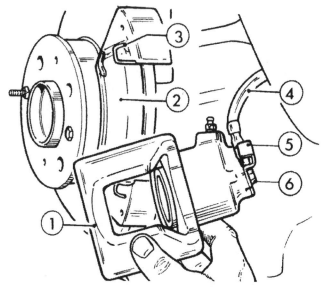

FIG 10:5   Removing brake pads

Key to Fig 10:5   1 Caliper   2 Brake pad   3 Spring
4 Brake hose   5 Mounting bracket   6 Bolt

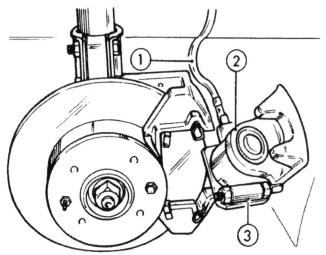

FIG 10:6   Disconnecting handbrake cable from caliper

Key to Fig 10:6 1 Brake hose 2 Caliper 3 Handbrake cable

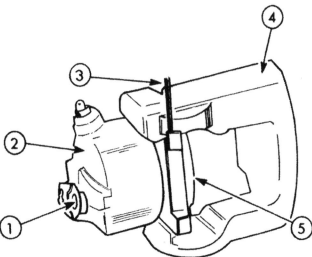

FIG 10:7   Removing caliper from yoke

Key to Fig 10:7 1 Hose connection 2 Cylinder 3 Thin rod
4 Yoke 5 Rubber boot

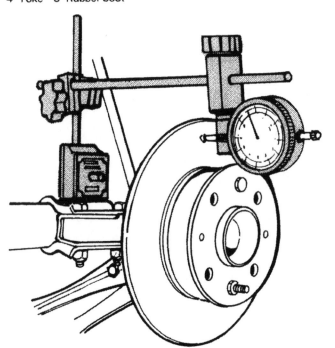

FIG 10:8   Checking brake disc for distortion

washers in place and that the hose is not twisted or strained when the caliper is refitted. On completion, bleed the brakes as described in **Section 10:5**.

Caliper overhaul:

Remove the caliper from mounting bracket as described previously.

Front brake unit:

Brush road dirt and rust from the caliper then clean the outside of the assembly using methylated spirits. Refer to **FIG 10:7**. Remove the rubber boot 5, then depress the dowel using a thin rod 3 and separate cylinder 2 from yoke 4. Use compressed air at brake hose connection 1 to eject the piston from caliper. Do this carefully to avoid excessive pressure which would cause the piston to be ejected at high speed, as this may cause accidental damage or injury.

Refer to **FIG 10:2** and use a thin plastic or wooden rod to remove seal 10 from cylinder bore, taking care not to damage bore surfaces. Clean all internal parts with methylated spirits or the correct grade of brake fluid. **Do not use any other cleaning fluid or solvent.** Examine for signs of wear or scoring on the cylinder and piston surfaces. Renew all rubber seals and dust boots and any other part found defective during inspection. Dip the internal parts in clean brake fluid and assemble them wet. Observe absolute cleanliness to prevent the entry of dirt or any trace of oil or grease. Use the fingers only to fit the rubber piston seals to prevent damage. Reassemble the remaining caliper components in the reverse order of dismantling, then refit the caliper as described previously.

Rear brake unit:

Rear brake calipers are dismantled in a similar manner to that described previously for front brake units, but note that the piston is threaded onto the handbrake mechanism plunger shown at 11 in **FIG 10:3**. To remove the piston, use a suitable screwdriver to turn the piston anticlockwise until it is free of the threads, then use compressed air as described previously to eject the piston.

Service the components as previously described for front brake units, additionally checking components for handbrake mechanism, as shown in **FIG 10:3**. When reassembling, note that the piston must be screwed fully into place then aligned as shown in **FIG 10:3**, with the mark (arrowed) towards bleed screw (20) side of caliper. This done, push piston to bottom of its bore. On completion, refit the caliper as described previously then adjust handbrake mechanism as described in **Section 10:2**.

Brake discs:

To remove a brake disc, raise and safely support the car then remove the road wheel. Remove the brake caliper complete with mounting bracket as described previously, then remove the fixing screw and stud and detach plate and brake disc.

Check the surface of the disc for excessive wear or damage. Light score marks are unimportant, but deep scoring will dictate resurfacing of the disc at a service station or renewal if this remedial treatment would require the removal of too much metal. Note that minimal allowable thickness of disc after resurfacing is 9.35mm (0.368in).

Brake discs should be checked for distortion while properly installed on the hub, using a dial gauge assembly as shown in **FIG 10:8**. Rotate the disc through one full turn and check maximum indicator reading, which should not exceed 0.15mm (0.06in). If distortion is excessive, it may be possible to resurface the disc as described previously, but excessive distortion which cannot be cured by this method will dictate renewal of the disc.

The thickness of new discs differs between 1300 and 1500 models (see **Technical Data**). Ensure, if new discs are required, that the correct type are obtained.

10:4 The master cylinder

Removal:

Use a suitable syringe to drain the contents of brake fluid reservoir, keeping the fluid perfectly clean if it is to be re-used, but noting that it is recommended that all used fluid be discarded and new fluid of the correct grade used for topping up later.

Refer to **Chapter 9** and remove the steering column assembly. Refer to **FIG 10:9** and disconnect the feed hoses from reservoir and master cylinder connections, catching any fluid spillage with a piece of rag to prevent damage to paintwork. Disconnect the three brake pipe connectors at the master cylinder, then plug all pipes to prevent the ingress of dirt.

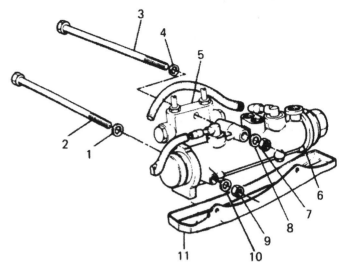

FIG 10:9   Master cylinder removal

Key to Fig 10:9 1 Washer 2, 3 Bolts 4 Washer 5 Switch 6 Master cylinder 7 Nut 8 Washer 9 Nut 10 Washer 11 Mounting bracket

Remove bolts 2 and 3 securing master cylinder to support bracket 11, then carefully pull master cylinder away from operating pushrod and remove from the car.

Servicing:

Refer to **FIG 10:10**. Remove the boot 2, then remove the primary piston, springs, washers and seals, then partially release the stop screw 8 and remove the

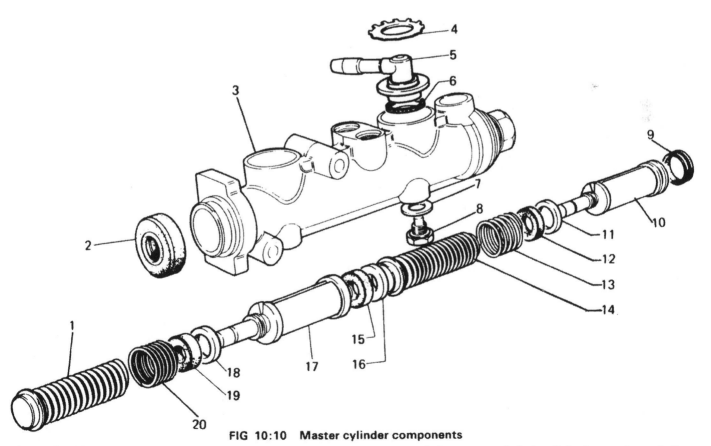

FIG 10:10   Master cylinder components

Key to Fig 10:10   1 Spring   2 Boot   3 Master cylinder   4 Lockplate   5 Connector   6 Seal   7 Sealing washer   8 Stop screw   9 Seal   10 Piston   11 Spacer   12 Seal   13,14 Springs   15 Seal   16 Spacer   17 Piston   18 Spacer   19 Seal   20 Spring

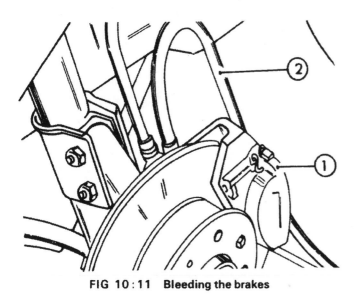

FIG 10:11   Bleeding the brakes

Key to Fig 10:11   1 Caliper being bled   2 Bleed tube

the bore to be honed at a service station, but note that bore diameter must not be increased.

Coat all parts with clean brake fluid and assemble them wet. Reassemble the secondary piston assembly and insert it into the cylinder bore, pressing down the bore with a suitable tool while the stop screw is tightened, taking care not to damage the bore. Refit the primary piston and all other components in the reverse order of dismantling. Use the fingers only to fit the new rubber parts to prevent damage and observe absolute cleanliness to avoid the entry of dirt or grease.

Refitting:

This is a reversal of the removal procedure, making sure that all pipes and hoses are properly reconnected in their correct positions. On completion, top up the fluid in the supply reservoir to the correct level, then bleed the brakes as described in the next section.

10:5 Bleeding the system

This is not routine maintenance and it is only necessary if air has entered the system due to parts being dismantled, or because the fluid level in the supply reservoir has been allowed to drop too low. The need for bleeding is indicated by a spongy feeling at the brake pedal accompanied by poor braking performance. This must not be confused with the sharp drop in brake efficiency accompanied by greater pedal travel which indicates that one of the dual braking circuits has failed. This latter condition must be investigated immediately and the fault rectified.

If work has been carried out on the front brakes only or the rear brakes only, then it will normally only be necessary to bleed the circuit (front or rear) that is affected, as the

secondary piston assembly. Note that secondary piston assembly components must be retained in the bore by the stop screw when the master cylinder is reassembled. If necessary, remove connector 5 with lockplate 4 and seal 6. Discard all rubber parts and thoroughly clean the remaining parts in methylated spirits or the correct grade of brake fluid only. Inspect all parts for scoring, wear or damage. Make sure that the compensating ports in the body are clear. Check the pistons and cylinder bores for rust marks and scoring, which would dictate renewal of the affected component. Always renew any part if its serviceability is in doubt. Cylinder bores should have a mirror finish, but if not perfectly smooth it is possible for

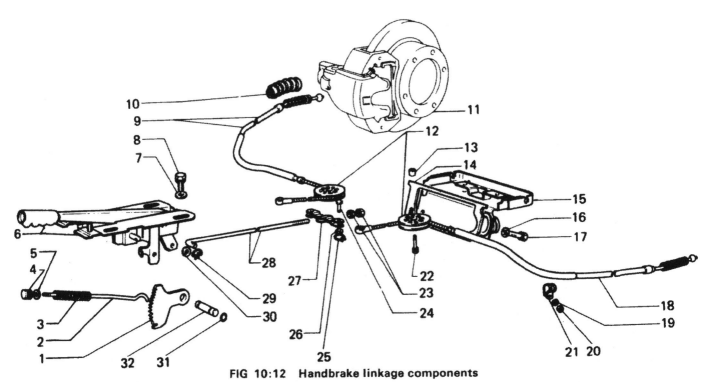

FIG 10:12   Handbrake linkage components

Key to Fig 10:12   1 Ratchet   2 Rod   3 Spring   4 Button   5 Rubber ring   6 Lever assembly   7 Washer   8 Bolt
9 cable   10 Boot   11 Disc   12 Pulleys   13 Spacer   14 Gasket   15 Support bracket   16 Washer   17 Bolt   18 Cable
19 Lockwasher   20 Nut   21 Clamp   22 Bolt   23 Nuts   24 Pin   25 Clip   26 Washer   27 Equaliser   28 Operating rod
29 Clip   30 Washer   31 Lock ring   32 Pin

other system should not have been disturbed. If both circuits have been disturbed, or if braking performance is poor, bleeding should be carried out at all four wheels. Bleeding must be carried out in the following sequence: rear wheel furthest from master cylinder, opposite rear wheel, front wheel furthest from master cylinder, opposite front wheel. **Do not bleed the brakes with any caliper removed or with any brake line disconnected.**

Check the fluid level in supply reservoir and top up if necessary. Clean the bleed screw dust caps and the area around the bleed screw to remove all dirt and rust. Remove the cap from bleed screw on the appropriate caliper 1 and attach a length of rubber tube 2 to the screw as shown in **FIG 10:11**. Lead the free end of the tube into a transparent container and add sufficient brake fluid to safely cover the end of the tube. Loosen the bleed screw and have an assistant press the brake pedal quickly to the floor and allow it to return slowly. Wait a few seconds for the master cylinder to refill with fluid then repeat the operation. Continue until no air bubbles can be seen in the fluid flowing from the tube into the container. Check and top up fluid level in the reservoir at frequent intervals during the operation, as if the level falls too low air will be drawn into the system and the operation will have to be restarted. When the fluid is free from air bubbles, hold the pedal to the floor at the end of a downstroke and tighten the bleed screw. Refit the dust cap and proceed to the next caliper in the correct sequence.

It is recommended that all fluid drained from the system be discarded and new fluid only used for topping up. However, if the drained fluid is new and perfectly clean, allow it to stand for at least 24 hours to ensure that it is free from air bubbles before re-use. Always store brake fluid in clean, sealed containers.

10:6 Handbrake linkage

Handbrake cable adjustment is described in **Section 10:2**.

Handbrake linkage components are shown in **FIG 10:12**. To renew a handbrake cable, fully release the handbrake and, if necessary, slacken the adjusting nut to release all tension from the cable. Disconnect the cable from equaliser and rear brake caliper and remove from beneath the car. Install the new cable, making sure that it passes correctly around the pulley, then carry out the adjustment procedure described in **Section 10:2**. Clean and lightly lubricate equaliser unit and cable pulleys.

10:7 Fault diagnosis

(a) Spongy pedal

1 Leak in the system
2 Worn master cylinder
3 Leaking caliper cylinder
4 Air in the fluid system

(b) Excessive pedal movement

1 Check 1 and 4 in (a)
2 Excessive wear of friction pads
3 Very low fluid level in supply reservoir

(c) Brakes grab or pull to one side

1 Distorted brake disc
2 Wet or oily friction pads
3 Loose caliper
4 Disc or hub loose
5 Worn suspension or steering connections
6 Mixed linings of different grades
7 Uneven tyre pressures
8 Seized handbrake caliper
9 Seized caliper piston

(d) Brakes partly or fully locked on

1 Swollen friction linings
2 Damaged brake pipes preventing fluid return
3 Master cylinder compensating hole blocked
4 Master cylinder piston seized
5 Pedal return spring broken
6 Dirt in the hydraulic system
7 Seized caliper piston
8 Seized handbrake mechanism

(e) Brake failure

1 Empty fluid reservoir
2 Broken hydraulic pipeline
3 Ruptured master cylinder seal
4 Ruptured caliper seal

(f) Reservoir empties too quickly

1 Leaks in pipelines
2 Deteriorated cylinder seals

(g) Pedal yields under continuous pressure

1 Faulty master cylinder seals
2 Faulty caliper seals
3 Leak in the system

Inches	Decimals	Milli-metres	Inches to Millimetres — Inches	Inches to Millimetres — mm	Millimetres to Inches — mm	Millimetres to Inches — Inches
1/64	.015625	.3969	.001	.0254	.01	.00039
1/32	.03125	.7937	.002	.0508	.02	.00079
3/64	.046875	1.1906	.003	.0762	.03	.00118
1/16	.0625	1.5875	.004	.1016	.04	.00157
5/64	.078125	1.9844	.005	.1270	.05	.00197
3/32	.09375	2.3812	.006	.1524	.06	.00236
7/64	.109375	2.7781	.007	.1778	.07	.00276
1/8	.125	3.1750	.008	.2032	.08	.00315
9/64	.140625	3.5719	.009	.2286	.09	.00354
5/32	.15625	3.9687	.01	.254	.1	.00394
11/64	.171875	4.3656	.02	.508	.2	.00787
3/16	.1875	4.7625	.03	.762	.3	.01181
13/64	.203125	5.1594	.04	1.016	.4	.01575
7/32	.21875	5.5562	.05	1.270	.5	.01969
15/64	.234375	5.9531	.06	1.524	.6	.02362
1/4	.25	6.3500	.07	1.778	.7	.02756
17/64	.265625	6.7469	.08	2.032	.8	.03150
9/32	.28125	7.1437	.09	2.286	.9	.03543
19/64	.296875	7.5406	.1	2.54	1	.03937
5/16	.3125	7.9375	.2	5.08	2	.07874
21/64	.328125	8.3344	.3	7.62	3	.11811
11/32	.34375	8.7312	.4	10.16	4	.15748
23/64	.359375	9.1281	.5	12.70	5	.19685
3/8	.375	9.5250	.6	15.24	6	.23622
25/64	.390625	9.9219	.7	17.78	7	.27559
13/32	.40625	10.3187	.8	20.32	8	.31496
27/64	.421875	10.7156	.9	22.86	9	.35433
7/16	.4375	11.1125	1	25.4	10	.39370
29/64	.453125	11.5094	2	50.8	11	.43307
15/32	.46875	11.9062	3	76.2	12	.47244
31/64	.484375	12.3031	4	101.6	13	.51181
1/2	.5	12.7000	5	127.0	14	.55118
33/64	.515625	13.0969	6	152.4	15	.59055
17/32	.53125	13.4937	7	177.8	16	.62992
35/64	.546875	13.8906	8	203.2	17	.66929
9/16	.5625	14.2875	9	228.6	18	.70866
37/64	.578125	14.6844	10	254.0	19	.74803
19/32	.59375	15.0812	11	279.4	20	.78740
39/64	.609375	15.4781	12	304.8	21	.82677
5/8	.625	15.8750	13	330.2	22	.86614
41/64	.640625	16.2719	14	355.6	23	.90551
21/32	.65625	16.6687	15	381.0	24	.94488
43/64	.671875	17.0656	16	406.4	25	.98425
11/16	.6875	17.4625	17	431.8	26	1.02362
45/64	.703125	17.8594	18	457.2	27	1.06299
23/32	.71875	18.2562	19	482.6	28	1.10236
47/64	.734375	18.6531	20	508.0	29	1.14173
3/4	.75	19.0500	21	533.4	30	1.18110
49/64	.765625	19.4469	22	558.8	31	1.22047
25/32	.78125	19.8437	23	584.2	32	1.25984
51/64	.796875	20.2406	24	609.6	33	1.29921
13/16	.8125	20.6375	25	635.0	34	1.33858
53/64	.828125	21.0344	26	660.4	35	1.37795
27/32	.84375	21.4312	27	685.8	36	1.41732
55/64	.859375	21.8281	28	711.2	37	1.4567
7/8	.875	22.2250	29	736.6	38	1.4961
57/64	.890625	22.6219	30	762.0	39	1.5354
29/32	.90625	23.0187	31	787.4	40	1.5748
59/64	.921875	23.4156	32	812.8	41	1.6142
15/16	.9375	23.8125	33	838.2	42	1.6535
61/64	.953125	24.2094	34	863.6	43	1.6929
31/32	.96875	24.6062	35	889.0	44	1.7323
63/64	.984375	25.0031	36	914.4	45	1.7717

UNITS	Pints to Litres	Gallons to Litres	Litres to Pints	Litres to Gallons	Miles to Kilometres	Kilometres to Miles	Lbs. per sq. In. to Kg. per sq. Cm.	Kg. per sq. Cm. to Lbs. per sq. In.
1	.57	4.55	1.76	.22	1.61	.62	.07	14.22
2	1.14	9.09	3.52	.44	3.22	1.24	.14	28.50
3	1.70	13.64	5.28	.66	4.83	1.86	.21	42.67
4	2.27	18.18	7.04	.88	6.44	2.49	.28	56.89
5	2.84	22.73	8.80	1.10	8.05	3.11	.35	71.12
6	3.41	27.28	10.56	1.32	9.66	3.73	.42	85.34
7	3.98	31.82	12.32	1.54	11.27	4.35	.49	99.56
8	4.55	36.37	14.08	1.76	12.88	4.97	.56	113.79
9		40.91	15.84	1.98	14.48	5.59	.63	128.00
10		45.46	17.60	2.20	16.09	6.21	.70	142.23
20				4.40	32.19	12.43	1.41	284.47
30				6.60	48.28	18.64	2.11	426.70
40				8.80	64.37	24.85		
50					80.47	31.07		
60					96.56	37.28		
70					112.65	43.50		
80					128.75	49.71		
90					144.84	55.92		
100					160.93	62.14		

UNITS	Lb ft to kgm	Kgm to lb ft	UNITS	Lb ft to kgm	Kgm to lb ft
1	.138	7.233	7	.967	50.631
2	.276	14.466	8	1.106	57.864
3	.414	21.699	9	1.244	65.097
4	.553	28.932	10	1.382	72.330
5	.691	36.165	20	2.765	144.660
6	.829	43.398	30	4.147	216.990

CHAPTER 11
THE ELECTRICAL SYSTEM

11:1 Description

All models covered by this manual have 12-volt electrical systems in which the negative terminal of the battery is earthed to the car bodywork.

There are wiring diagrams in **Technical Data** at the end of this manual which will enable those with electrical experience to trace and correct faults.

Some items of electrical equipment can be serviced to repair minor faults or renew worn components, but others can only be renewed complete if defective. In either case, items that are seriously defective, electrically or mechanically, should be replaced by new units, or reconditioned units which can be obtained on an exchange basis should be fitted.

11 : 2 The battery

The negative terminal is earthed. **Do not, under any circumstances, reverse the terminal connections.**

To maintain the performance of the battery, it is essential to carry out the following operations, particularly in winter when heavy current demands must be met.

Keep the top and surrounding parts of the battery dry and clean, as dampness can cause current leakage. Clean off corrosion from the metal parts of the battery mounting with diluted ammonia and coat them with anti-sulphuric paint. Clean the terminal posts and smear them with petroleum jelly, tightening the terminal fixings securely. High electrical resistance due to corrosion of the battery terminals can be responsible for a lack of sufficient current to operate the starter motor.

Regularly check the electrolyte level in the battery cells and top up with distilled water, if necessary, to the correct level. Fill to the level mark on the case if one is provided, or follow the filling instructions printed on the battery or its cover. If neither case applies to the battery which is fitted, top up until the internal separators are just covered.

If a battery fault is suspected, test the condition of the cells with a hydrometer. **Never add neat acid to the battery. If it is necessary to prepare new electrolyte due to loss of spillage, add sulphuric acid to distilled water. It is highly dangerous to add water to acid.** It is safest to have the battery refilled with electrolyte by a service station, if it is necessary.

The indications from the hydrometer readings of the specific gravity are as follows:

For climates below 27°C (80°F)			*Specific gravity*
Cell fully charged..	..	..	.. 1.270 to 1.290
Cell half discharged	..	..	.. 1.190 to 1.210
Cell discharged ..	..	..	.. 1.110 to 1.130

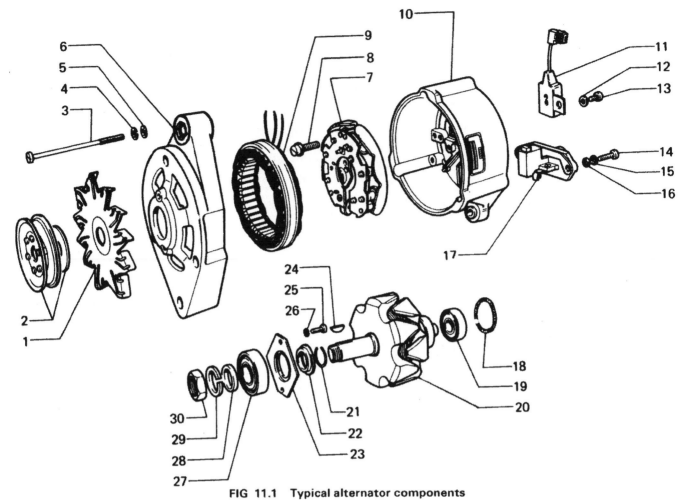

FIG 11.1   Typical alternator components

Key to Fig 11:1   1 Cooling fan   2 Pulley   3 Through bolt   4 Lockwasher   5 Washer   6 End bracket   7 Plate   8 Screw
9 Stator   10 Housing   11 Capacitor   12 Washer   13, 14 Screws   15 Lockwasher   16 Washer   17 Brush holder
18 Seal   19 Bearing   20 Rotor   21 Clip   22 Seal   23 Retainer   24 Key   25 Screw   26 Washer   27 Bearing
28 Seal   29 Lockwasher   30 Nut

For climates above 27°C (80°F)

Cell fully charged..	..	..	.. 1.210 to 1.230
Cell half discharged	..	..	.. 1.130 to 1.150
Cell discharged ..	..	..	.. 1.030 to 1.070

These figures assume an electrolyte temperature of 16°C (60°F). If the temperature exceeds this, add 0.002 to the readings for each 3°C (5°F) rise. Subtract 0.002 for any corresponding drop below the stated temperature.

If the battery is in a low state of charge, take the car for a long daylight run or put the battery on a charger at 5 amps, until it gases freely. If an auto-fill type of battery is installed, the battery cover should be left in place during charging to prevent loss of electrolyte. If the battery is fitted with screw caps, these should be removed during charging. Do not use a naked light near the battery as the gas is inflammable. If the battery is to stand unused for long periods, give a refreshing charge every month. It will be ruined if it is left in a discharged state. Always disconnect the battery from the car electrical system when it is being charged from an outside source, to prevent damage to alternator internal components.

11:3 The alternator

The alternator provides current for the various items of electrical equipment and to charge the battery, the unit operating at all engine speeds. The current produced is alternate, this being rectified to direct current supply by diodes mounted in the alternator casing. Alternator drive is by belt from the crankshaft pulley. Very little maintenance is needed, apart from the occasional check on belt tension as described later, and on the condition and security of wiring connections.

The alternator must never be run with the battery disconnected, nor must the battery cables be reversed at any time. Test connections must be carefully made, and the battery and alternator must be completely disconnected before any electric welding is carried out on any part of the car. The engine must never be started with a battery charger still connected to the battery, although it is in order to use a second, fully charged battery to boost the one in the car in order to start the engine. In the latter case, make sure that the jump leads are connected positive to positive and negative to negative. These warnings must be observed, otherwise extensive damage to the alternator components, particularly the diodes, will result.

The alternator is designed and constructed to provide many years of trouble free service. If a fault should develop in the unit, it should be checked and serviced by a fully equipped service station or a reconditioned unit obtained and fitted.

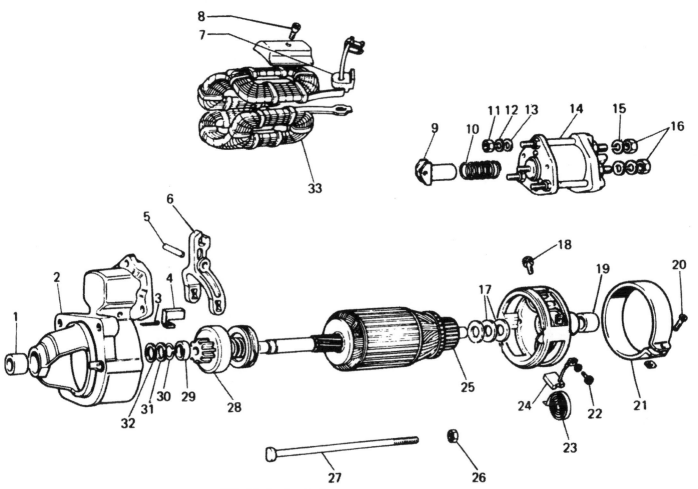

FIG 11:2 Typical starter motor components

Key to Fig 11:2   1 Bush   2 End bracket   3 Cotter pin   4 Rubber block   5 Pivot pin   6 Engagement lever   7 Insulator
8 Screw   9 Plunger   10 Spring   11 Nut   12 Lockwasher   13 Washer   14 Solenoid   15 Lockwasher   16 Nut
17 Washers   18 Screw   19 Bush   20 Screw   21 Cover   22 Screw   23 Brush spring   24 Carbon brush   25 Armature
26 Nut   27 Bolt   28 Drive pinion assembly   29 Stop ring   30 Circlip   31, 32 Washers   33 Field coils

Checking alternator operation:

A simple check on alternator charging can be carried out after dark by switching on the headlamps and starting the engine. If the alternator is charging, the headlamps will brighten considerably as the system voltage rises from the nominal battery voltage to the higher figure produced by the alternator.

If the alternator is not charging, check the wiring and connections in the charging circuit, then check the brush gear as described later. If these are in order, the alternator or regulator is at fault, so checks and any necessary repairs should be carried out by a service station.

Carbon brush renewal:

This work can be carried out without the need for alternator removal. Disconnect the battery earth cable then disconnect the wiring from alternator. **FIG 11:1** shows typical alternator components. Remove brush holder 17, then remove and discard the old brushes. Clean the brush holder and install the new brushes.

The slip rings on rotor 20 on which the brushes operate should be cleaned with a petrol-moistened cloth. Hold the cloth through the brush holder mounting hole. To facilitate cleaning, slacken the drive belt as described in **Chapter 4**,

then remove the belt from the alternator pulley so that the pulley can be turned by hand.

On completion, refit the brush holder assembly, reconnect the wiring then reconnect battery earth cable. Reset belt tension as described in **Chapter 4**.

Alternator removal:

Disconnect the battery, then disconnect cables to the alternator. Slacken and remove the drive belt as described in **Chapter 4**. Unbolt and remove the alternator.

Refitting is a reversal of the removal procedure, adjusting belt tension as described in **Chapter 4**.

Alternator bearing removal:

Remove the alternator as described previously. Refer to **FIG 11:1**. Mark the relationships of end bracket 6 and housing 10 to maintain alignment when reassembling. Remove the securing nut, then remove pulley and washer 2 and cooling fan 1 from the shaft. Collect locating key 24.

Remove the three through bolts 3 and separate end bracket from housing. Hold the shaft of rotor 20 and carefully tap housing with a soft-faced hammer to remove the rotor. Remove the screws and detach bearing retainer 23, then remove the bearing assembly. Use a suitable

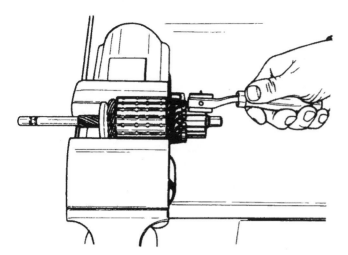

FIG 11:3 Undercutting commutator insulation

puller to remove rear bearing 19 from the rotor shaft. If the bearings are obviously defective, discard them, otherwise clean the bearings in a suitable solvent and check for wear or damage by rotating by hand. If faults are found the bearing should be renewed. Fit the bearings and reassemble the components in the reverse order of removal, using new bearing seals if the originals are not in good condition. The bearings should be lubricated with grease. Do not overlubricate and take care to avoid lubricant contamination of rotor slip rings or brush gear.

11:4 The starter motor

The starter is a brush type series wound motor equipped with an overrunning clutch and operated by a solenoid. The armature shaft is supported in metal bushes which require no routine servicing.

When the starter is operated from the switch, the engagement lever moves the pinion into mesh with the engine ring gear. When the pinion meshes with the ring gear teeth, the solenoid contact closes the circuit and the starter motor operates to turn the engine. When the engine starts, the speed of the rotating ring gear causes the pinion to overrun the clutch and armature. The pinion continues in engagement until the switch is released, when the engagement lever returns it to the rest position under spring pressure.

On models so equipped, the seat belt interlock system prevents current from reaching the starter solenoid, thereby preventing starter operation, unless the seat belts are correctly fastened.

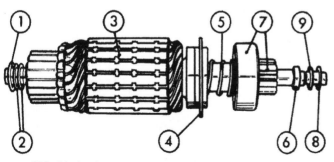

FIG 11:4 Armature and drive pinion assembly

Key to Fig 11:4   1 Thrust washer   2 Plain washers
3 Armature   4 Sleeve   5 Spring   6 Stop ring   7 Drive
pinion   8, 9 Plain washers

Tests for a starter which does not operate:

Check that the battery is in good condition and fully charged and that its connections are clean and tight. Switch on the headlamps and operate the starter switch. Current is reaching the starter if the lights dim when the starter is operated, in which case it will be necessary to remove the starter for servicing. If the lights do not dim significantly, switch them off and operate the starter switch while listening for a clicking sound at the starter motor, which will indicate that the starter solenoid is operating. If no sound can be heard at the starter when the switch is operated, check the wiring and connections between the battery and the starter switch, and between the switch and the solenoid. If a seat belt interlock system is incorporated, use a test lamp to check for current supply to the solenoid feed terminal while the ignition switch is turned to the starting position. If no current is available, either the wiring or connections are defective as just described, or there is a fault in the interlock system which should be checked and repaired at a service station.

If the solenoid can be heard operating when the starter switch is operated, check the wiring and connections between the battery and the main starter motor terminal, taking care not to accidentally earth the main battery to starter motor lead which is live at all times. If the wiring is not the cause of the trouble, the fault is internal and the starter motor must be removed and serviced.

Removing the starter:

Disconnect the battery then disconnect the wiring from starter to motor terminals. Remove the three fixing screws securing the starter to the engine block, then withdraw the unit by sliding it horizontally from its mountings.

Refitting is a reversal of this procedure.

Dismantling starter motor:

FIG 11:2 shows starter motor internal components. Remove the nut and detach the terminal which connects solenoid to starter motor, then remove nuts 11 and detach solenoid 14. Slacken screw 20 and remove cover 21. Remove screws 22 securing brush terminals, then release springs 23 and lift brushes 24 slightly in their holders. Position springs against sides of brushes to hold them in this position, then remove the screws securing brush holder assembly and detach from starter body. Collect thrust washers. Remove nuts 26 on through bolts 27, then remove starter body from end bracket 2. Remove cotter pin 3 and pivot pin 5, then pull armature assembly 25 from end bracket. Note location of rubber block 4.

Servicing components:
Cleaning:

Blow away all loose dust and dirt with an air-line. Use a small brush to clean out crevices. Petrol or methylated spirits may be used to help in cleaning the metal parts, but the field coils, armature and drive pinion assembly must under no circumstances be soaked with solvent.

Brush gear:

Check the brushes for wear or contamination. Clean the brushes and holders with a petrol-moistened cloth and check that the brushes move freely in their holders. If a brush sticks, ease the sides of the brush by polishing with a smooth file. If any brush is excessively worn or damaged in any way, all brushes should be renewed as a set.

The commutator:

The commutator on which the carbon brushes operate should have a smooth polished surface which is dark in appearance. Wiping over with a piece of cloth moistened with methylated spirits or petrol is usually sufficient to clean the surface. Light burn marks or scores can be polished off with fine grade glass paper (do not use emery cloth as this leaves particles embedded in the copper). Deeper damage may be skimmed off in a lathe, at high speed and using a very sharp tool. A diamond-tipped tool should be used for a light final cut. On completion, the mica between commutator segments must be undercut to a minimum depth of 1.0mm (0.04in), using a special tool as shown in **FIG 11:3** or a hacksaw blade ground to the width of the insulation. Make sure that all dust is cleaned from the commutator when the work is complete.

The armature:

Check the armature for charred insulation, loose segments or laminations and for scored laminations. Short circuited windings may be suspected if individual commutator segments are badly burned. If the armature is damaged in any way it should be renewed. If an electrical fault in the armature is suspected, have it tested on special equipment at a service station.

Field coils:

The field coils and pole pieces are held in place by special screws. To ensure correct installation and alignment it is recommended that field coil checking and servicing be carried out at a service station.

The field coils can be checked for continuity using a test lamp and battery. A better method is to check the resistance using an ohmmeter. The resistance can also be checked using a 12-volt battery and ammeter (voltage divided by a current equals resistance).

Bearings:

If the bearing bushes are excessively worn, they should be renewed at a service station, as press equipment and very accurate mandrels are required to install the new bushes. If the bearings are in good condition, they should be lightly lubricated with engine oil during reassembly.

Drive pinion assembly:

The starter drive pinion and clutch assembly must not be washed in solvents, as this would wash away the internal lubricant. Cleaning should be confined to wiping away dirt with a cloth. Light damage to the pinion teeth which engage the engine ring gear can be cleaned off with a fine file or oilstone, deeper damage necessitates the renewal of the complete drive assembly. Check that the clutch takes up the drive instantaneously but slips freely in the opposite direction. The complete assembly must be renewed if the clutch is defective.

To remove the starter drive, refer to **FIG 11:4** and use a suitable piece of metal tube to drive the stop ring 6 down the shaft to free the circlip, then remove the circlip and pull

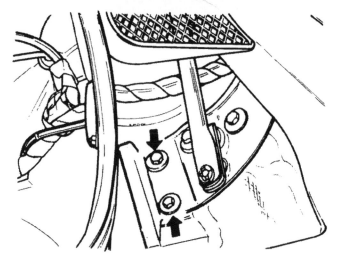

FIG 11:5 Wiper motor removal

off the stop ring and drive pinion assembly. Refit in the reverse order of removal, making sure that the stop ring is pulled over the circlip to retain it securely.

Reassembly:

This is a reversal of the removal procedure. Lubricate the bearing bushes and the splines on the starter drive assembly with a thin coating of engine oil and the face of stop ring for drive pinion with lithium based grease. Do not over-lubricate and take care not to contaminate commutator, brush gear or electrical winding with lubricant.

11:5 Fuses

The fuses which protect the main electrical circuits are mounted in a fusebox situated beneath the instrument panel and provided with a snap-on cover.

If a fuse blows, briefly check the circuit that it protects and install a new fuse. Check each circuit in turn and if the new fuse does not blow, it is likely that the old one had weakened with age. If the new fuse blows, carefully check the circuit that was live at the time and do not fit another fuse until the fault has been found and repaired. A fuse that blows intermittently will make it more difficult to correct the fault, but try shaking the wiring loom, as the fault is likely to be caused by chafed insulation making intermittent contact.

Never fit a fuse of higher rating than that specified, and never use anything as a substitute for a fuse of the correct type. The fuse is designed to be the weak link in the circuit and if a higher rated fuse or an incorrect substitute is installed the wiring may fail instead.

Unprotected circuits, 1300 models:

The following circuits are unprotected: ignition, charging, starting, charging warning light, radiator fan motor relay, side light warning light, panel lights and steering column switches relay.

Unprotected circuits, 1500 models:

The following circuits are unprotected: ignition, charging and starting.

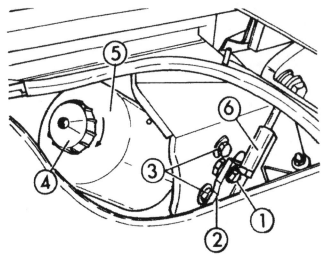

FIG 11:6 Headlamp motor removal

Key to Fig 11:6   1 Bolt   2 Arm   3 Bolts   4 Tilting
manual control   5 Motor   6 Adjuster for headlamp
vertical alignment

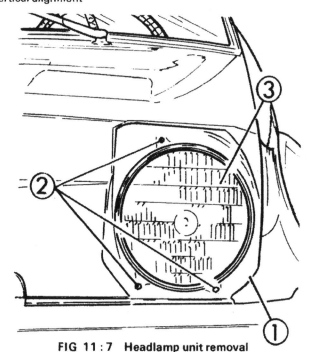

FIG 11:7 Headlamp unit removal

Key to Fig 11:7   1 Frame   2 Screws   3 Headlamp unit

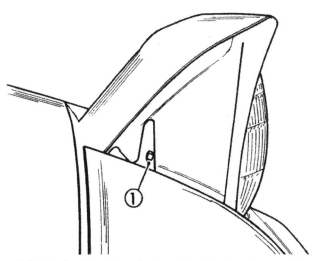

FIG 11:8 Headlamp horizontal adjustment screw 1

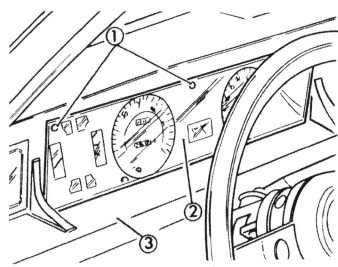

FIG 11:9 Instrument panel removal

Key to Fig 11:9   1 Screws   2 Instrument panel
3 Facia

11:6 Windscreen wipers

The windscreen wipers are operated by a two-speed
electric motor incorporating a self-parking switch.

If wiper operation is sluggish, check the linkage for
binding. If the motor is inoperative, check the fuse first,
then check the wiring and connections between the
battery and switch and between the switch and wiper
motor. If the motor unit is defective, a new or exchange
unit should be obtained and fitted.

Wiper motor removal:

Remove the wiper arms by carefully levering the
mountings from splined shafts. Open the front
compartment lid, then disconnect the wiper wiring
connector. Remove the two bolts shown in **FIG 11:5**, then
unscrew the nut which attaches linkage to wiper motor
arm. Separate linkage from motor and remove the motor.
Operate linkage by hand to check for wear or binding and
renew parts if necessary.

Install the motor in the reverse order of removal,
lubricating linkage joints with waterproof grease. On
completion, use the screenwasher or plain water to wet the
screen, then check wiper operation. If the sweep area of
any wiper is incorrect, or if a wiper blade contacts the
screen surround at any point, reposition the arm on the
shaft as necessary.

11:7 Headlamps

If the motors fail to raise or lower the headlamp units,
check the fuses first. If these are in order, check the wiring
and connections in the operating circuit. If a motor is faulty
a new or exchange unit should be obtained and fitted.
Check that the headlamp hinges are free and lubricated.

**Care should be taken when working on the head-
lamp units, for if the battery is not disconnected
slight movement may start the motor and the fingers
may be trapped in the mechanism.**

Headlamp motor removal:

Refer to **FIG 11:6**. Take care not to turn control 4,
otherwise the motor, if operative, will retract the headlamp

unit. Remove bolt 1 securing arm 2 to motor shaft. Remove three bolts and washers 3 securing motor 5, then disconnect the electrical connector and remove the motor.

Refit in the reverse order of removal, making sure that motor earth wire is fitted under the appropriate mounting bolt 3. On completion, it is recommended that headlamp beam setting be checked as described later.

Headlamp unit removal:

Refer to **FIG 11:7**. Remove the three screws securing frame 1 to body, then remove the frame. Loosen the three screws 2 securing headlamp ring, then turn ring to left and remove. Remove plug from rear of headlamp unit 3, then remove the unit.

Installation is a reversal of the removal procedure. On completion, it is recommended that headlamp beam setting be checked as described next.

Headlamp beam setting:

Correct headlamp beam setting is now a legal requirement in many countries and checking by an optical beam setter is part of the vehicle's annual road worthiness certification. Each headlamp is provided with a vertical and a horizontal adjuster. The vertical adjuster is shown at 6 in **FIG 11:6** and the horizontal adjuster at 1 in **FIG 11:8**. To adjust the setting of the beam, loosen the locknuts, turn the adjusters as necessary and retighten the locknuts. If the beams have been disturbed, pending optical setting, they may be temporarily reset as follows.

Position the unladen car on level ground (with the tyres correctly inflated) facing a wall at a distance of 5m (16.4ft) and use the adjusters to set the **undipped** beams parallel to each other and having the centre of the beams 35mm (1.38in) lower than the height of the centre of the headlamps from the ground.

11:8 Instrument panel

Removal:

Refer to **FIG 11:9**. Disconnect the battery to prevent accidental shortcircuits, then remove five screws 1 (two of these are marked), securing instrument panel 2 to facia 3. Pull the panel out slightly, then reach behind it and disconnect the three electrical connectors and the speedometer cable. Remove the instrument panel from the facia.

Refitting is a reversal of the removal procedure. On completion, reconnect the battery and check operation of instruments, gauges and warning lights.

11:9 Fault diagnosis

(a) Battery discharged

1 Terminal connections loose or dirty
2 Shorts in lighting circuits
3 Alternator not charging
4 Regulator faulty
5 Battery internally defective

(b) Insufficient charge rate

1 Check 1 and 4 in (a)
2 Drive belt slipping
3 Alternator defective

(c) Battery will not hold charge

1 Low electrolyte level
2 Electrolyte leakage from cracked case
3 Battery internally defective

(d) Battery overcharged

1 Regulator faulty

(e) Alternator output low or nil

1 Drive belt broken or slipping
2 Regulator faulty
3 Brushes sticking, springs weak or broken
4 Faulty internal windings
5 Defective diode(s)

(f) Starter motor lacks power or will not turn

1 Battery discharged, loose cable connections
2 Starter switch or solenoid faulty
3 Brushes worn or sticking, leads detached or shorting
4 Commutator dirty or worn
5 Starter shaft bent
6 Engine abnormally stiff

(g) Starter runs but does not turn engine

1 Pinion engagement mechanism faulty
2 Broken teeth on pinion or engine ring gear

(h) Starter motor rough or noisy

1 Mounting bolts loose
2 Pinion engagement mechanism faulty
3 Damaged pinion or engine ring gear teeth

(j) Noisy starter when engine is running

1 Pinion return mechanism faulty
2 Mounting bolts loose

(k) Starter motor inoperative

1 Check 1, 2 and 3 in (f)
2 Armature or field coils faulty
3 Seat belt interlock circuit faulty (where fitted)

(l) Lamps inoperative or erratic

1 Battery low, bulbs burned out
2 Faulty earthing of lamps or battery
3 Lighting switch faulty, loose or broken connections

(m) Wiper motor sluggish, taking high current

1 Wiper motor internally defective
2 Wiper motor fixings loose
3 Linkage worn or binding

Inches	Decimals	Milli-metres	Inches to Millimetres		Millimetres to Inches	
			Inches	mm	mm	Inches
1/64	.015625	.3969	.001	.0254	.01	.00039
1/32	.03125	.7937	.002	.0508	.02	.00079
3/64	.046875	1.1906	.003	.0762	.03	.00118
1/16	.0625	1.5875	.004	.1016	.04	.00157
5/64	.078125	1.9844	.005	.1270	.05	.00197
3/32	.09375	2.3812	.006	.1524	.06	.00236
7/64	.109375	2.7781	.007	.1778	.07	.00276
1/8	.125	3.1750	.008	.2032	.08	.00315
9/64	.140625	3.5719	.009	.2286	.09	.00354
5/32	.15625	3.9687	.01	.254	.1	.00394
11/64	.171875	4.3656	.02	.508	.2	.00787
3/16	.1875	4.7625	.03	.762	.3	.01181
13/64	.203125	5·1594	.04	1.016	.4	.01575
7/32	.21875	5.5562	.05	1.270	.5	.01969
15/64	.234375	5.9531	.06	1.524	.6	.02362
1/4	.25	6.3500	.07	1.778	.7	.02756
17/64	.265625	6.7469	.08	2.032	.8	.03150
9/32	.28125	7.1437	.09	2.286	.9	.03543
19/64	.296875	7.5406	.1	2.54	1	.03937
5/16	.3125	7.9375	.2	5.08	2	.07874
21/64	.328125	8.3344	.3	7.62	3	.11811
11/32	.34375	8.7312	.4	10.16	4	.15748
23/64	.359375	9.1281	.5	12.70	5	.19685
3/8	.375	9.5250	.6	15.24	6	.23622
25/64	.390625	9.9219	.7	17.78	7	.27559
13/32	.40625	10.3187	.8	20.32	8	.31496
27/64	.421875	10.7156	.9	22.86	9	.35433
7/16	.4375	11.1125	1	25.4	10	.39370
29/64	.453125	11.5094	2	50.8	11	.43307
15/32	.46875	11.9062	3	76.2	12	.47244
31/64	.484375	12.3031	4	101.6	13	.51181
1/2	.5	12.7000	5	127.0	14	.55118
33/64	.515625	13.0969	6	152.4	15	.59055
17/32	.53125	13.4937	7	177.8	16	.62992
35/64	.546875	13.8906	8	203.2	17	.66929
9/16	.5625	14.2875	9	228.6	18	.70866
37/64	.578125	14.6844	10	254.0	19	.74803
19/32	.59375	15.0812	11	279.4	20	.78740
39/64	.609375	15.4781	12	304.8	21	.82677
5/8	.625	15.8750	13	330.2	22	.86614
41/64	.640625	16.2719	14	355.6	23	.90551
21/32	.65625	16.6687	15	381.0	24	.94488
43/64	.671875	17.0656	16	406.4	25	.98425
11/16	.6875	17.4625	17	431.8	26	1.02362
45/64	.703125	17.8594	18	457.2	27	1.06299
23/32	.71875	18.2562	19	482.6	28	1.10236
47/64	.734375	18.6531	20	508.0	29	1.14173
3/4	.75	19.0500	21	533.4	30	1.18110
49/64	.765625	19.4469	22	558.8	31	1.22047
25/32	.78125	19.8437	23	584.2	32	1.25984
51/64	.796875	20.2406	24	609.6	33	1.29921
13/16	.8125	20.6375	25	635.0	34	1.33858
53/64	.828125	21.0344	26	660.4	35	1.37795
27/32	.84375	21.4312	27	685.8	36	1.41732
55/64	.859375	21.8281	28	711.2	37	1.4567
7/8	.875	22.2250	29	736.6	38	1.4961
57/64	.890625	22.6219	30	762.0	39	1.5354
29/32	.90625	23.0187	31	787.4	40	1.5748
59/64	.921875	23.4156	32	812.8	41	1.6142
15/16	.9375	23.8125	33	838.2	42	1.6535
61/64	.953125	24.2094	34	863.6	43	1.6929
31/32	.96875	24.6062	35	889.0	44	1.7323
63/64	.984375	25.0031	36	914.4	45	1.7717

UNITS	Pints to Litres	Gallons to Litres	Litres to Pints	Litres to Gallons	Miles to Kilometres	Kilometres to Miles	Lbs. per sq. In. to Kg. per sq. Cm.	Kg. per sq. Cm. to Lbs. per sq. In.
1	.57	4.55	1.76	.22	1.61	.62	.07	14.22
2	1.14	9.09	3.52	.44	3.22	1.24	.14	28.50
3	1.70	13.64	5.28	.66	4.83	1.86	.21	42.67
4	2.27	18.18	7.04	.88	6.44	2.49	.28	56.89
5	2.84	22.73	8.80	1.10	8.05	3.11	.35	71.12
6	3.41	27.28	10.56	1.32	9.66	3.73	.42	85.34
7	3.98	31.82	12.32	1.54	11.27	4.35	.49	99.56
8	4.55	36.37	14.08	1.76	12.88	4.97	.56	113.79
9		40.91	15.84	1.98	14.48	5.59	.63	128.00
10		45.46	17.60	2.20	16.09	6.21	.70	142.23
20				4.40	32.19	12.43	1.41	284.47
30				6.60	48.28	18.64	2.11	426.70
40				8.80	64.37	24.85		
50					80.47	31.07		
60					96.56	37.28		
70					112.65	43.50		
80					128.75	49.71		
90					144.84	55.92		
100					160.93	62.14		

UNITS	Lb ft to kgm	Kgm to lb ft	UNITS	Lb ft to kgm	Kgm to lb ft
1	.138	7.233	7	.967	50.631
2	.276	14.466	8	1.106	57.864
3	.414	21.699	9	1.244	65.097
4	.553	28.932	10	1.382	72.330
5	.691	36.165	20	2.765	144.660
6	.829	43.398	30	4.147	216.990

CHAPTER 12

THE BODYWORK

12:1 Bodywork finish

Large scale repairs to body panels are best left to expert panel beaters. Even small dents can be tricky, too much hammering will stretch the metal and make things worse instead of better. If panel beating is to be attempted, use a dolly on the opposite side of the panel. The head of a large hammer will suffice for small dents, but for large dents, a block of metal will be necessary. Use light hammer blows to reshape the panel, pressing the dolly against the opposite side of the panel to absorb the blows. If this method is used to reduce the depth of dents, final smoothing with a suitable filler will be easier, although it may be better to avoid hammering minor dents and just use the filler.

Clean the area to be filled, making sure that it is free from paint, rust and grease, then roughen the area with emerycloth to ensure a good bond. Use a proprietary fibreglass filler paste mixed according to the manufacturer's instructions and press it into the dent with a putty knife or similar flat-bladed tool. Allow the filler to stand proud of the surrounding area to allow for rubbing down after hardening. Use a file and emerycloth or a disc sander to blend the repaired area to the surrounding bodywork, using finer grade abrasive as the work nears completion. Apply a coat of primer surfacer and, when it is

dry, rub down with 'Wet or Dry' paper lubricated with soapy water, finishing with 400 grade. Apply more primer and repeat the operation until the surface is perfectly smooth. Take time on achieving the best finish possible at this stage as it will control the final effect.

The touching-up of paintwork can be carried out with self-spraying cans of paint, these being available in a wide range of colours. Use a piece of newspaper or board as a test panel to practise on first, so that the action of the spray will be familiar when it is used on the panel. Before spraying the panel, remove all traces of wax polish. Mask off large areas such as windows with newspaper and masking tape. Small areas such as trim strips or door handles can be wrapped with masking tape or carefully coated with grease or Vaseline. Apply the touching-up paint, spraying with short bursts and keeping the spray moving. Do not attempt to cover the area in one coat, applying several coats with a few minutes' drying time between each. If too much paint is applied at one time, runs may develop. If so, do not try to remove the run by wiping but wait until it is dry and rub down as before.

After the final coat has been applied, allow a few hours of drying time before blending the new finish to the old with fine cutting compound, buffing with a light, circular motion. Finish with the application of a good quality polish.

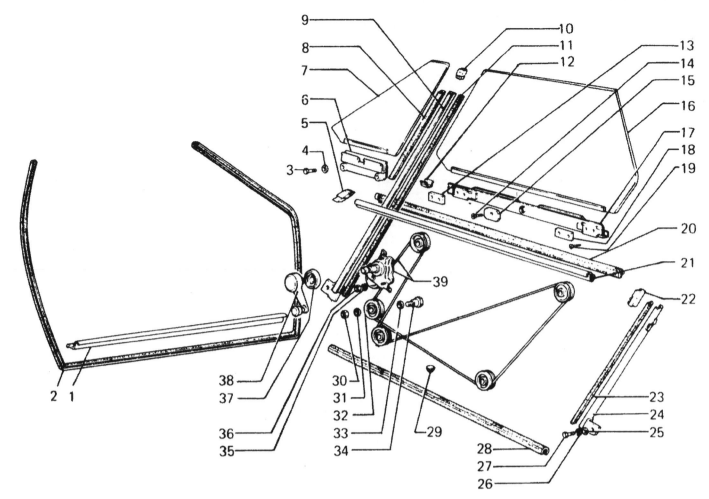

FIG 12:1 Door glass and regulator mechanism components

Key to Fig 12:1 1 Doorsill moulding   2 Weatherstrip   3 Bolt   4 Washer   5 Boot   6 Channel   7 Glass   8 Weatherstrip
9 Pillar   10 Pad   11 Weatherstrip   12 Clip   13 Plate   14 Screw   15 Pad   16 Glass   17 Guide   18 Plate   19 Screw
20 Weatherstrip   21 Cover   22 Boot   23 Weatherstrip   24 Channel   25 Washer   26 Lockwasher   27 Screw
28 Weatherstrip   29 Pad   30 Nut   31 Washer   32 Pulley   33 Washer   34 Bolt   35 Lockwasher   36 Nut   37 Bezel
38 Handle   39 Window regulator

12:2 Door components

Door window glass and regulator mechanism components are shown in **FIG 12:1**, door lock and operating mechanism components in **FIG 12:2**.

Door trim panel removal:

Refer to **FIG 12:3**. Carefully lever plug 1 from armrest 2, then remove three screws and detach armrest from door. Remove screw and lock operating handle 4. Unscrew and remove lock button 3 from lockrod. Lever cover 5 away from handle 6 and push the handle towards the regulator to remove. Carefully lever the trim panel 7 from door inner panel to release the retaining clips, using a large screwdriver or suitable flat-bladed tool.

Refitting is a reversal of the removal procedure.

Window glass adjustment:

Remove the trim panel as described previously. Wind the window glass down fully, then refer to **FIG 12:1**. Slacken the screws securing clamp plates 13 and 18, then allow the window to rest on the rubber pad provided. In this position firmly retighten the clamp plate screws. Check that the glass can be operated smoothly through its

full range of movement and that the control cable winds and unwinds properly on the regulator pulley. If necessary, make further fine adjustments to correct any faults.

Regulator cable tensioning:

If the regulator cable slackens in service and slips on the pulleys, retension in the following manner:

Remove the trim panel as described previously. Refer to **FIG 12:4** and loosen nut 2 securing idler pulley. Move idler pulley in slot 3 until tension of cable 1 is correct, then firmly retighten nut. Check operation of window through full range of movement.

Door lock adjustment:

If the door lock does not operate correctly from the outside handle, remove the trim panel as described previously and disconnect the upper end of rod shown at 24 in **FIG 12:2**. Rotate the connector as necessary to modify the length of the rod, temporarily reconnecting and checking after each adjustment. When correct, reconnect and secure the rod then refit the trim panel.

If the lock does not operate correctly from the inside handle, remove the trim panel as described previously then

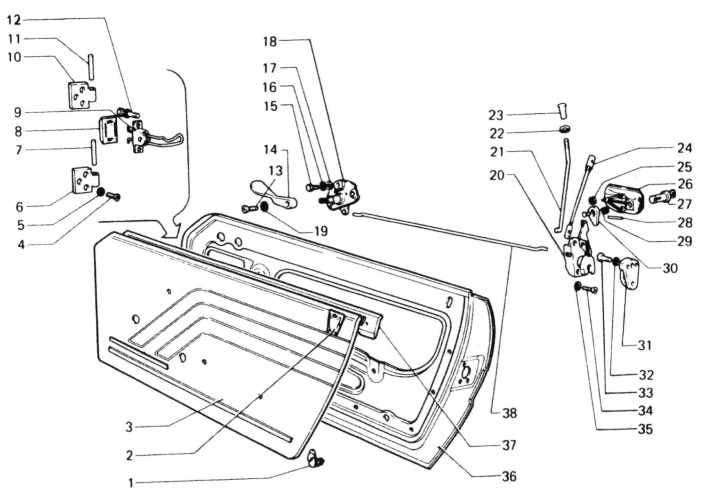

FIG 12:2   Door lock and operating mechanism components

Key to Fig 12:2   1 Clip   2 Lock cover   3 Door trim panel   4 Screw   5 Lockwasher   6 Hinge half   7 Pin   8 Lining
9 Door check   10 Hinge half   11 Pin   12 Bolt   13 Screw   14 Handle   15 Bolt   16 Lockwasher   17 Washer
18 Lever   19 Lockwasher   20 Lock   21 Rod   22 Rubber ring   23 Knob   24 Rod   25 Nut   26 Handle   27 Lock
cylinder   28 Pin   29 Spring   30 Pawl   31 Striker plate   32 Lockwasher   33, 34 Screws   35 Lockwasher   36 Door
37 Channel   38 Rod

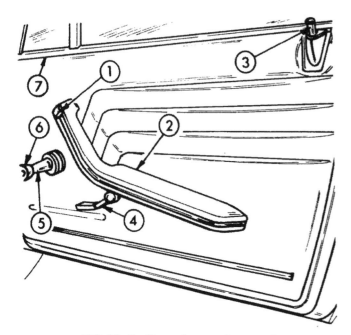

FIG 12:3   Door trim panel removal

Key to Fig 12:3   1 Plug   2 Armrest   3 Lock button
4 Handle   5 Cover   6 Handle   7 Trim panel

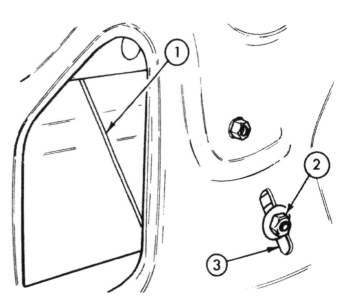

FIG 12:4   Adjusting regulator cable tension

Key to Fig 12:4   1 Cable   2 Nut   3 Slot

FIG 12 : 5   Door lock striker adjustment

Key to Fig 12 : 5   1 Striker plate   2 Screws

slacken the screws 15 securing lock 18 to door panel (see **FIG 12 : 2**). Move the lock as necessary within the range allowed by the mounting holes, then retighten the bolts and refit the trim panel.

If a door does not close fully when shut or needs excessive slamming to close fully, the position of the lock striker plate can be modified to cure the fault. Refer to **FIG 12 : 5**. Scribe around the striker plate so that its original position is known, then slacken screws 2 and move plate 1 in or out as necessary. Firmly retighten the screws, then check that the door closes correctly. Note that it is essential for the door to close with two distinct clicks, in the safety catch and fully locked position. The striker plate must never be adjusted so that the door closes in the safety catch position only.

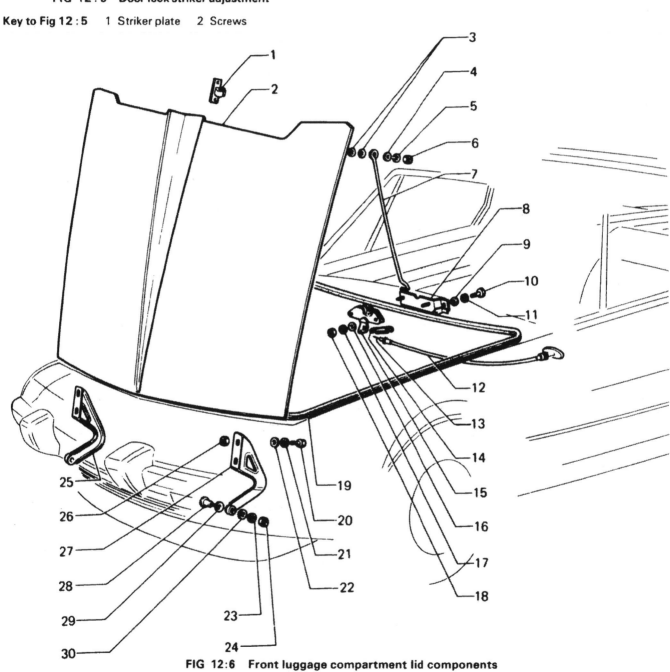

FIG 12:6   Front luggage compartment lid components

Key to Fig 12:6   1 Striker plate   2 Lid   3 Spring washers   4 Washers   5 Lockwasher   6 Nut   7 Rod   8 Lock bracket
9 Washers   10 Bolt   11 Washer   12 Outer sleeve   13 Lock cable   14 Spring   15 Lock   16 Washer   17 Lockwasher
18 Nut   19 Compartment rubber seal   20 Bolt   21 Lockwasher   22 Washer   23 Lockwasher   24 Nut   25 Hinge
26 Nut   27 Hinge   28 Bolt   29, 30 Washers

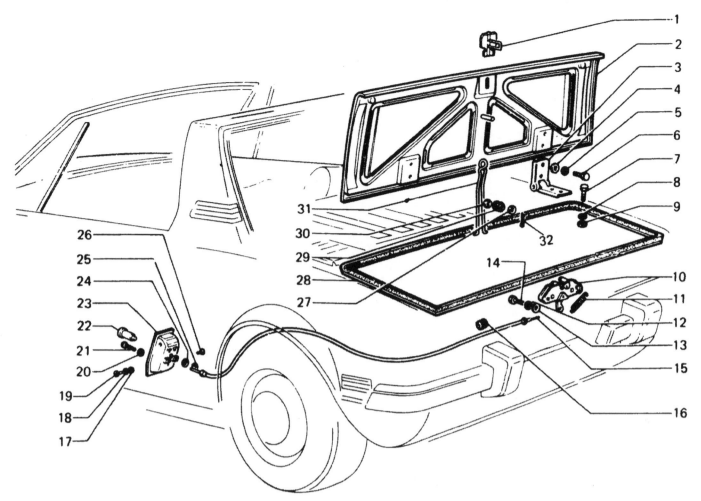

FIG 12:7   Rear luggage compartment lid components

Key to Fig 12:7   1 Striker plate   2 Lid   3 Hinge   4 Washer   5 Lockwasher   6,7 Bolts   8 Lockwasher   9 Washer
10 Lock   11 Spring   12 Lockwasher   13 Washer   14 Bolt   15 Cable   16 Rubber ring   17 Washer   18 Lockwasher
19 Screw   20 Lockwasher   21 Screw   22 Lock cylinder   23 Handle   24 Washer   25 Fork   26 Screw   27 Washer
28 Weatherstrip   29 Bushing   30 Washer   31 Stay

12:3 Engine and luggage compartment lids

Front luggage compartment lid:

Front luggage compartment lid, hinge and lock components are shown in **FIG 12:6**.

Lid (bonnet) removal:

Raise the lid and scribe the hinge positions on the panel to facilitate refitting. Disconnect stay 7 from lid. Slacken the four bolts 20, then have an assistant steady the panel while the bolts, lockwashers and plain washers are removed. Lift off the lid.

Refit the lid in the reverse order of removal, aligning the hinges with the scribe marks previously made before tightening the bolts. Close the lid and check for a correct fit. If misalignment is evident, slacken the retaining bolts again sufficiently to allow the panel to be moved on the hinges, re-align as necessary, then retighten the bolts.

If, when closed, the panel is above the adjacent bodywork at the rear, or if the bonnet closes too tightly, slacken the lock retaining bolts and move the lock assembly slightly to correct. Tighten the bolts firmly on completion.

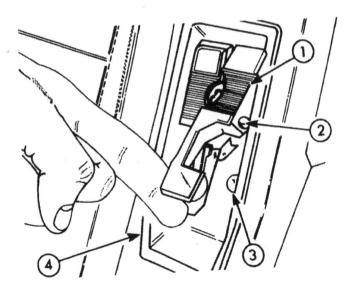

FIG 12:8   Cable operating lever removal

Key to Fig 12:8   1 Lever   2 Screw   3 Screw
4 Lever assembly

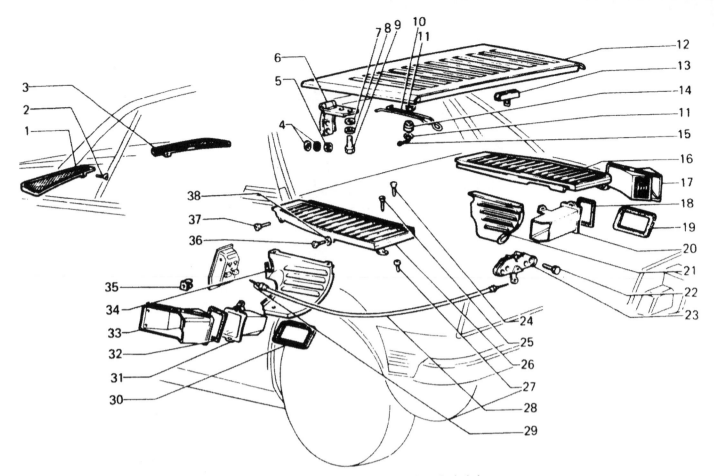

FIG 12:9   Engine compartment lid and air inlets

Key to Fig 12:9   1 Grille   2 Screw   3 Grille   4 Washers   5 Nut   6 Hinge   7 Washer   8 Lock washer   9 Bolt
10 Stay   11 Washer   12 Lid   13 Striker plate   14 Bushing   15 Cotter pin   16 Grille   17 Conveyor   18, 19 Gaskets
20, 21 Ducts   22 Bolt   23 Lock   24, 25 Screws   26 Grille   27 Screw   28 Outer sleeve   29 Lock cable   30 Gasket
31 Duct   32 Gasket   33 Air intake   34 Duct   35 Clip   36, 37 Screws   38 Washer

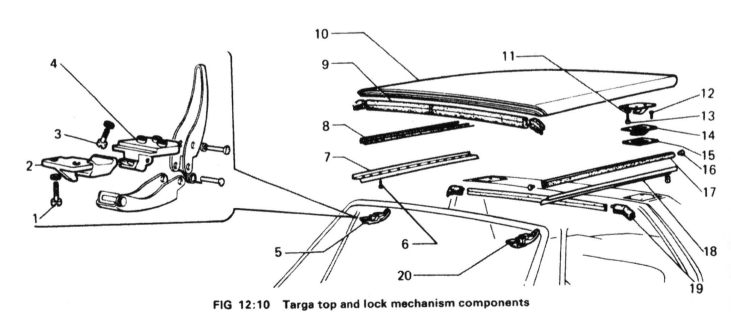

FIG 12:10   Targa top and lock mechanism components

Key to Fig 12:10   1 Screw   2 Striker plate   3 Screw   4 Support   5 Lock   6 Screw   7 Moulding   8, 9 Weatherstrips
10 Targa top   11 Lug   12, 13 Screws   14 Striker plate   15 Covering   16 Plug   17 Weatherstrip   18 Moulding
19 Joint   20 Lock

Lid lock removal:

For access to the lock, the air intake grille in front of the windscreen on the righthand side of the car must first be removed. To do this, remove the four screws and the bolt then lift off the grille. Remove the two bolts and washers securing the lock, then work the lock out through the grille opening. Disconnect the operating cable from the lock. Remove the two nuts and washers securing lock to mounting bracket.

Refit in the reverse order of removal, leaving the lock to bracket mounting bolts loose to enable any necessary adjustments to be carried out. Reconnect the cable and refit the lock, being sure to check that the lock can be correctly operated from the cable release before closing the lid. Adjust lock position as necessary for correct closing of lid, then firmly tighten the mounting bolts.

Rear luggage compartment lid:

Rear luggage compartment lid and lock mechanism components are shown in FIG 12:7.

Lid removal:

Open the lid, then scribe around the hinge plates to mark their positions on the panel to facilitate refitting. Slacken bolts 6 securing hinge plates to panel (see FIG 12:7), then squeeze the legs of stay 31 together to release from the mountings. Have an assistant steady the lid, then remove the mounting bolts, lock washers and plain washers and remove the lid.

Refit in the reverse order of removal, aligning the scribe marks previously made. If the lid is not correctly aligned in the aperture, slacken the hinge securing bolts and move the lid as necessary before retightening the bolts. If, when locked, the lid is too tight or too loose, slacken the lock mounting bolts, move the lock as necessary, then retighten the bolts.

Lid lock removal:

Open the lid, then remove the two bolts with washers securing the lock in place. Disconnect operating cables from lock, then remove through panel aperture.

Refit in the reverse order of removal. Leave the mounting bolts loose to allow for any necessary adjustments. Reconnect the cable and check that the lock operates correctly from the cable release before shutting the lid. Adjust position of lock as necessary, then firmly tighten mounting bolts.

Operating lever removal:

Refer to FIG 12:8. Remove screw 2 securing cable in lever 1. Remove screw 3 holding the lever assembly 4 to door frame, then remove the assembly.

To refit, feed the cable into the lever. Hold the lever in the open position as shown, then pull the cable through until the lock operates to open the lid. Holding both lever and cable in this position, tighten the screw securing cable to lever. Install screw 3 and tighten to secure assembly to door frame. Before closing the lid again, check operation of lock.

Engine compartment lid:

The operations of lid removal, lock removal and cable operating lever removal are carried out in the same manner as that previously described for rear luggage compartment

components. Refer to FIG 12:9 for component identification.

12:4 Targa top

Removal of targa top lock mechanism and related components is a straightforward operation, referring to FIG 12:10 for component identification. If the top is misaligned when fitted and locked, adjust with the top open by slackening screws 1 securing striker plate 2, moving the striker plate as necessary then firmly retightening the screws.

12:5 Bumpers and spoilers

Models produced up to 1978 are fitted with quarter bumpers front and rear with the front spoiler integral with the front lower valance. Later models are provided with USA federal reinforced type bumpers front and rear and the front spoiler is larger and separate from the valance. On 1500 models the front and rear bumpers are USA federal type and the front spoiler is combined with the bumper.

Front bumper removal and refitment (federal type):

Refer to FIG 12:11. Remove the twelve screws marked 1, 2 and 3 and dismount the radiator grille 4. Remove the four screws 7 which secure the centre section of the spoiler 5. Remove four screws from each bumper end cap 6 and remove the end caps. Refer to FIG 12:12. Disconnect the cable 5 from the side/direction indicator lights 6 at each side. Remove the two bolts 4 at each side and dismount the bumper. If necessary, remove five bolts and dismount the upper moulding.

To refit, reverse the removal sequence.

Rear bumper removal and refitment (federal type):

Remove two retaining screws from each bumper end cap and remove the end caps. Refer to FIG 12:13. Disconnect the number plate illumination lights cable 4. Remove the two bolts 6 at each side and dismount the bumper. If necessary, remove three bolts and dismount the upper moulding.

To refit, reverse the removal sequence.

Front quarter bumper removal and refitment:

Remove the radiator grille. Remove the screws (if fitted) which retain the side of the quarter bumper. Remove two bolts which secure the quarter bumper to the support (as in FIG 12:12) and dismount the bumper.

To refit, reverse this sequence.

Rear quarter bumper removal and refitment:

Remove the screws (if fitted) which retain the side of the quarter bumper. Remove two bolts which secure the quarter bumper to the support (as in FIG 12:13) and dismount the quarter bumper.

To refit, reverse this sequence.

12:6 Front wheelbox linings

Each front wheelbox lining is made up of two removable sections. Each section is bolted and rivetted to the body.

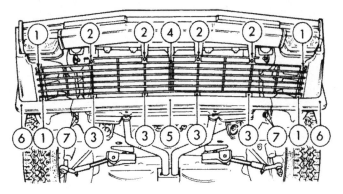

FIG 12:11 Removing the radiator grille

Key to Fig 12:11   1 Grille to bumper cap screws
2 Grille to body screws   3 Grille to spoiler screws
4 Grille   5 Spoiler   6 Bumper cap   7 Spoiler to body
screws

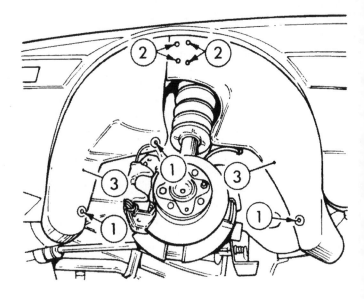

FIG 12:14 Removing the wheelbox linings

Key to Fig 12:14   1 Bolts   2 Rivets   3 Lining

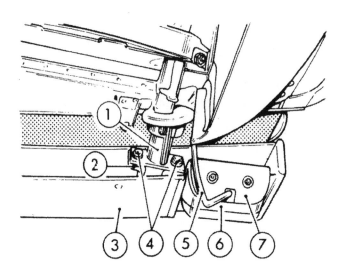

FIG 12:12 Removing the front bumper (federal type)

Key to Fig 12:12   1 Bumper support (anchored to
body)   2 Bumper support (anchored to bumper)   3 Bumper
4 Bolts   5 Cable   6 Side/indicator lights   7 Side/
indicator lights support

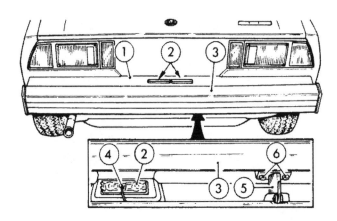

FIG 12:13 Removing the rear bumper (federal type)

Key to Fig 12:13   1 Bumper moulding   2 Number
plate illumination lights   3 Bumper   4 Cable   5 Bumper
support (anchored to body)   6 Bolts

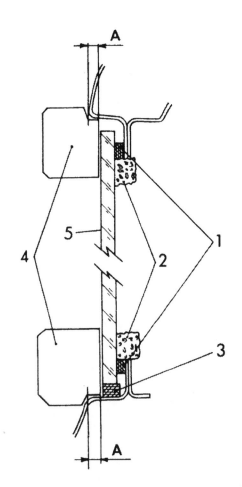

FIG 12:15 Fitting a new windscreen glass

Key to Fig 12:15   1 Spacers   2 Moltoprene   3 Spacer
4 Gauges   5 Glass   **A** Gauged recess of glass

Removal :

Raise the front of the car and remove the relevant road wheel. Refer to **FIG 12 : 14**. Carefully drill out the four rivets 2. Remove the bolts 1 and dismount the linings 3.

Refitment :

Reverse the removal sequence. Leave the bolts 1 loose until the rivet holes have been aligned and the new rivets fitted. The bolts may now be tightened. Refit the road wheel and lower the car.

12 : 7 The windscreen and backlight

Windscreen renewal :

The windscreen renewal procedure requires various primers, sealant, adhesive, etc., plus reference gauges, a sealant gun and a spring type fixture. Although the procedure can be performed by an owner, it is recommended that, in view of the complexity, renewal of a windscreen should be carried out by an authorised agent or a specialist. The procedure is as follows.

1 Remove the wiper blades. Refer to **Chapter 11, Section 11 : 8** and remove the instrument panel. Remove the exterior moulding. Cut the layer of sealant between the glass and the opening flange with steel wire. Remove the broken windscreen. Clean the weatherstrip and the opening flange thoroughly.

2 Refer to **FIG 12 : 15**. Centre the new glass in and against the opening flange and fit spacers 1 (at least four should be used) using adhesive to retain them to the flange. Use gauges 4 to determine their thickness. Check that the glass is centred correctly.

3 Again using adhesive, insert at least four spacers 3 to hold the glass. Ensure that they are the right size to enable a continuous bead of sealant to be applied.

4 For alignment purposes, apply four strips of tape across the glass and the body and cut the tapes at the edge of the glass. Remove the glass and lay it on a protected surface with the inner side upwards.

5 Apply self-adhesive moltoprene of 10mm x 10mm (0.39in x 0.39in) section along the inside perimeter of the glass and about 15mm (0.6in) from the edge so that, at operation 8, sealant will not get into the car.

6 Using a gun, apply sealant along the inside perimeter of the glass. This must form a bead of about 10mm (0.39in) in diameter and **care must be taken to avoid variations in the section of the bead. Ensure that there are no air bubbles between the sealant and the glass.**

7 Using the gun, apply sealant along the inner part of the exterior weatherstrip. Again be careful to avoid variations in the bead section and air bubbles between the sealant and the glass. Position the prepared glass into the body opening and rest it on the spacers 3.

8 Check that the tapes on the glass and the body align. The tapes may now be removed. Apply a thin coating of primer of about 10mm (0.39in) in width to the outer edge of the glass. Fit the exterior weatherstrips and join the ends with butt joints. Press the strips into place. Use a spring type fixture to apply pressure to the weatherstrips.

9 After 24 hours, remove the strip of moltoprene. Remove excess sealant. Remove the spring type fixture. Clean the interior and exterior of the glass. Refit the instrument panel and the wiper blades.

Backlight renewal :

1 Remove the engine compartment lid as described in **Section 12 : 3**. Remove the air scoops on either side by removing eight screws. Remove the fuel tank cap. Remove the six bolts which retain the weatherstrip to the body.

2 If the backlight is the heated type, disconnect the wiring at each side. Pull the rubber seal towards the centre of the glass and off the perimeter of the glass. If the glass was broken, ensure that fragments do not enter either the car or the engine compartment.

3 Place the rubber seal on top of the new glass. Position the glass in the opening and push it up into place. Slide the seal under the glass. Ensure that the glass is centred in the seal and that the seal overlaps the frame.

4 Install the weatherstrip and retain it with six bolts. Refit the air scoops. On relevant models connect up the wiring at each side. Install the engine compartment lid. Clean both sides of the glass.

NOTES

APPENDIX

TECHNICAL DATA

Engine   Fuel system   Ignition system   Cooling system
Clutch and transmission   Suspension   Steering   Braking system
Electrical equipment   Capacities   Dimensions   Oils and fluids
Torque wrench settings

WIRING DIAGRAMS

MAINTENANCE SUMMARY

HINTS ON MAINTENANCE AND OVERHAUL

GLOSSARY OF TERMS

INDEX

Inches	Decimals	Millimetres	Inches to Millimetres — Inches	Inches to Millimetres — mm	Millimetres to Inches — mm	Millimetres to Inches — Inches
1/64	.015625	.3969	.001	.0254	.01	.00039
1/32	.03125	.7937	.002	.0508	.02	.00079
3/64	.046875	1.1906	.003	.0762	.03	.00118
1/16	.0625	1.5875	.004	.1016	.04	.00157
5/64	.078125	1.9844	.005	.1270	.05	.00197
3/32	.09375	2.3812	.006	.1524	.06	.00236
7/64	.109375	2.7781	.007	.1778	.07	.00276
1/8	.125	3.1750	.008	.2032	.08	.00315
9/64	.140625	3.5719	.009	.2286	.09	.00354
5/32	.15625	3.9687	.01	.254	.1	.00394
11/64	.171875	4.3656	.02	.508	.2	.00787
3/16	.1875	4.7625	.03	.762	.3	.01181
13/64	.203125	5.1594	.04	1.016	.4	.01575
7/32	.21875	5.5562	.05	1.270	.5	.01969
15/64	.234375	5.9531	.06	1.524	.6	.02362
1/4	.25	6.3500	.07	1.778	.7	.02756
17/64	.265625	6.7469	.08	2.032	.8	.03150
9/32	.28125	7.1437	.09	2.286	.9	.03543
19/64	.296875	7.5406	.1	2.54	1	.03937
5/16	.3125	7.9375	.2	5.08	2	.07874
21/64	.328125	8.3344	.3	7.62	3	.11811
11/32	.34375	8.7312	.4	10.16	4	.15748
23/64	.359375	9.1281	.5	12.70	5	.19685
3/8	.375	9.5250	.6	15.24	6	.23622
25/64	.390625	9.9219	.7	17.78	7	.27559
13/32	.40625	10.3187	.8	20.32	8	.31496
27/64	.421875	10.7156	.9	22.86	9	.35433
7/16	.4375	11.1125	1	25.4	10	.39370
29/64	.453125	11.5094	2	50.8	11	.43307
15/32	.46875	11.9062	3	76.2	12	.47244
31/64	.484375	12.3031	4	101.6	13	.51181
1/2	.5	12.7000	5	127.0	14	.55118
33/64	.515625	13.0969	6	152.4	15	.59055
17/32	.53125	13.4937	7	177.8	16	.62992
35/64	.546875	13.8906	8	203.2	17	.66929
9/16	.5625	14.2875	9	228.6	18	.70866
37/64	.578125	14.6844	10	254.0	19	.74803
19/32	.59375	15.0812	11	279.4	20	.78740
39/64	.609375	15.4781	12	304.8	21	.82677
5/8	.625	15.8750	13	330.2	22	.86614
41/64	.640625	16.2719	14	355.6	23	.90551
21/32	.65625	16.6687	15	381.0	24	.94488
43/64	.671875	17.0656	16	406.4	25	.98425
11/16	.6875	17.4625	17	431.8	26	1.02362
45/64	.703125	17.8594	18	457.2	27	1.06299
23/32	.71875	18.2562	19	482.6	28	1.10236
47/64	.734375	18.6531	20	508.0	29	1.14173
3/4	.75	19.0500	21	533.4	30	1.18110
49/64	.765625	19.4469	22	558.8	31	1.22047
25/32	.78125	19.8437	23	584.2	32	1.25984
51/64	.796875	20.2406	24	609.6	33	1.29921
13/16	.8125	20.6375	25	635.0	34	1.33858
53/64	.828125	21.0344	26	660.4	35	1.37795
27/32	.84375	21.4312	27	685.8	36	1.41732
55/64	.859375	21.8281	28	711.2	37	1.4567
7/8	.875	22.2250	29	736.6	38	1.4961
57/64	.890625	22.6219	30	762.0	39	1.5354
29/32	.90625	23.0187	31	787.4	40	1.5748
59/64	.921875	23.4156	32	812.8	41	1.6142
15/16	.9375	23.8125	33	838.2	42	1.6535
61/64	.953125	24.2094	34	863.6	43	1.6929
31/32	.96875	24.6062	35	889.0	44	1.7323
63/64	.984375	25.0031	36	914.4	45	1.7717

UNITS	Pints to Litres	Gallons to Litres	Litres to Pints	Litres to Gallons	Miles to Kilometres	Kilometres to Miles	Lbs. per sq. In. to Kg. per sq. Cm.	Kg. per sq. Cm. to Lbs. per sq. In.
1	.57	4.55	1.76	.22	1.61	.62	.07	14.22
2	1.14	9.09	3.52	.44	3.22	1.24	.14	28.50
3	1.70	13.64	5.28	.66	4.83	1.86	.21	42.67
4	2.27	18.18	7.04	.88	6.44	2.49	.28	56.89
5	2.84	22.73	8.80	1.10	8.05	3.11	.35	71.12
6	3.41	27.28	10.56	1.32	9.66	3.73	.42	85.34
7	3.98	31.82	12.32	1.54	11.27	4.35	.49	99.56
8	4.55	36.37	14.08	1.76	12.88	4.97	.56	113.79
9		40.91	15.84	1.98	14.48	5.59	.63	128.00
10		45.46	17.60	2.20	16.09	6.21	.70	142.23
20				4.40	32.19	12.43	1.41	284.47
30				6.60	48.28	18.64	2.11	426.70
40				8.80	64.37	24.85		
50					80.47	31.07		
60					96.56	37.28		
70					112.65	43.50		
80					128.75	49.71		
90					144.84	55.92		
100					160.93	62.14		

UNITS	Lb ft to kgm	Kgm to lb ft	UNITS	Lb ft to kgm	Kgm to lb ft
1	.138	7.233	7	.967	50.631
2	.276	14.466	8	1.106	57.864
3	.414	21.699	9	1.244	65.097
4	.553	28.932	10	1.382	72.330
5	.691	36.165	20	2.765	144.660
6	.829	43.398	30	4.147	216.990

TECHNICAL DATA

Manufacturer's spares are in millimetre sizes. Dimensions in the following tabulations are also in millimetres unless otherwise stated

ENGINE

	1300	1500
Nominal engine capacity	*1300*	*1500*
Bore and stroke	86.0 x 55.5	86.4 x 63.9
Capacity	1290cc	1498cc
Compression ratio:		
European:		
Before January 1977	8.9:1	–
After January 1977	9.2:1	9.2:1
USA models	8.5:1	8.5:1
Cylinder block:		
Cylinder bore:	86.000 to 86.050	86.400 to 86.450
Gradings	0.01 between each grade	
Oversizes	0.20, 0.40 and 0.60	
Main bearing housing bores:	54.507 to 54.520	
Bearing thickness	1.825 to 1.831	
Width between thrust washers	22.140 to 22.200	
Auxiliary shaft bearings:		
Drive end:		
Bush housing bore	38.700 to 38.730	
Bush bore	35.664 to 35.684	
Inner end:		
Bush housing bore	35.036 to 35.066	
Bush bore	32.000 to 32.020	
Crankshaft:		
Main journal diameter, standard:	50.785 to 50.805	50.775 to 50.795
Undersizes	0.254, 0.508, 0.762 and 1.016	
Eccentricity	0.03 maximum	
Misalignment	0.35 maximum	
Ovality	0.005 maximum	
Taper	0.005 maximum	
Running clearance	0.040 to 0.085	0.032 to 0.077
End float	0.055 to 0.265	
Thrust washers, fitted at:	No 5 bearing	
Standard thickness	2.310 to 2.360	
Oversize thickness range	2.437 to 2.487	
Crankpin diameter, standard:	45.498 to 45.518	
Undersizes	0.254, 0.508, 0.762 and 1.016	
Eccentricity, misalignment, ovality and taper	As for main journals	
Auxiliary shaft:		
Journal diameter:		
Drive end	35.593 to 35.618	
Inner end	31.940 to 31.960	
Running clearance:		
Drive end	0.046 to 0.091	
Inner end	0.040 to 0.080	
Camshaft:	Toothed belt driven	
Journal bore diameter:		
Drive end	29.989 to 30.014	
Intermediate 1	47.980 to 48.005	
Centre	48.180 to 48.205	
Intermediate 2	48.380 to 48.405	
Flywheel end	48.580 to 48.605	

Journal diameter :							
Drive end	..	..	..	..	..		29.944 to 29.960
Intermediate 1		..	..	..	..		47.935 to 47.950
Centre		..	..	..	..		48.135 to 48.150
Intermediate 2		..	..	..	..		48.335 to 48.350
Flywheel end	..	..	..	..	..		48.535 to 48.550
Running clearance	..	..	..	..			0.030 to 0.070
Cam lift :							
Inlet	..	..	..	..	..	9.20	9.85
Exhaust	..	..	..	..	..	9.25	9.90
Valve timing :							
Inlet opens °BTDC	..	..	..	..		12	24
Inlet closes °ABDC	..	..	..	..		52	68
Exhaust opens °BBDC		..	..	..	..	52	64
Exhaust closes °ATDC		..	..	..	..	12	28

Connecting rods :

Big-end bearing thickness :		..	..	1.531 to 1.538
Undersizes	..	..	..	0.254, 0.508, 0.762 and 1.016
Running clearance	..	..		0.036 to 0.086
Small-end bore diameter :		..	..	23.939 to 23.972
Bush interference fit	..	..	..	0.044 to 0.102
Bush bore :				
Grade 1	..	..	..	22.004 to 22.007
Grade 2	..	..	..	22.007 to 22.010

Pistons :

					*	**
Grade :						
A diameter	..	..	..	..	85.920 to 85.930	86.360 to 86.370
C diameter	..	..	..	..	85.940 to 85.950	86.380 to 86.390
E diameter	..	..	..	..	85.960 to 85.970	86.400 to 86.410
Clearance in cylinder bore		..	..		0.050 to 0.070	0.030 to 0.050
Undersizes	..	..	..		0.254, 0.508, 0.762 and 1.016	
Piston pin bore :						
Grade 1	..	..	..		21.996 to 21.999	
Grade 2	..	..	..		21.999 to 22.002	
Weight variation per set		..	..		± 2.5 grams maximum	
Ring groove widths :						
Top	..	..	..		1.535 to 1.555	
Centre	..	..	..		2.030 to 2.050	
Bottom	..	..	..		3.967 to 3.987	
Ring thickness :						
Top	..	..	..		1.478 to 1.490	
Centre	..	..	..		1.978 to 1.990	
Bottom	..	..	..		3.925 to 3.937	
Ring clearance in groove :						
Top	..	..	..		0.045 to 0.077	
Centre	..	..	..		0.040 to 0.072	
Bottom	..	..	..		0.030 to 0.062	
Ring gap (fitted) :						
Top and centre	..	..	..		0.30 to 0.45	
Bottom	..	..	..		0.25 to 0.40	
Ring oversizes	..	..	..		0.20, 0.40 and 0.60	

*Measured 27.5 from skirt edge
**Measured 27.5 (Borgo pistons) or 20 (Mondial pistons) from crown

Pistons (gudgeon) pins :

Diameter :					
Grade 1	..	..	..	..	21.991 to 21.994
Grade 2	..	..	..	..	21.994 to 21.997

Oversize	0.20
Clearance in piston	0.002 to 0.008
Clearance in small-end	0.010 to 0.016

Cylinder head :

Valve guide housing bore	13.950 to 13.977
Guide outside diameter	14.040 to 14.058
Interference fit in head	0.063 to 0.108
Guide inside diameter	8.022 to 8.040
Valve seat diameter :	
Inlet	30.90 to 31.10
Exhaust	28.50 to 28.70
Valve seat angle	45° ± 5′

Valves :

Stem diameter	7.974 to 7.992
Stem to guide clearance	0.030 to 0.066
Head diameter :	
Inlet	35.850 to 36.150
Exhaust	32.850 to 33.450
Face angle	45° 30′ ± 5′
Face contact width	2.0 approximately

Valve springs :

	Inner	Outer
Height under load :		
14 to 15daN (31 to 33lbf)	31	–
37 to 40daN (82 to 88lbf)	–	36
Minimum load for height	13.2daN (29lbf)	35.2daN (78lbf)

Tappets :

Bore diameter	37.000 to 37.025
Outside diameter	36.975 to 36.995
Bore to tappet clearance	0.005 to 0.050
Shim thickness	3.25 to 4.70 in 0.05 steps

Valve clearances :

	1300	1500
Inlet (cold)	0.40	0.45
Exhaust (cold)	0.50	0.60

Oil pump :

Pressure at 100°C (212°F)	3.4 to 4.9 bars at 4000r/min
Clearance :	
Gears to cover	0.020 to 0.105 (wear limit 0.15)
Gears to housing	0.110 to 0.180 (wear limit 0.25)
Backlash between gears	0.15 (wear limit 0.25)

FUEL SYSTEM

Air cleaner	Renewable paper element
Fuel pump :	Diaphragm type (mechanical)
Delivery pressure	0.18 bar at 4000r/min
Output per hour	75 litres at 4000r/min
Idling speed :	Engine at normal operating temperature
1300 models	875 ± 25r/min*
1500 models	875 ± 25r/min*
Idling mixture (CO%) :	Engine at normal operating temperature
1300 models	4.0 ± 0.5*
1500 models	1.75 ± 0.25*

Depends on pollution regulations – refer to Regulation Conformity Tag on underside of engine compartment lid of USA models

Model :	1300	1500
Carburetter manufacturer	Weber	Weber
Carburetter types :	Weber	–
European models :		
Before January 1977	32 DMTR 22	–
After January 1977	32 DMTR 34/250	–
USA models :		
1974	32 DMTRA 200	–
1975-76	32 DATRA 1/100	–
1977 onwards :		
Standard version without air conditioning	32 DATRA 201	–
Standard version with air conditioning ..	32 DATRA 101	–
Catalytic version without air conditioning	32 DATRA 10/200	–
Catalytic version with air conditioning ..	32 DATRA 10/100	–
From model introduction	–	34 DATR 7/250

32 DMTR 22 :	Primary	Secondary
Main venturi	22	22
Main jet	1.10	1.15
Idle jet	0.50	0.70
Main air corrector	2.10	1.90
Idle air corrector	1.10	0.70
Accelerator pump jet	0.40	–
Emulsion tube type		F30
Extra fuel device :		
Air jet	–	1.10
Fuel jet	–	1.00
Partial primary throttle opening (choke on) ..	0.80 to 0.85	–
Needle valve seat		1.50
Float level		6

32 DMTR 34/250 :	Primary	Secondary
As 32 DMTR 22 except :		
Idle jet	0.50	0.50
Air corrector	2.20	1.90
Accelerator pump jet	–	2.0
Accelerator excess orifice	0.40	–
Anti-syphon bleed	1.00	–
Float level		7 ± 0.25

32 DMTRA 200 :	Primary	Secondary
Main venturi	22	22
Main jet	1.10	1.10
Idle jet	0.45	0.60
Main air corrector	2.00	1.95
Idle air corrector	1.10	0.70
Accelerator pump jet	0.50	–
Emulsion tube type		F30
Extra fuel device :		
Air jet	–	0.70
Fuel jet	–	0.85
Partial primary throttle opening (choke on) ..	0.90 to 10.0	–
Needle valve seat		1.50
Float level		6

32 DATRA 1/100 :

	Primary	Secondary
Main venturi	22	22
Main jet	1.10	1.05
Emulsion tube type		F30
Choke calibration		25°C (77°F)
Needle valve seat		1.50
Float level		7 ± 1.0

USA models from 1977 :

32 DATRA 201, 101, 10/200, 10/100 .. As 32 DATRA 1/100

34 DATR 7/250 :

	Primary	Secondary
Main venturi	23	26
Auxiliary venturi	4	4
Main jet	1.07	1.30
Air correction jet	1.60	1.50
Emulsion tube type	F30	F30
Idle jet	0.47	0.70
Idle air bleed	1.10	0.70
Accelerator pump jet	0.40	–
Accelerator excess orifice	0.40	–
Power jet	–	0.80
Power mixture outlet	–	2.0
First progression diameter	0.80	1.00
Second progression diameter	1.10	1.00
Third progression diameter	1.00	–
Anti-syphon bleed	1.00	–
Idling adjustment diameter	1.40	–
Mixture bush	1.10	–
Needle valve seat		1.75
Float level		7 ± 0.25
Throttle valve minimum opening		1.00
Pneumatic weakening valve :		
Minimum		4.5 ± 0.25
Maximum		6.5 ± 0.25

IGNITION SYSTEM

Firing order .. ..   1–3–4–2 (No 1 is the righthand cylinder)

Ignition timing (static) :

Euopean models :
- Before February 1977 .. .. ..   10° BTDC
- After February 1977 .. ..   5° BTDC including 1500 models

USA 1974 models .. ..   0° (TDC)

All other models .. ..   10° BTDC

Distributor :

European 1300 models :
- Before February 1977 .. .. .. · Ducellier S135B
- After February 1977 .. .. Marelli S135F or Ducellier 4526A

USA models :
- 1974–76 .. .. Ducellier 4481A
- 1977 onwards .. .. Ducellier 525047A

1500 models :
- From introduction .. .. .. Marelli S135LX or Ducellier 5251A

Contact breaker points gap :

- Ducellier 4526A .. .. 0.35 to 0.50 (0.014 to 0.019in)
- All other Ducellier .. .. 0.37 to 0.43 (0.015 to 0.017in)
- All Marelli .. .. 0.37 to 0.43 (0.015 to 0.017in)

Dwell angle .. .. 55° ± 3°

Capacitor (mf) :
Ducellier .. .. 0.22 to 0.23
Marelli .. .. 0.20 to 0.22
Ignition coil :
All European models .. .. Marelli BE200B or Martinetti G52S
USA models :
1974 .. .. Marelli BE200B or Martinetti G52S
1975-76 .. .. Marelli BE200A or Martinetti G37SU
1977 onwards .. .. Martinetti G37SU
Sparking plugs :
1300 European models .. .. .. Marelli CW78LP, Champion N7Y or
Bosch W200T30

USA models :
Without resistor .. .. AC Delco 42XLS, Marelli CW7LP or
Champion N9Y

With resistor .. .. AC Delco R42XLS, Marelli CW7LPR
or Champion RN9Y
1500 models .. .. Champion RN7Y, Marelli CW78LPR
or Bosch WR6D

Sparking plug gap :
All models before February 1977 .. .. 0.5 to 0.6 (0.020 to 0.024in)
1300 models after February 1977 .. .. 0.6 to 0.7 (0.024 to 0.027in)
1500 models .. .. 0.7 to 0.8 (0.027 to 0.031in)

COOLING SYSTEM

Thermostat :	Opens at	Fully open at
1300 models :		
1974	80° to 84°C	96°C
Before January 1977	73° to 77°C	85°C
After January 1977	82° to 84°C	96°C
1500 models	73° to 77°C	85°C
Valve travel to fully open	7.5 minimum	

Cooling fan :	Cuts in at	Cuts out at
1300 models :		
Before January 1977	92° ± 2°C	87° ± 2°C
After January 1977	87° ± 2°C	82° ± 2°C
1500 models	92° ± 2°C	87° ± 2°C

System pressure .. .. 0.78 bar

CLUTCH AND TRANSMISSION

Clutch type : .. .. Dry, single plate
Spring .. .. Diaphragm
Release mechanism .. .. Hydraulic actuation
Diameter :
1300 models 181.5
1500 models 190.0

Clutch pedal :	Travel	Free play
1300 models :		
Before January 1977	170	30
After January 1977	160	30
1500 models	120	Nil

Gearbox ratios :	1300 (4-speed)	1500 (5-speed)
First	3.583:1	3.583:1
Second	2.235:1	2.235:1
Third	1.454:1	1.454:1
Fourth	0.959:1	1.042:1
Fifth	–	0.863:1
Reverse	3.714:1	3.714:1
Final drive ratio	4.077:1	4.077:1

SUSPENSION

		Laden*		Unladen	
		1300	1500	1300	1500
Front and rear	Independent, MacPherson type struts				
Dampers	Double-acting telescopic, hydraulic				
Caster, front		7° ± 30'	7° ± 30'	7° ± 30'	6° 50' ± 30'
Camber:					
Front		−1° ± 20'	−1° ± 30'	−30' ± 30'	−30' ± 30'
Rear		−2° ± 20'	−1° 15' ± 30'	−1° 40' ± 30'	−1° 15' ± 30'
Wheel alignment:					
Front toe-in		3 ± 1	3 ± 2	4 ± 2	4 ± 2
Rear toe-in		5 ± 1	6 ± 2	6 ± 2	7 ± 2

		Front	Rear
Springs:		Coil	Coil
Load for:			
170 length		196daN minimum	–
200 length		–	230.5daN minimum
Tyre pressures:			
Bars (lbf/in²)		1.8 (26)	2.0 (28)

*Two persons, plus luggage, total of 190daN (420lbf)

STEERING

Type		Rack and pinion
Turns lock to lock		Approximately 3
Turning circle		Approximately 10m
Rack travel		117

Steering angles:	1300	1500
Inner wheel	32° 40'	33° 30'
Outer wheel	28°	30°

BRAKING SYSTEM

Type	Dual line hydraulic
Discs:	Front and rear
Diameter	227
Thickness (new):	
1300 models	9.95 to 10.15
1500 models	10.70 to 10.90
Machining limit	9.35 minimum (all models)
Wear limit	9.0 minimum (all models)
Runout	0.15 maximum at disc periphery
Calipers	Floating single cylinder
Adjustment	Automatic
Pad lining thickness	2.0 minimum front and rear
Handbrake	Mechanical on rear wheels

ELECTRICAL EQUIPMENT

Battery	12-volt 45Ah
Polarity	Negative earth
Starter motor:	
1300 models	Fiat E84-0.8/12 Var.1
1500 models	Marelli E 95-0.9/12

Alternator :
  1300 models :
    European :

Before January 1977	Bosch G1-14V33A27 (40amps)	
After January 1977	FIMM A124-14V-44A Var.3 (53amps)	
USA 1974-76 :	FIMM A124-14V-44A Var.3 (53amps)	
1977 onward	FIMM A124-14V-60A Var.1 (70amps)	
1500 models	Marelli AA125-14V-45A or Bosch K1-14V-45A20	

Regulator :

1300 models	Bosch AD1/14V or FIMM RC 2/12D
1500 models	Integral with alternator
Fuses :	Refer to circuit/wiring diagrams
1300 models	12 in fuse box and one in-line
1500 models	16 in fuse box and two in-line
Relays	Refer to circuit/wiring diagrams

CAPACITIES

	Imperial	USA	Litres
Fuel tank, including reserve :			
1300 models	10.6gals	12.7gals	48
1500 models	10.8gals	13.0gals	49
Engine, including filter :	Pints	Pints	Litres
Total from dry	8.8	10.6	5.0
Oil change	7.5	9.0	4.25
Transmission :			
1300 4-speed	5.5	6.6	3.15
1500 5-speed	5.3	6.4	3.0
Cooling system, including heater :			
1300 models	19.4	23.3	11.0
1500 models	20.4	24.5	11.6
Hydraulic fluid :			
Brakes reservoir :			
Front section	0.28	0.34	0.16
Rear section	0.28	0.34	0.16
Clutch reservoir	0.32	0.38	0.18

DIMENSIONS

	Upto 1978	From 1978
Overall length	3830(150.8in)	3969(156.3in)
Overall width	1570(61.8in)	1570(61.8in)
Overall height	1170(46.1in)	1180(46.5in)
Track :		
Front	1335(52.6in)	1355(53.3in)
Rear	1343(52.9in)	1350(53.0in)
Wheelbase	2202(86.7in)	2202(86.7in)

OILS AND FLUIDS

	Single grade*	Multi-grade*
Engine oil :		
Below –15°C	SAE. 10W	–
–15°C to 0°C	SAE. 20W)	
Up to 35°C	SAE. 30)	15W/40
Above 35°C	SAE. 40)	
Transmission oil	Oliofiat ZC90 or equivalent*	

Cooling system antifreeze	Water and Fiat Paraflu or equivalent*
Steering rack and pinion	Oliofiat W90/M or equivalent*
Constant velocity joints	Grassofiat MRM2 or equivalent*
Hydraulic fluid :	
Brakes and clutch	Fiat DOT3 or equivalent*

Of reputable brand

TORQUE WRENCH SETTINGS

Figures are given in daNm (lbf ft)

Engine :

Main bearing cap bolt	8.0 (59)
Cylinder head to block bolts	9.3 (69)
Cylinder head stud nut (M12)	9.3 (69)
Camshaft cover bolts	2.0 (15)
Manifold nuts	2.7 (20)
Big-end cap nuts	5.1 (38)
Flywheel to crankshaft bolts	8.3 (61)
Pulley to camshaft bolt	8.3 (61)
Tensioner nut	4.4 (32)
Pulley to auxiliary shaft bolt	13.7 (100)
Mounting to crankcase	5.9 (44)
Mounting pad nut, engine side	3.4 (25)
Sidemember to body	2.0 (15)
Lower support to transmission	2.5 (18)
Upper support to transmission	2.5 (18)
Pad to crossmember bolt	1.5 (11)

Transmission :

Clutch cover to flywheel bolts	1.6 (12)
Fork retaining bolt	2.6 (19)
Slave cylinder retaining bolts and nut	2.6 (19)
Bellhousing to engine nuts	7.8 (58)
Bellhousing to gearbox	2.5 (18)
Exhaust to bellhousing bolt	2.5 (18)
Ring nut main and countershaft (5-speed) . .	11.8 (87)
Reversing shaft plate bolt	1.0 (7)
Gearbox cover bolts	1.0 (7)
Ring gear retaining bolts (5-speed)	6.8 (50)
Ring gear retaining bolts (4-speed)	6.8 (50)
Boot cover to casing nuts (4-speed)	1.0 (7)
Boot cover to casing bolts (5-speed)	1.0 (7)
Constant velocity joint bolts (5-speed) . .	3.4 (25)

Suspension :

Hub nut (M18), front and rear	13.5 (100)
Hub nut (M20), front and rear	21.6 (160)
Hub carrier ball joint nut (front)	5.4 (40)
Control arm to body	4.0 (30)
Damper to hub carrier, front and rear	5.9 (44)
Damper to body mounting, front and rear . .	5.9 (44)
Damper mounting to body, front and rear . .	1.2 (9)
Hub carrier ball joint nut (rear)	8.3 (61)
Wheel bearing ring nut (rear)	5.9 (44)
Reaction strut to control arm and support (front)	6.9 (51)
Reaction strut ball joint nut (rear)	5.9 (44)

Steering:

Steering wheel nut	4.9 (36)
Joint yoke nut	2.7 (20)
Steering unit mounting nuts	2.5 (18)
Steering arm ball joint nut	4.9 (36)
Column mounting nuts	1.5 (11)

Braking:

Caliper to hub carrier (front) bolts	4.7 (35)
Caliper to hub support (rear) bolts	4.7 (35)
Brake hose union	1.8 (13)
Hose to caliper	2.7 (20)
Handbrake support bolt	1.5 (11)
Master cylinder to pedal support nuts	2.5 (18)

Electrical equipment:

Alternator upper and lower support nuts	4.9 (34)
Alternator to cylinder block support bolt	4.9 (34)

Sparking plugs	3.7 (27)
Road wheel bolts	8.6 (63)

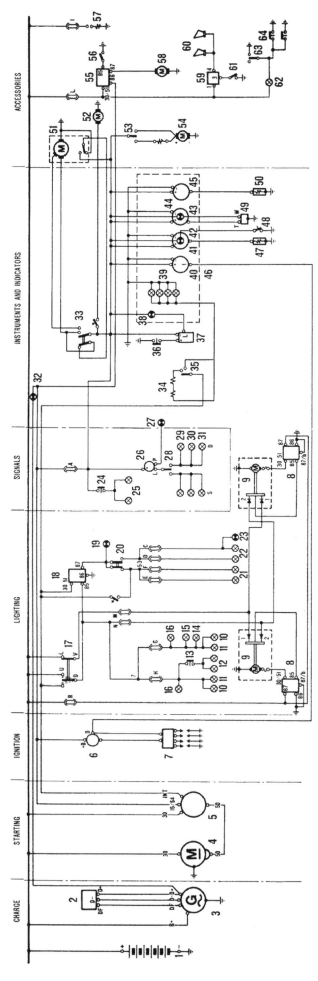

FIG 13:1 Circuit diagram, European 1300 models

Key to Fig 13:1   1 Battery   2 Voltage regulator   3 Alternator   4 Starting motor   5 Ignition switch   6 Ignition switch   7 Distributor and sparking plugs   8 Retractable headlamps control relays   9 Retractable headlamps actuators   10 Rear tail lights   11 Front side lights   12 Reversing lights   13 Reversing lights press switch   14 Optical fibre light source   15 Cigar lighter spot light   16 Number plate lights   17 Rocker switch, lighting and headlamps   18 Relay, dipswitch/headlamp flasher   19 Side and tail lights switch   20 Dipswitch and headlamp flasher   21 Headlamp dipped beam   22 Headlamp main beam   23 Main beam telltale   24 Stop lights switch   25 Rear stop lights   26 Direction indicators flasher unit   27 Direction indicators telltale   28 Direction indicators switch   29 Front direction indicators   30 Side direction indicators   31 Rear direction indicators   32 No charge warning light   33 Screen washer and wiper switch   34 Resistor, panel lighting switch   35 Three-position rocker switch, panel lighting   36 Handbrake warning light switch   37 Handbrake warning light flasher unit   38 Handbrake warning light   39 Instrument panel lamps   40 Three-position rocker switch, panel lighting   41 Oil pressure gauge   42 Oil pressure warning light   43 Fuel gauge   44 Fuel reserve warning light   45 Water temperature gauge   46 Instrument panel   47 Oil pressure sender unit   48 Oil pressure warning light switch   49 Blower   gauge tank unit   50 Water temperature gauge sender unit   51 Screen wiper unit   52 Screen washer pump   53 Three-position rocker switch, blower   54 Blower   two-speed motor   55 Radiator fan motor relay   56 Radiator fan motor thermostatic switch   57 Cigar lighter   58 Radiator fan motor   60 Horns   61 Horn button   62 Courtesy light   63 Courtesy light switch   64 Courtesy light door switches   59 Horns relay

131

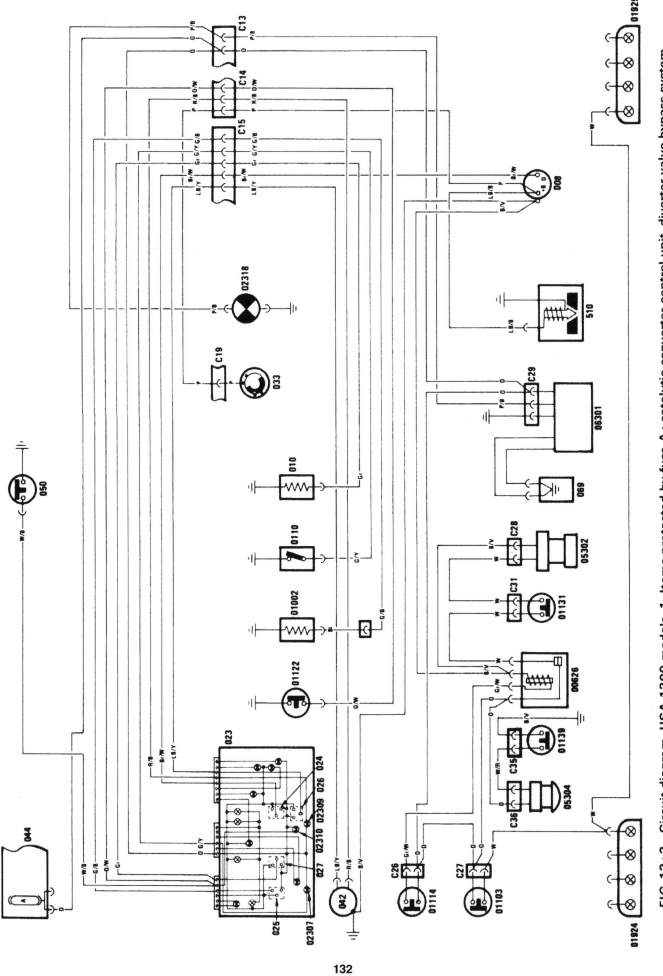

FIG 13:2 Circuit diagram, USA 1300 models, 1. Items protected by fuse A : catalytic converter control unit, diverter valve bypass system, instruments and warning lights, distributor vacuum bypass system

132

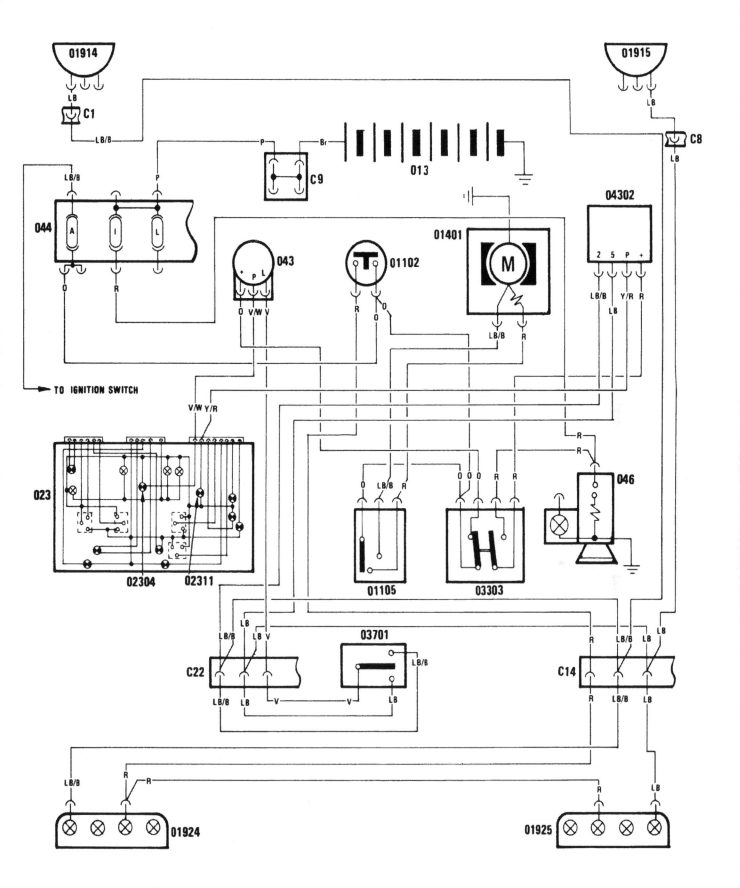

FIG 13 : 3 Circuit diagram, USA 1300 models, 2. Items protected by fuses A and I : stoplights, direction indicators, heater fan, cigarette lighter, hazard signals

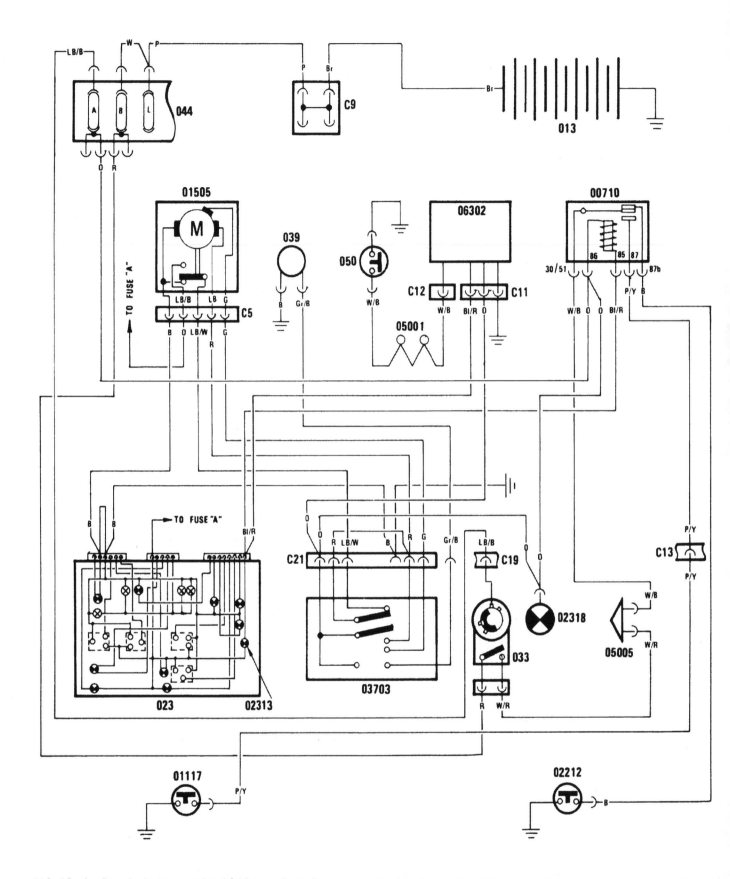

FIG 13:4 Circuit diagram, USA 1300 models, 3. Items protected by fuses A and B : seat belt interlock system, windshield washer and wipers, catalytic converter indicator, remove key system

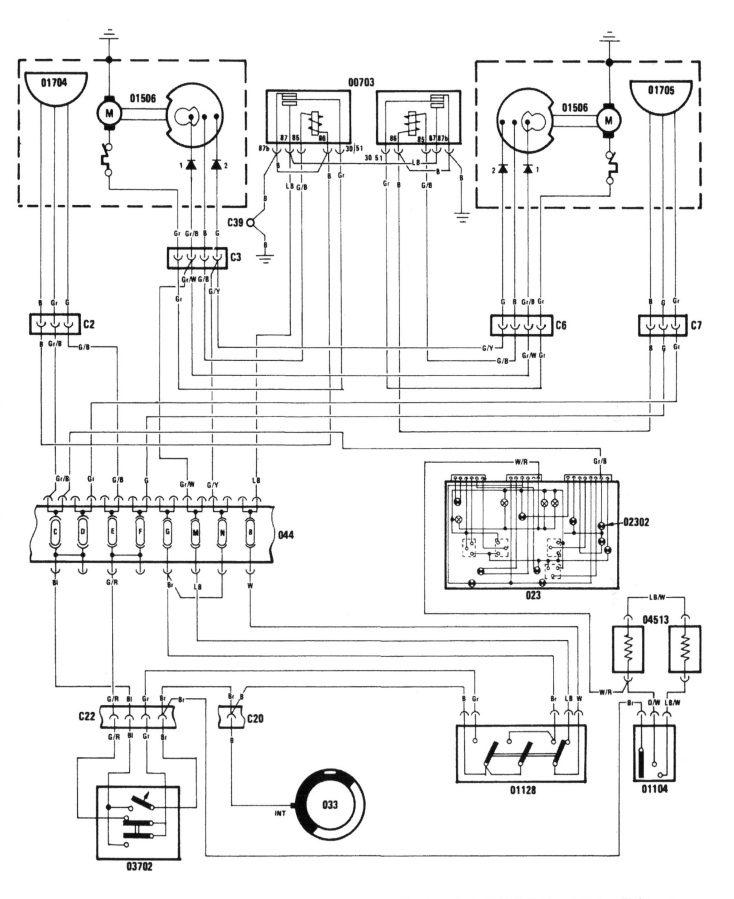

FIG 13 : 5   Circuit diagram, USA 1300 models, 4. Items protected by fuses B, C, D, E, F, G, M and N : headlight system

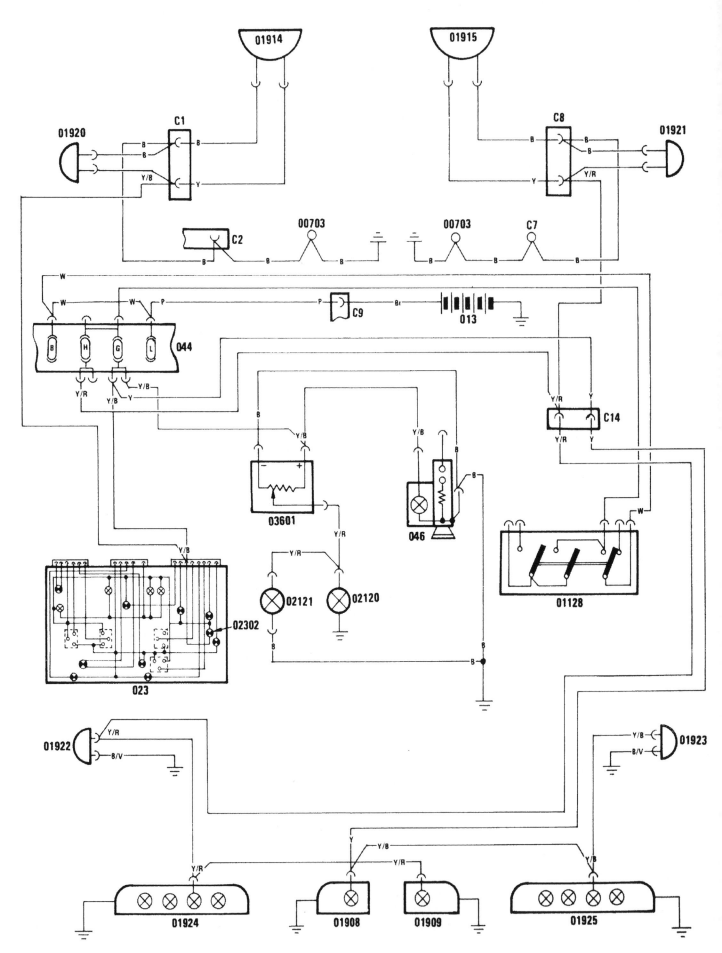

FIG 13 : 6   Circuit diagram, USA 1300 models, 5. Items protected by fuses G and H : external lighting

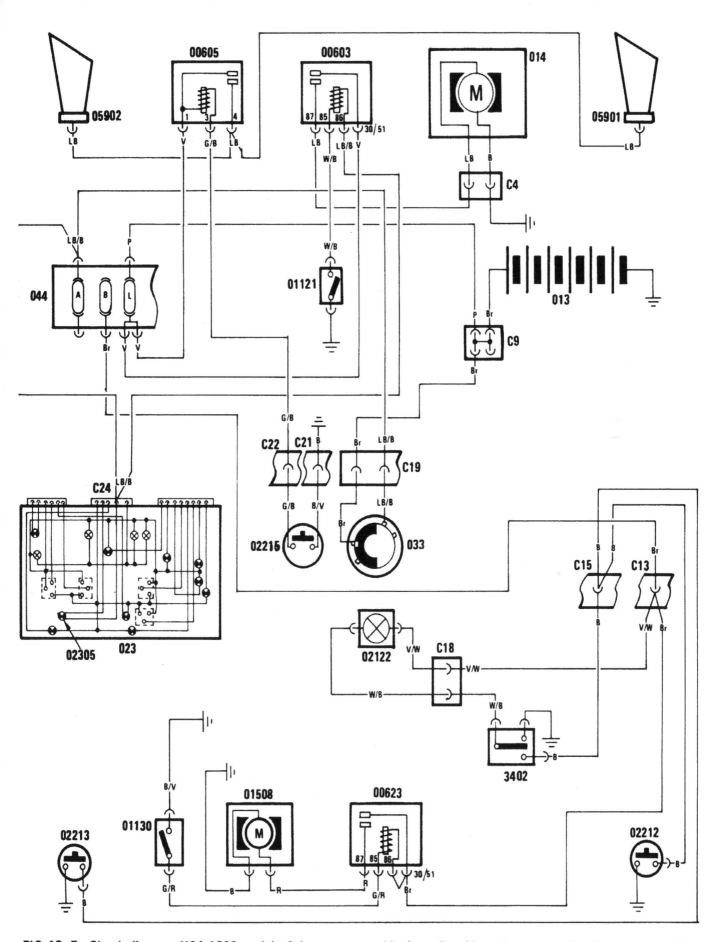

FIG 13 : 7 Circuit diagram, USA 1300 models, 6. Items protected by fuses B and L : carburetter cooling fan, radiator cooling fan, horns, courtesy light

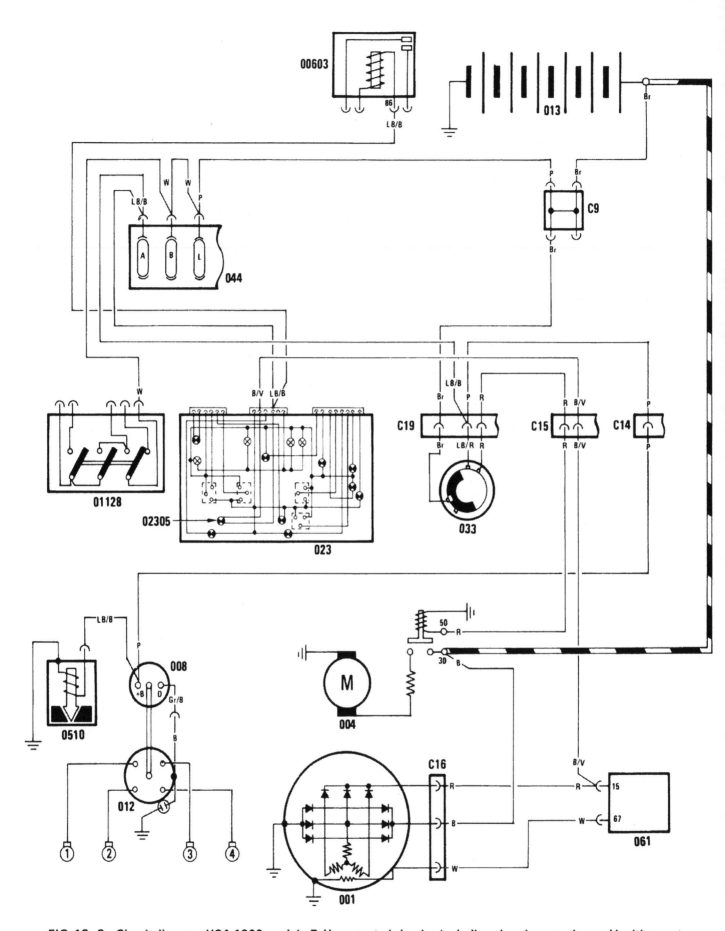

FIG 13 : 8   Circuit diagram, USA 1300 models, 7. Unprotected circuits, including charging, starting and ignition systems

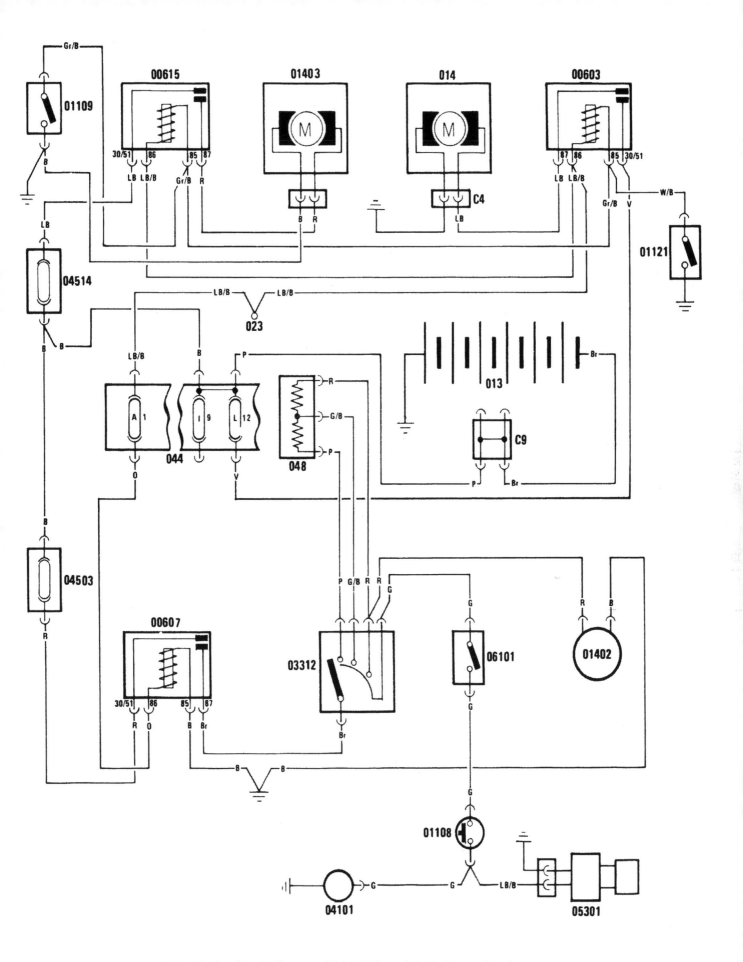

FIG 13 : 9   Circuit diagram, USA 1300 models, 8. Air conditioning system

Key to circuit diagrams, USA 1300 models :

Components   001 Alternator   004 Starter motor   00603 Radiator fan motor relay   00605 Horn relay   00607 Air conditioner control relay   00616 Condenser fan relay   00623 Carburetter fan motor relay   00626 Diverter valve by-pass system relay   00703 Concealed left headlights relay   00704 Concealed right headlights relay   00710 Seat belt relay   008 Ignition coil   010 Engine water temperature sending unit   01002 Oil pressure gauge sending unit   0110 Low oil pressure indicator sending unit   01102 Stop light switch   01103 Back-up light switch   01104 Instrument cluster lighting three-position switch   01105 Heater fan three-position switch   01108 Low pressure switch   01109 Condenser fan switch   01114 Diverter valve by-pass system gear engaged switch   01117 Switch on driver's belt   01121 Radiator thermostatic switch   01122 Handbrake on switch   01128 Outer lighting three-position switch   01130 Carburetter fan motor thermstatic switch   01131 Diverter valve by-pass system thermostatic switch   01139 Switch on transmission for 4th gear   012 Ignition distributor   013 Battery   014 Radiator fan motor   01401 Heater fan two-speed motor   01402 Air conditioner blower motor   01403 Condenser fan motor   01505 Windshield wiper motor   01506 Concealed headlight motors   01508 Carburetter fan motor   01704 Left high/low beam concealed headlight   01705 Right high/low beam concealed headlight   01908 Left number plate light   01909 Right number plate light   01914 Left front turn signal and parking light   01915 Right front turn signal and parking light   01920 Left side marker light   01921 Right side marker light   01922 Left rear side marker light   01923 Right rear side marker light   01924 Left tail, turn signal, back-up, and stop lights unit   01925 Right tail, turn signal, back-up, and stop lights unit   02120 Ideogram lamp   02121 Control panel light   02122 Courtesy light   02212 Courtesy light right door switch   02213 Courtesy light left door switch   02215 Horn button   023 Instrument cluster   02301 Tail light indicator   02302 High beam indicator   02304 Turn signal indicator   02305 Battery charge indicator   02307 Low oil pressure indicator   02309 Fuel reserve indicator   02310 Brake warning indicator   02311 Vehicular hazard warning indicator   02312 Rear window defroster indicator   02313 Fasten belts indicator   02318 Catalytic converter temperature warning indicator   024 Tachometer   025 Oil pressure gauge   026 Fuel gauge   027 Engine water temperature gauge   033 Steering lock ignition switch   03303 Hazard warning signal switch   03312 Air conditioner control switch   03402 Courtesy light switch   03601 Ideogram illumination dimmer   03701 Turn signal indicator switch   03702 High/low beams changeover switch   03703 Wiper/washer three-position switch   039 Windshield washer pump   04101 Compressor clutch   042 Fuel gauge sending unit   043 Turn signal flasher   04302 Hazard signal flasher   044 Fuse box   04401 3A. fuse   04402 16A. fuse   04503 Air conditioner control fuse   04513 Instrument cluster lights resistors   04514 Condenser fan fuse   046 Lighter   048 Blower resistor   050 Brake warning indicator switch   05001 Brake fluid level switch   05005 Fasten belts and remove key buzzer   0510 Idle fuel flow shut-off solenoid   05301 Fast-idle electrovalve   05302 Diverter valve by-pass system electrovalve   05304 Ignition delay cut-off electrovalve   05901 Right horn   05902 Left horn   061 Voltage regulator   06101 Air conditioner temperature switch   06301 Catalytic converter temperature control unit   06302 Seat belt indicator delay switch   069 Thermocouple for catalytic converter

Connector locations   C1, C2, C3 Left headlight motor compartment   C4 Behind radiator fan motor   C5 Under grille in front of windshield, left   C6, C7, C8 Right headlight motor compartment   C9 Inside car in front of heater   C11, C12 Right side of right foot well   C13, C14, C15 Inside car in front of heater   C16 Engine compartment, right rear   C18 Spare wheel compartment, left   C19, C20, C21, C22 Under steering column cover   C23, C24, C25 Behind instrument panel   C26, C27 Engine compartment, front centre bottom   C28 Engine compartment, left, below expansion tank   C29 Spare wheel compartment, left   C31 Engine compartment, top centre rear   C35, C36 Engine compartment, left

Wiring colour code   **B** Black   **Bl** Blue   **Br** Brown   **G** Grey   **Gr** Green   **LB** Light blue   **O** Orange   **P** Pink   **R** Red   **V** Violet   **W** White   **Y** Yellow
Where a wire has two colour codes the first indicates the main colour, the second the tracer stripe

FIG 13 : 10   Circuit diagram, 1500 models

Key to Fig 13 : 10   1 Front direction indicators (21W, spherical)   2 Side lights (5W, spherical)   3 Pop-up headlamps (45/40W, spherical, double filament)   4 Supplementary headlamp, main beam (optional)   5 Screen washer pump   6 Horns   7 Radiator fan motor   8 Radiator fan thermostatic switch   9 Pop-up headlamp motors   10 Repeater lights (4W, tubular)   11 Low brake fluid level signal switch   12 Wiper motor   13 Windscreen wiper interrupter   14 In-line fuse (8amps), courtesy light   15 Fuse unit   16 Left pop-up headlamp motor diverter relay   17 Right pop-up headlamp motor diverter relay   18 Pop-up headlamp shut-down and side light diverter relay   19 Headlamp change-over relay   20 Radiator fan relay   21 Horn relay   22 Heated backlight relay   23 Battery   24 Stop light switch   25 Handbrake warning flasher   26 Direction indicator/hazard warning flasher   27 Handbrake 'ON'/low brake fluid level w/l (1.2W, w/b)   28 Panel connectors   29 Spare w/l socket   30 Panel lights (3W, w/b)   31 Direction indicator w/l (1.2W, w/b)   32 Spare w/l socket   33 Hazard w/l (1.2W, w/b)   34 Side light w/l (1.2W, w/b)   35 Main beam w/l (1.2W, w/b)   36 Electronic tachometer   37 Fuel w/l (1.2W, w/b)   38 Fuel gauge   39 Water temperature gauge   40 Ignition w/l (3W, w/b)   41 Heated backlight w/l (1.2W, w/b)   42 Oil pressure w/l (1.2W, w/b)   43 Oil pressure gauge   44 Preset connection for radio set   45 Lighting/headlamp raise switch   46 Ignition switch   47 Wiper/washer switch   48 Headlamp switch   49 Direction indicator switch   50 Horn switch   51 Heater fan motor   52 Heater fan switch   53 Cigar lighter/lamp (4W, tubular)   54 Preset connection for clock   55 Door switches   56 Heater controls light bulb (1.2W, w/b)   57 Ideogram illumination optical fibre light source (3W, tubular bulb)   58 Panel light ballast resistors   59 Hazard warning switch   60 Heated backlight switch   61 Panel light switch   62 Preset connection for loudspeakers   63 Fuel transmitter   64 Reversing light switch   65 Handbrake 'ON' signal switch   66 Courtesy light (5W, tubular) and switch   67 Carburetter cooling fan motor relay   68 Heated backlight (optional)   69 Ignition coil   70 Starter   71 Oil pressure w/l transmitter   72 Water temperature transmitter   73 Oil pressure gauge transmitter   74 Distributor   75 Spark plugs   76 Carburetter cooling fan motor   77 Thermostatic switch for carburetter cooling fan motor   78 Alternator   79 Rear direction indicators (21W, spherical)   80 Rear lights (5W, spherical)   81 Stop lights (21W, spherical)   82 Reversing lights (21W, spherical)   83 Number plate lights (5W, spherical)

Lamp wattages and types in brackets

w/l   Warning light
w/b   Wedge-base

Wiring colour code   **A** Light blue   **B** White   **C** Amber   **G** Yellow   **H** Grey   **L** Blue   **M** Brown   **N** Black   **R** Red   **S** Pink   **V** Green   **Z** Mauve

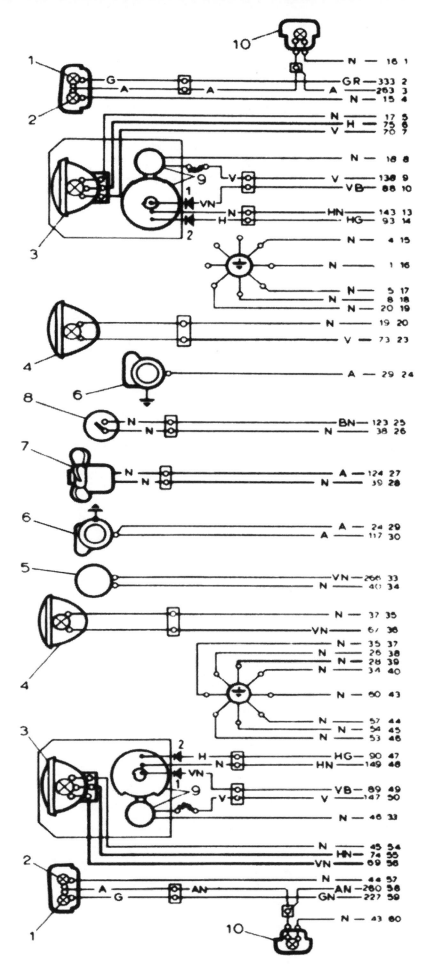

FIG 13:10   Circuit diagram, 1500 models

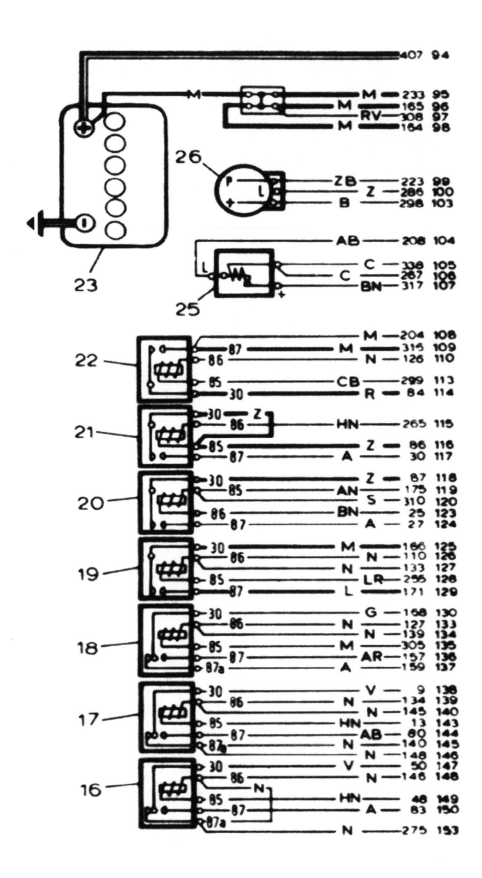

FIG 13 : 10   Circuit diagram, 1500 models

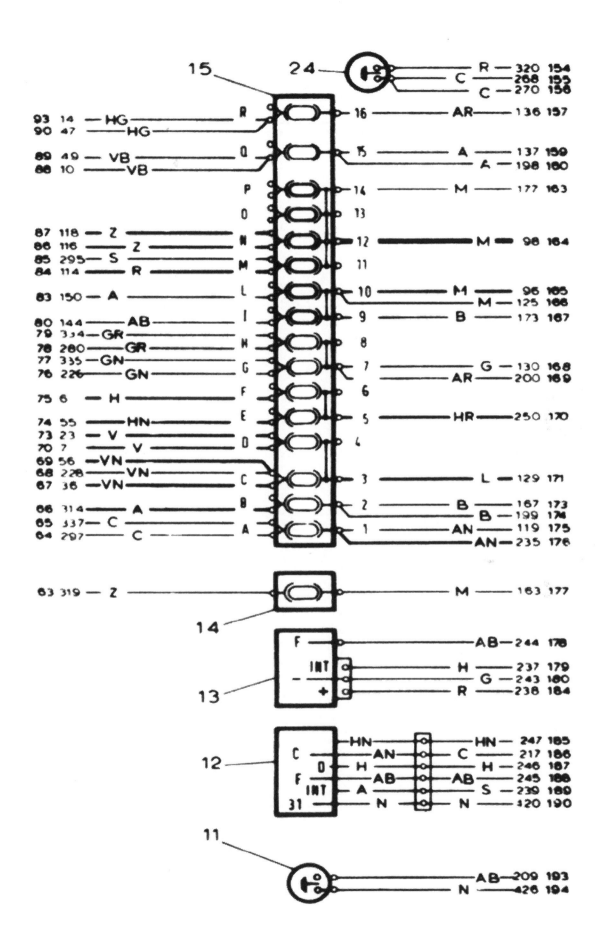

FIG 13 : 10   Circuit diagram, 1500 models

143

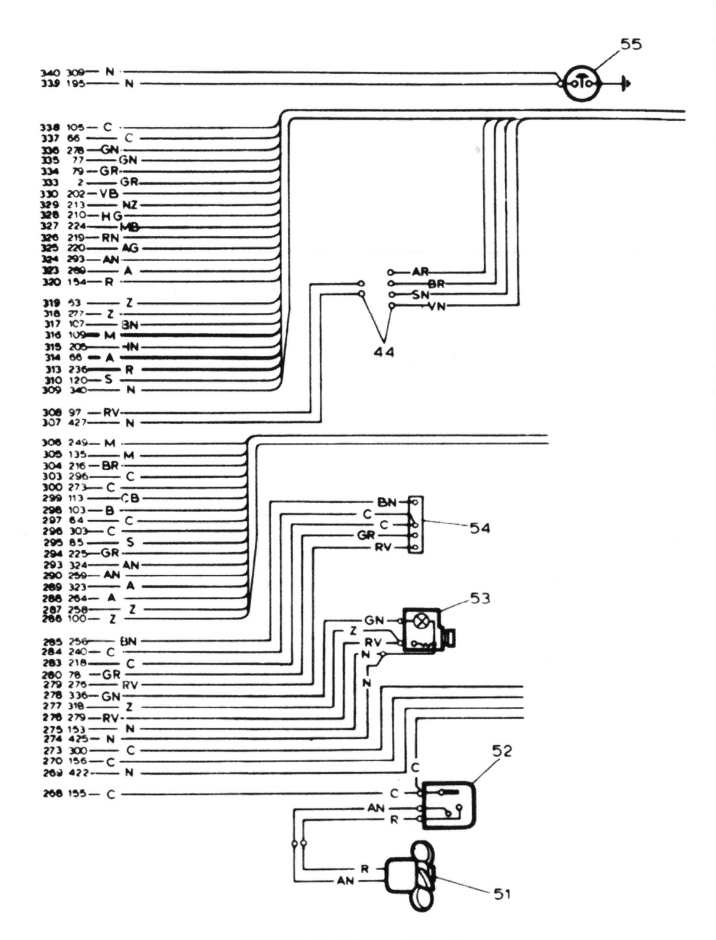

FIG 13 : 10   Circuit diagram, 1500 models

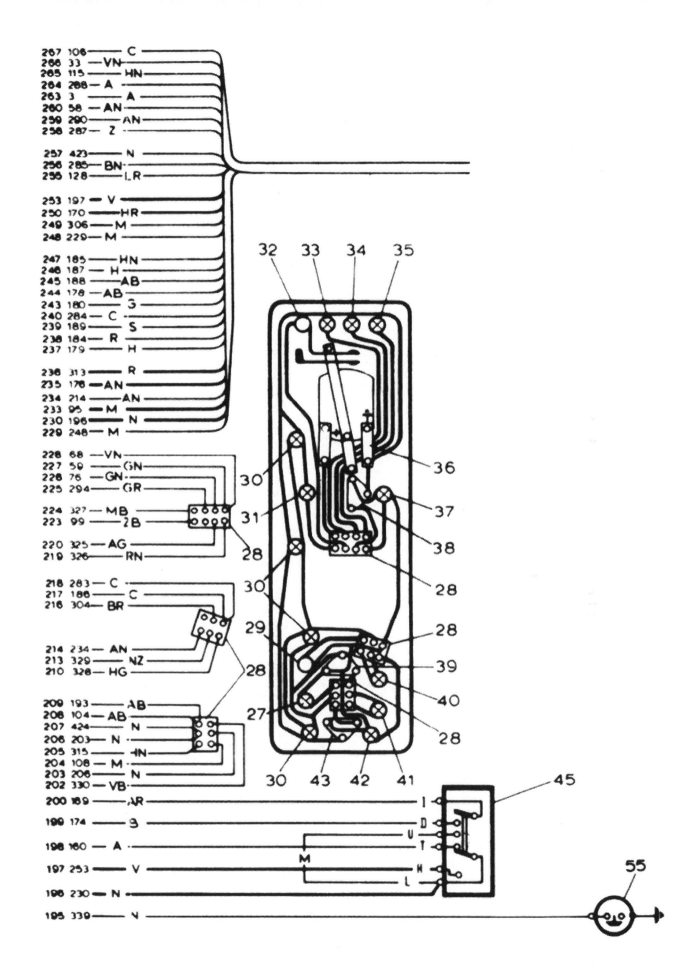

FIG 13 : 10   Circuit diagram, 1500 models

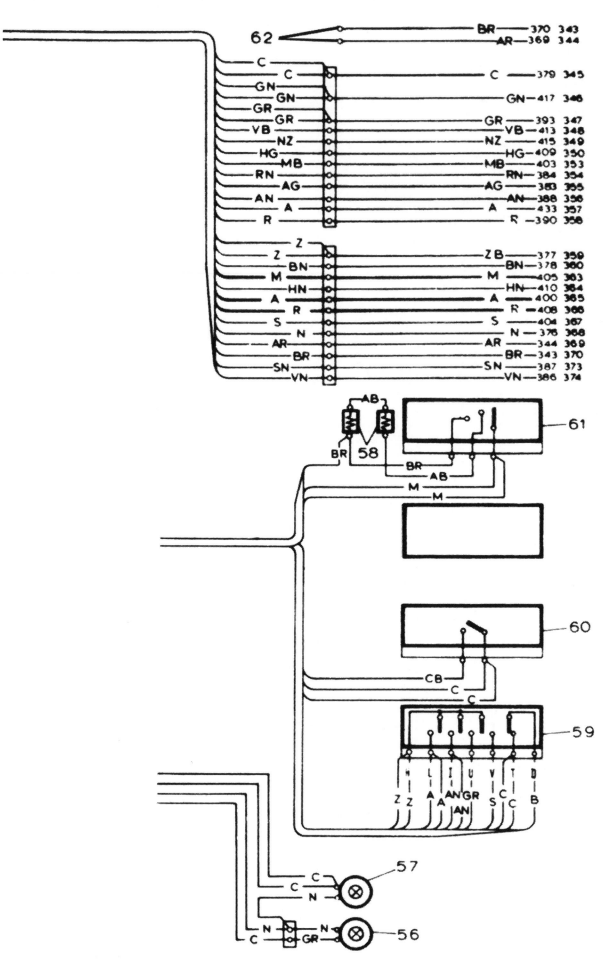

FIG 13:10   Circuit diagram, 1500 models

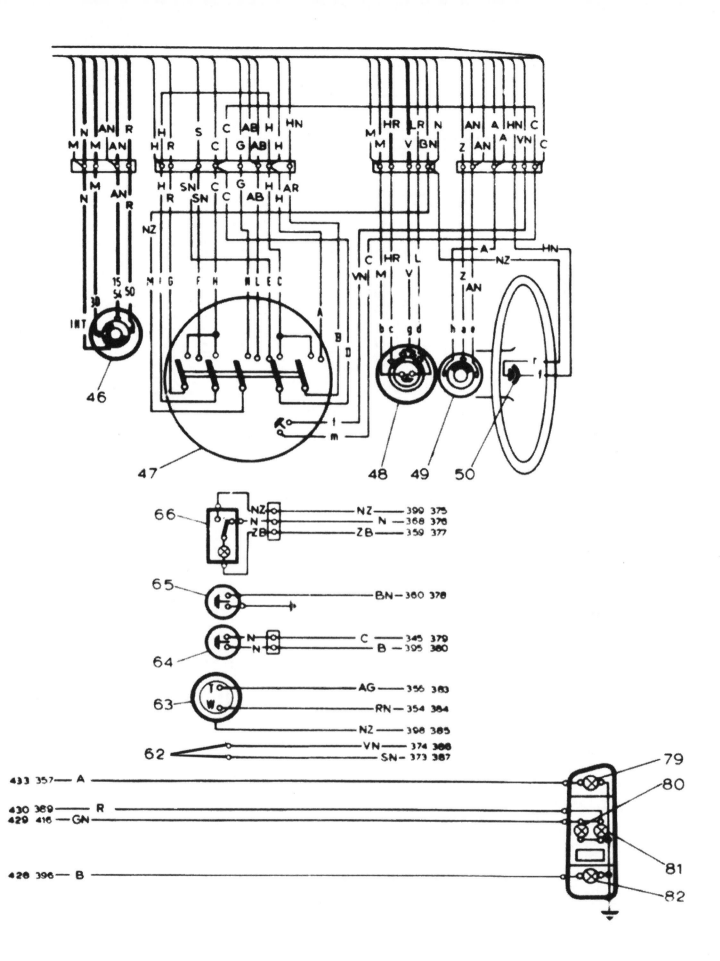

FIG 13 : 10   Circuit diagram, 1500 models

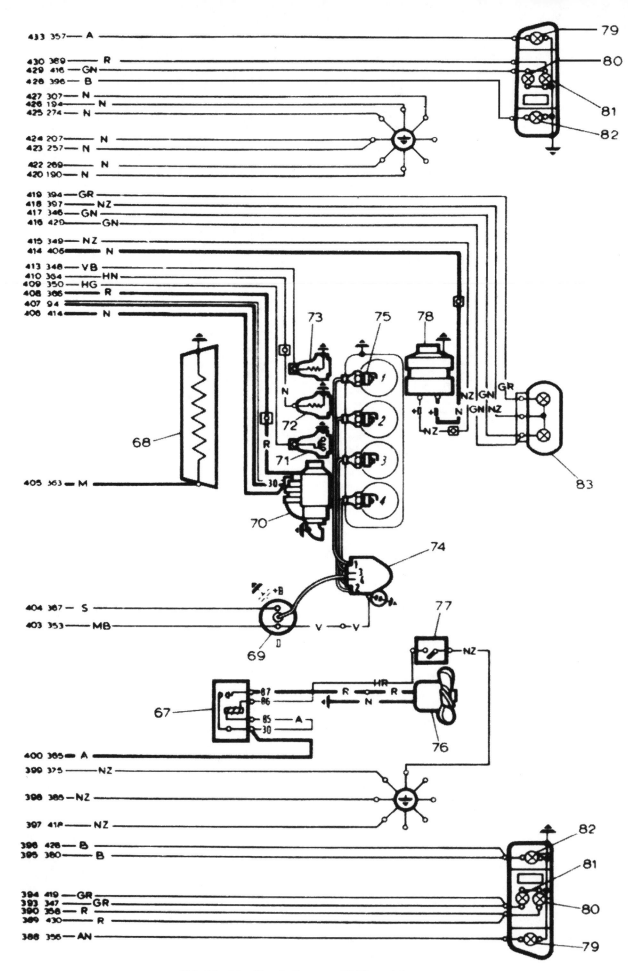

FIG 13:10   Circuit diagram, 1500 models

MAINTENANCE SUMMARY

It is in the interest of the owner/driver to perform regular maintenance checks to his vehicle or, alternatively, to pass the vehicle to an authorised dealer for jobs considered too complex to handle himself. Regular maintenance, using the correct parts, fluids and lubricants, at the specified intervals, is the key to economy, safety and reliability.

The following tabulations summarise the maintenance operations and the recorded mileage and/or time intervals at which (as quoted in the chapter texts) they should be carried out. The chapter section in which each operation is described or indicated, is quoted against each tabulated item. The arrows in **FIGS 13 : 11** and **13 : 12** are numbered to correspond with the tabulated item numbers.

Every 500km (300 miles) or weekly	Reference
1 Check engine oil level	Section 1 : 2
2 Check coolant level	Section 4 : 2
3 Check clutch hydraulic fluid level	Section 5 : 2
4 Check tyre pressures	Sections 7 : 2, 8 : 2 and Technical Data
5 Check the brake hydraulic fluid level	Section 10 : 2
6 Check the battery electrolyte level	Section 11 : 2

As required	
7 Adjust the handbrake	Section 10 : 2
8 Renew the alternator/coolant pump drive belt	Section 4 : 5
9 Renew the air pump drive belt	Section 1 : 15

Every 5000km (3000 miles)	
10 Visually check the front suspension	Section 7 : 2
11 Visually check the rear suspension and drive shaft boots	Section 8 : 2
12 Visually check the steering gear bellows and linkage	Section 9 : 2

Every 10,000km (6000 miles)	
13 Renew the engine oil	Section 1 : 2
14 Renew the oil filter	Section 1 : 13
15 Check the air pump drive belt tension	Section 1 : 15
16 Check the idling speed	Section 2 : 7
17 Renew air cleaner element	Section 2 : 3
18 Renew fuel filter	Section 2 : 5
19 Lubricate the ignition distributor	Section 3 : 2
20 Adjust contact breaker points gap	Section 3 : 2
21 Check ignition timing	Section 3 : 5
22 Clean and regap the sparking plugs	Section 3 : 6
23 Adjust clutch pedal travel and free play	Section 5 : 2
24 Interchange road wheels, inspect tyre treads	Sections 7 : 2 and 8 : 2
25 Check wheel alignment	Section 9 : 7
26 Check caliper pads	Section 10 : 2

Every 20,000km (12,000 miles)	
27 Renew air pump filter	Section 1 : 15
28 Adjust valve clearances	Section 1 : 11
29 Service the emission control systems	Section 1 : 15
30 Check operation of throttle and choke controls	Section 2 : 7
31 Service the evaporative emission control system	Section 2 : 10
32 Renew distributor contact breaker points	Section 3 : 2
33 Renew sparking plugs	Section 3 : 2
34 Check coolant hoses and joints	Section 4 : 2
35 Check transmission oil level	Section 6 : 2
36 Lubricate the gearchange linkage	Section 6 : 3
37 Lubricate the constant velocity joints	Section 8 : 6

Every 40,000km (24,000 miles)	Reference
38 Renew activated carbon trap	Section 2 : 10
39 Renew distributor cap and rotor, check HT cables	Section 3 : 2
40 Service spark control modulation device	Section 3 : 7
41 Renew transmission oil	Section 6 : 2
42 Check starter motor brushes	Section 11 : 4
43 Check alternator brushes	Section 11 : 3
Annually (or as necessary)	
44 Check headlamp alignment	Section 11 : 7
45 Lubricate headlamp hinges	Section 11 : 7
Every 60,000km (36,000 miles) or every two years	
46 Drain, flush and refill the cooling system	Section 4 : 2
Every 60,000km (36,000 miles) or every three years	
47 Overhaul clutch hydraulic system, renew hose	Section 5 : 5
48 Overhaul brakes hydraulic system, renew hoses	Sections 10 : 3 and 10 : 4
49 Renew clutch hydraulic fluid	Section 5 : 5
50 Renew brakes hydraulic fluid	Section 10 : 5

Oil of the recommended specification and grade should always be used in the engine and transmission. The use of oil to the incorrect grade or specification can lead to high oil and fuel consumption and, ultimately, damaged components. This also applies to clutch and brake hydraulic fluid.

WARNING:

Many liquids and other substances used are poisonous and should, under no circumstances, be consumed and should, so far as possible, be kept away from open wounds. These substances, amongst others, include antifreeze, hydraulic fluid, fuel, windscreen washer additives, lubricants and various adhesives. Hydraulic fluid can damage paintwork and, if spilt, should immediately be washed off with cold water applied copiously.

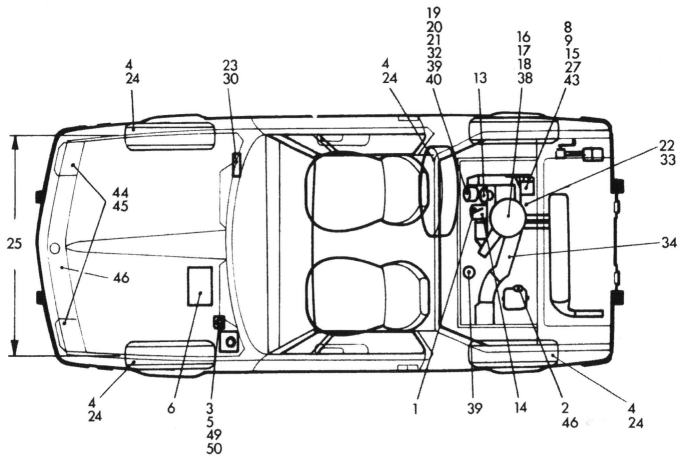

FIG 13 : 11   Location of maintenance summary points

Key to Fig 13 : 11   Numerals relate to maintenance summary tabulation

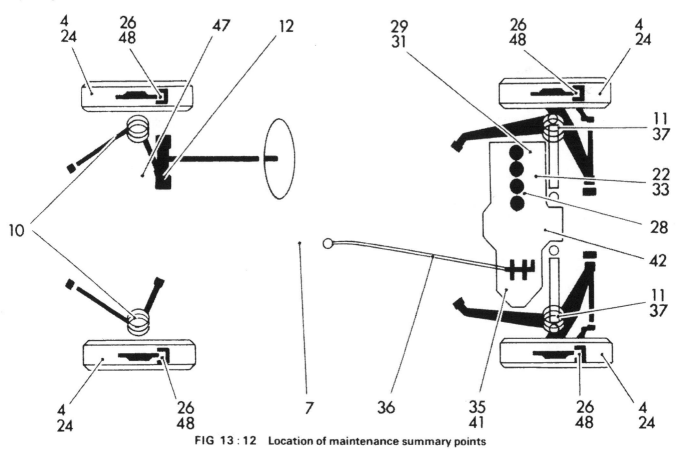

FIG 13 : 12   Location of maintenance summary points

Key to Fig 13 : 12   Numerals relate to maintenance summary tabulation

Glossary of Terms

Allen key — Cranked wrench of hexagonal section for use with socket head screws.

Alternator — Electrical generator producing alternating current. Rectified to direct current for battery charging.

Ambient temperature — Surrounding atmospheric temperature.

Annulus — Used in engineering to indicate the outer ring gear of an epicyclic gear train.

Armature — The shaft carrying the windings, which rotates in the magnetic field of a generator or starter motor. That part of a solenoid or relay which is activated by the magnetic field.

Axial — In line with, or pertaining to, an axis.

Backlash — Play in meshing gears.

Balance lever — A bar where force applied at the centre is equally divided between connections at the ends.

Banjo axle — Axle casing with large diameter housing for the crownwheel and differential.

Bendix pinion — A self-engaging and self-disengaging drive on a starter motor shaft.

Bevel pinion — A conical shaped gearwheel, designed to mesh with a similar gear with an axis usually at 90 deg. to its own.

bhp — Brake horse power, measured on a dynamometer.

bmep — Brake mean effective pressure. Average pressure on a piston during the working stroke.

Brake cylinder — Cylinder with hydraulically operated piston(s) acting on brake shoes or pad(s).

Brake regulator — Control valve fitted in hydraulic braking system which limits brake pressure to rear brakes during heavy braking to prevent rear wheel locking.

Camber — Angle at which a wheel is tilted from the vertical.

Capacitor — Modern term for an electrical condenser. Part of distributor assembly, connected across contact breaker points, acts as an interference suppressor.

Castellated — Top face of a nut, slotted across the flats, to take a locking splitpin.

Castor — Angle at which the kingpin or swivel pin is tilted when viewed from the side.

cc — Cubic centimetres. Engine capacity is arrived at by multiplying the area of the bore in sq. cm by the stroke in cm by the number of cylinders.

Clevis — U-shaped forked connector used with a clevis pin, usually at handbrake connections.

Collet — A type of collar, usually split and located in a groove in a shaft, and held in place by a retainer. The arrangement used to retain the spring(s) on a valve stem in most cases.

Commutator — Rotating segmented current distributor between armature windings and brushes in generator or motor.

Compression ratio — The ratio, or quantitative relation, of the total volume (piston at bottom of stroke) to the unswept volume (piston at top of stroke) in an engine cylinder.

Condenser — See 'Capacitor'.

Core plug — Plug for blanking off a manufacturing hole in a casting.

Crownwheel — Large bevel gear in rear axle, driven by a bevel pinion attached to the propeller shaft. Sometimes called a 'ring gear'.

'C'-spanner — Like a 'C' with a handle. For use on screwed collars without flats, but with slots or holes.

Damper — Modern term for shock absorber, used in vehicle suspension systems to damp out spring oscillations.

Depression — The lowering of atmospheric pressure as in the inlet manifold and carburetter.

Dowel — Close tolerance pin, peg, tube or bolt which accurately locates mating parts.

Drag link — Rod connecting steering box drop arm (pitman arm) to nearest front wheel steering arm in certain types of steering systems.

Dry liner — Thinwall tube pressed into cylinder bore.

Dry sump — Lubrication system where all oil is scavenged from the sump and returned to a separate tank.

Dynamo — See 'Generator'

Electrode — Terminal part of an electrical component such as the points or 'Electrodes' of a sparking plug.

Electrolyte — In lead-acid car batteries a solution of sulphuric acid and distilled water.

End float — The axial movement between associated parts, end play.

EP — Extreme pressure. In lubricants, special grades for heavily loaded bearing surfaces, such as gear teeth in a gearbox, or crown wheel and pinion in a rear axle.

Fade — Of brakes. Reduced efficiency due to overheating.

Field coils — Windings on the polepieces of motors and generators.

Fillets — Narrow finishing strips usually applied to interior bodywork.

First motion shaft — Input shaft from clutch to gearbox.

Fullflow filter	Filters in which all the oil is pumped to the engine. If the element becomes clogged, a bypass valve operates to pass unfiltered oil to the engine.	**lb ft**	A measure of twist or torque. A pull of 10lb at a radius of 1 ft is a torque of 10 lb ft.
FWD	Front wheel drive.	**lb/sq in**	Pounds per square inch.
Gear pump	Two meshing gears in a close fitting casing. Oil is carried from the inlet round the outside of both gears in the spaces between the gear teeth and casing to the outlet. The meshing gear teeth prevent oil passing back to the inlet and the oil is forced through the outlet port.	**Little-end**	The small, or piston end of a connecting rod. Sometimes called the 'small-end'.
		LT	Low Tension. The current output from the battery.
		Mandrel	Accurately manufactured bar or rod used for test or centring purposes.
Generator	Modern term for 'Dynamo'. When rotated produces electrical current.	**Manifold**	A pipe, duct, or chamber, with several branches.
Grommet	A ring of protective or sealing material. Can be used to protect pipes or leads passing through bulkheads.	**Needle rollers**	Bearing rollers with a length many times their diameter.
Grubscrew	Fully threaded headless screw with screwdriver slot. Used for locking or alignment purposes.	**Oil bath**	Reservoir which lubricates parts by immersion. In air filters, a separate oil supply for wetting a wire mesh element to hold the dust.
Gudgeon pin	Shaft which connects a piston to its connecting rod. Sometimes called 'wrist pin' or 'piston pin'.	**Oil wetted**	In air filters, a wire mesh element lightly oiled to trap and hold airborne dust.
Halfshaft	One of a pair transmitting drive from the differential.	**Overlap**	Period during which inlet and exhaust valves are open together.
Helical	In spiral form. The teeth of helical gears are cut at a spiral angle to the side faces of the gearwheel.	**Panhard rod**	Bar connected between fixed point on chassis and another on axle to control sideways movement.
Hot spot	Hot area that assists vapourisation of fuel on its way to cylinders. Often provided by close contact between inlet and exhaust manifolds.	**Pawl**	Pivoted catch which engages in the teeth of a ratchet to permit movement in one direction only.
HT	High Tension. Applied to electrical current produced by the ignition coil for the sparking plugs.	**Peg spanner**	Tool with pegs, or pins, to engage in holes or slots in the part to be turned.
		Pendant pedals	Pedals with levers that are pivoted at the top end.
Hydrometer	A device for checking specific gravity of liquids. Used to check specific gravity of electrolyte.	**Phillips screwdriver**	The cross-point screwdriver for using with the cross-slotted heads of Phillips screws.
Hypoid bevel gears	A form of bevel gear used in the rear axle drive gears. The bevel pinion meshes below the centre line of the crownwheel, giving a lower propeller shaft line.	**Pinion**	A small gear in relation to another gear.
		Piston-type damper	Shock absorber in which damping is controlled by a piston working in a closed oil-filled cylinder.
Idler	A device for passing on movement. A free running gear between driving and driven gears. A lever transmitting track rod movement to a side rod in steering gear.	**Preloading**	Preset static pressure on ball or roller bearings not due to working loads.
		Radial	Radiating from a centre, like the spokes of a wheel.
Impeller	A centrifugal pumping element. Used in water pumps to stimulate flow.	**Radius rod**	Pivoted arm confining movement of a part to an arc of fixed radius.
Journals	Those parts of a shaft that are in contact with the bearings.	**Ratchet**	Toothed wheel or rack which can move in one direction only, movement in the other being prevented by a pawl.
Kingpin	The main vertical pin which carries the front wheel spindle and permits steering movement. May be called 'steering pin' or 'swivel pin'.	**Ring gear**	A gear tooth ring attached to outer periphery of flywheel. Starter pinion engages with it during starting.
Layshaft	The shaft which carries the laygear in the gearbox. The laygear is driven by the first motion shaft and drives the third motion shaft according to the gear selected. Called the 'countershaft' or 'second motion shaft'.	**Runout**	Amount by which rotating part is out of true.
		Semi-floating axle	Outer end of rear axle halfshaft is carried on bearing inside axle casing. Wheel hub is secured to end of shaft.

Servo	A hydraulic or pneumatic system for assisting, or, augmenting a physical effort. See 'Vacuum Servo'.
Setscrew	One which is threaded for the full length of the shank.
Shackle	A coupling link, used in the form of two parallel pins connected by side plates to secure the end of the master suspension spring and absorb the effects of deflection.
Shell bearing	Thinwalled steel shell lined with anti-friction metal. Usually semi-circular and used in pairs for main and big-end bearings.
Shock absorber	See 'Damper'.
Silentbloc	Rubber bush bonded to inner and outer metal sleeves.
Socket-head screw	Screw with hexagonal socket for an Allen key.
Solenoid	A coil of wire creating a magnetic field when electric current passes through it. Used with a soft iron core to operate contacts or a mechanical device.
Spur gear	A gear with teeth cut axially across the periphery.
Stub axle	Short axle fixed at one end only.
Tachometer	An instrument for accurate measurement of rotating speed. Usually indicates in revolutions per minute.
TDC	Top Dead Centre. The highest point reached by a piston in a cylinder, with the crank and connecting rod in line.
Thermostat	Automatic device for regulating temperature. Used in vehicle coolant systems to open a valve which restricts circulation at low temperature.
Third motion shaft	Output shaft of gearbox.
Three-quarter floating axle	Outer end of rear axle half-shaft flanged and bolted to wheel hub,which runs on bearing mounted on outside of axle casing. Vehicle weight is not carried by the axle shaft.
Thrust bearing or washer	Used to reduce friction in rotating parts subject to axial loads.
Torque	Turning or twisting effort. See 'lb ft'.
Track rod	The bar(s) across the vehicle which connect the steering arms and maintain the front wheels in their correct alignment.
UJ	Universal joint. A coupling between shafts which permits angular movement.
UNF	Unified National Fine screw thread.
Vacuum servo	Device used in brake system, using difference between atmospheric pressure and inlet manifold depression to operate a piston which acts to augment brake pressure as required. See 'Servo'.
Venturi	A restriction or 'choke' in a tube, as in a carburetter, used to increase velocity to obtain a reduction in pressure.
Vernier	A sliding scale for obtaining fractional readings of the graduations of an adjacent scale.
Welch plug	A domed thin metal disc which is partially flattened to lock in a recess. Used to plug core holes in castings.
Wet liner	Removable cylinder barrel, sealed against coolant leakage, where the coolant is in direct contact with the outer surface.
Wet sump	A reservoir attached to the crankcase to hold the lubricating oil.

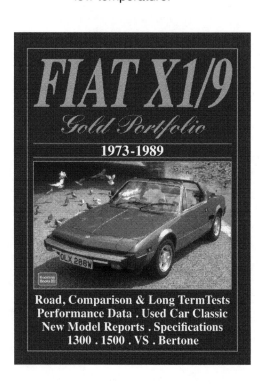

Fiat X1/9 Gold Portfolio 1973-1989

Covering the Fiat X1/9 from 1973 to 1989. 1300, 1500, VS, Bertone to the end of production in 1989. This book is a portfolio of contemporary reports featuring road and comparison tests, long term tests, performance data, used car classic and new model reports.

ISBN 9781855203563

Available from Amazon

Printed in Great Britain
by Amazon

46422718R00086